Chronic Acting-Out Students and Child Abuse

Chronic Acting-Out Students and Child Abuse

A Handbook for Intervention

David N. Sandberg

Program on Law and Child Maltreatment
Boston University School of Law

With contributions by

Henry Beyer
Judianne Densen-Gerber
Cynthia Mowles

Lexington Books

D.C. Heath and Company/Lexington, Massachusetts/Toronto

Library of Congress Cataloging-in-Publication Data

Sandberg, David N.
Chronic acting-out students and child abuse.

Bibliography: p.
Includes index.
1. Problem children—Education   Handbooks, manuals,
etc. 2. Abused children—Services for—Handbooks,
manuals, etc. 3. Juvenile delinquency—Prevention—
Handbooks, manuals, etc. I. Title. II. Title: Acting-out
students and child abuse.
LC4801.S26   1987   371.93   86-27403
ISBN 0-669-14736-2 (pbk. : alk. paper)

Published simultaneously in Canada
Printed in the United States of America
Paperbound International Standard Book Number: 0-669-14736-2
Library of Congress Catalog Card Number: 86-27403

The paper used in this publication meets the minimum requirements of
American National Standard for Information Sciences—Permanence of
Paper for Printed Library Materials, ANSI Z39.48-1984. ∞™

87 88 89 90 8 7 6 5 4 3 2 1

To Sally, Shawn, and Kelley

Contents

Preface

The Genesis of This Handbook

Every attempt to forge improvements, however modest, is shaped by what has come before. This Handbook is no different. Because the chapters that follow address two subject areas (child maltreatment and chronic acting-out behaviors) that are not yet linked in the public eye, we feel that there is a special reason for informing the reader about the genesis of this Handbook. The following are summary descriptions of the more significant influences on our work.

The 1982–83 National Center on Child Abuse and Neglect Project[1]

This research undertaking, entitled "The Role of Child Abuse in Delinquency and Juvenile Court Decision-Making" (HHS Grant No. 90CA901/01), reported the following findings:

Of 150 delinquents studied, 98 (65 percent) had child abuse histories, commencing, on the average, at age 7.

All of the abused youth experienced multiple problems and came from multiple-problem homes.

Specific abuse experiences (e.g., physical abuse) did not tend to result in specific types of later delinquency (e.g., assault).

Of all the adverse impacts on child development among the delinquents studied, child abuse was the most devastating, resulting in (among other things) major confusion over what nurturance is, what violence is, and what sexual exploitation is.

The juvenile justice system, nationally, has a low level of awareness of the abuse–delinquency relationship. (*Note:* In the intervening years, this has changed considerably.)

The abused children were typically filled with rage, including parricidal feelings.

Abused delinquents are both victims *and* offenders.

It is legally feasible and desirable to amend delinquency statutes to require that courts make abuse probes before making dispositions.

In the course of conducting the project, especially when reviewing the extensive medical, psychiatric, school, and family histories of the youths studied, we repeatedly asked, "What if major interventions had been made earlier in their lives, instead of waiting until they were 16 and in the delinquency court?" Most people who work with delinquent children and have witnessed how difficult it is for children at this late stage to curb ingrained patterns of destructive behavior are haunted by this question.

In time, this became the impetus for a second proposal to the National Center on Child Abuse and Neglect (NCCAN). We prefaced the proposal with comments by Judge David Bazelon to a gathering of juvenile and family court judges in Atlanta, Georgia, in 1970:

> Although the schools are plagued by bureaucracy, by lack of resources . . . still only the schools have a chance of reaching the millions of deprived children who pass through the system each year, unnoticed or singled out for the wrong reasons. We turn them out onto our city streets without education, and with ill-disguised contempt for the social institutions they know best. They come before the juvenile courts in spiralling numbers each year, accused of ugly street crimes, victims of heroin addiction, or just plain beyond control. You can probably do little for most of them. But you can do a great deal for their younger brothers and sisters, if you insist that your communities begin the hard uphill fight to convert our archaic schools into centers that can provide the full range of services that children need to become decent and law-abiding adults.

In the NCCAN proposal, we stated our agreement with Judge Bazelon that only the schools have a chance of preventing significant numbers of children from continuing on a track of school failure, juvenile delinquency, and, ultimately, adult criminality or dysfunction. In 1970, when he addressed the National Council of Juvenile Court Judges, no data existed on the relationship between child abuse and chronic deviant behavior including delinquency, so it is not surprising that he did not reference child abuse. However, in the intervening years, considerable research and direct service observation have linked a substantial amount of serious deviant behavior with underlying child abuse histories.

Yet aside from a reasonably good reporting rate of suspected child abuse, the public schools have not made much headway in the type of early intervention Judge Bazelon envisioned. He further stated to judges in attendance at the 1970 conference:

> Almost every juvenile court client has a poor school record, truancy, poor grades, misbehavior with teachers and classmates. What is the school's response now? Usually to single him out very early for the wrong kind of attention: bad marks, reprimands, petty scoldings and humiliations. Later come the "special adjustment classes," the "twilight schools," the suspensions and expulsions, finally the referrals to juvenile court. In between may come some sporadic, hurried, and usually unsuccessful counselling. The child's miserable record follows him from teacher to teacher and becomes its own self-fulfilling prophecy.

With the exception of advances spawned by Public Law 94-142 (the Education for All Handicapped Children Act), the situation Judge Bazelon described in 1970 fits today. Evidence of this was seen in the 150 delinquent children studied in the 1982–83 NCCAN project. It was striking how many of the abused members of the sample (98 of 150) were tipping off their abused condition during their elementary and/or secondary school years. Common examples included repeated fighting with peers, hitting teachers, continued academic difficulties, suspensions, and expulsions. More than a few had been referred to a school counselor, and some had been coded educationally handicapped. But not one of the ninety-eight children had been identified as an abused child through a school-initiated probe. Fewer than ten had been identified as abused by anyone before their involvement with delinquency courts and referral to treatment; the abuse was uncovered by treatment staff who have long been trained to identify child abuse histories.

In our proposal to NCCAN, we stated further that public schools offer society its best opportunity to identify abuse cases that we have been unable to prevent in the first instance. Although educators in some states report abuse at a higher rate than other professionals do, many chronic acting-out children are never the subject of abuse reports unless they evidence more traditional abuse symptoms, such as suspicious bruises or shabby clothing. What is remarkable about this is that the acting-out child probably gets more attention from teachers, school administrators, counselors, special education personnel, and even school board members than any other type of student. Unfortunately, this considerable attention, even when it is positive, is not apt to have lasting effect unless the underlying abuse is also addressed. Furthermore, these children, like many who have been abused, are very difficult, even offensive people to work with, thereby increasing the temptation for educators to remove them from their system.

Other barriers to child abuse and predelinquency interventions in public schools also come into play, and we proposed addressing some of the more important ones. Until they are properly identified and addressed, it is very unlikely that public schools will realize their excellent opportunity to intervene in the lives of acting-out children as well as other types of abused children. Thus, we noted that although the project's focus was to be abuse victims who feature pervasive acting out and failure in school, some of the project's analysis would have relevance to all abused children.

We also stated in the NCCAN proposal that it is crucial to realize just how important schools and educational success are to abused children in particular. It is likely that, for most children, their relationship with their school (which encompasses peer relationships) is second in importance only to their relationship with their parents. We know that abused children internalize a parent's abusive treatment, believing that they must be very bad, indeed, to warrant such treatment. Research is only just beginning to document the long-term harm that abuse causes. Common sense suggests that a successful school experience can mitigate some of the damage, especially in the areas of self-esteem, perceptions of adults and governmental systems, and the development of interpersonal relationships.

Conversely, public school failure—one of the distinguishing characteristics of the abused children considered in the proposed project—reinforces the family failure and, as much as anything else, may reduce these children's chances of ever overcoming the abuse experience. Child abuse, ingrained patterns of failure, and resultant anger and low self-esteem are primary ingredients for delinquency and adult dysfunction.

Thus, we concluded, societal objectives of early child abuse interventions and the reduction of crime and delinquency are closely related to the chronic acting-out student with underlying abuse. To be more successful, we will necessarily have to effect closer ties among the educational, child protection, and juvenile justice systems, reflecting the truly interdisciplinary nature of the child abuse–chronic acting out relationship.

Our proposal was eventually funded by NCCAN and became the project reported in this Handbook. We take some comfort in realizing that the situation looks more hopeful now than we had originally thought, and we refer the reader especially to Chapter 18, "What Others Are Doing."

Juvenile Delinquency Research Literature

Among the many themes, hypotheses, and recommendations found in the very large body of delinquency research begun in earnest in the 1930s by Eleanor and Sheldon Glueck, two are of particular interest to us:

1.   Repeated findings that most delinquents exhibit maladaptive behaviors very early on in school (and even prior to entry in school) and that it is essential to intercede before these behaviors become fixed patterns.
2.   Repeated findings that delinquents uniformly have histories of school failure.

In reflecting upon their research on 500 delinquent and 500 nondelinquent children the Gluecks concluded:

> It is [essential] for schools, particularly, to be equipped to discover potential delinquents before the trends of maladapted behavior become too fixed, and to distinguish among children already "acting up," the true delinquent from the pseudo-delinquent. For the schools are in a strategic position to note such marked deviations and difficulties of adaptation at the age of five or six, or earlier, when children first enter. (Glueck and Glueck, 1968)

Also significant was the Gluecks' conviction that problems of delinquency involve both biological or genetic and social influences, especially the family. They stated: "There can be little doubt . . . that it is almost futile to treat the child apart from the parents who contribute so much to make him what he is."

Many delinquency researchers have identified school failure as a significant variable in the lives of delinquent children. As noted by Michael Rutter and Henn Griller (1984) in their review of the delinquency literature: "Our link between education retardation [i.e., difficulties] and delinquency is one of the most consistent of all associations in the literature."

Thus, the notion of enhancing the educational prospects for chronic acting-out students as a way of lessening their risk for later delinquency appears to be a sound one; indeed, it has been attempted sporadically over the past 30 years. The only contradictory information appears in research reported by Elliot and Voss (1974), who found that delinquency rates may actually go down when delinquency-prone youth are out of school. The police contact rate among the delinquents they studied declined in the period after dropout and continued to decline in subsequent periods; that is, their involvement with delinquency began in school and was primarily a response to school and school failure. This finding led Elliott and Voss to call into question programs that are designed to keep many of these youths in school; indeed, they question "whether dropouts necessarily suffer all of the negative consequences usually ascribed to dropouts."

Given national statistics on such factors as lifetime income of high school graduates versus dropouts, especially when race is considered, it is difficult for us to accept the Elliott and Voss position. Even more central is that given what is now known about individual and family factors associated with delinquency, it is difficult to view schools and the pressures of school failure as the primary cause of delinquency. Perhaps most significant is that the Elliott and Voss position fails to consider the potential of a positive educational experience, be it academic or vocationally oriented, in ameliorating the effects of a disastrous family experience.

Child Abuse Research Literature

Compared to delinquency research, child abuse research is still in its infancy. In fact, recognition of child abuse as a specific medical condition only began in 1962 when Dr. Henry Kempe and colleagues presented their now-famous paper on the battered child syndrome.

David Gill (1969), a noted child abuse researcher, made the point early on that schools could be valuable screening and reporting centers for detecting child abuse. However, researchers have tended to focus more on the damaging effects of child abuse on a child's educational prospects. Dr. Kempe and his pediatrician wife, Dr. Ruth Kempe, described the abused school-age child well in their book, *Child Abuse* (1978):

> Regardless of their initial intelligence or socioeconomic background, abused children often perform poorly at communicative skills such as reading and writing. Not surprisingly, oppressed children for whom abuse is the reward for depression or initiative have difficulty with learning that requires exactly those behaviors. A child who is overly compulsive about getting approval and doing things right will tend to fail because of anxiety, while a child who has learned that communication leads to attention and receiving attention leads to being bashed would prefer to be essentially invisible and inactive. In either case he will not perform well in groups. This helps to explain why it is not only children who have been brain-damaged through head injuries who show poor school performance, but far more often children whose physical abuse has actually been stopped. Intervention may have managed to prevent permanent physical injury, but will not have produced the nurturing home environment that is so important for successful learning.

Dr. Brandt Steele, well-known colleague of the Kempes at the C. Henry Kempe Center for Child Abuse and Neglect in Denver, has made similar observations based on his direct service experiences. He notes that many abused and neglected children have problems with learning in general and language in particular. These children, he concludes, are the ones who fail in the early elementary years, and make up a significant proportion of those enrolled in special education classes.

We refer the reader to a more comprehensive assessment of the effects of child abuse and neglect in Chapter 3.

Schools as Mental Health Intervention Units

All that has been said thus far either directly points to or suggests that public schools can and should be more than just places where the "basics" are taught; they must also be directly involved with identifying and remediating assorted problems, including child abuse, that seriously jeopardize a child's opportunity to learn. Schools first began to move in this direction with employment of school nurses and guidance counselors years ago. Court decisions such as *Brown v. Education* and government programs such as Head Start lent additional impetus. But it was not until passage of the Education for All Handicapped Children Act in 1975 that public schools in America really began to take on a social service role.

It is safe to say, however, that more than ten years later, there is a great deal of disagreement over how broadly or narrowly the Act should be construed, including whether conduct-disordered children should be identified as educationally handicapped. Moreover, this uneasiness within the special educator sector is part of a larger uneasiness about just how much of a social service intervention role educators are willing to accept. We refer the reader to Chapters 11 and 19 for more extensive analysis of these issues.

The Indianapolis Conference

An undertaking similar to ours was a 1981 conference in Indianapolis entitled "Juvenile Delinquency and Early Childhood Intervention." (The conference proceedings, entitled *Early Childhood Intervention and Juvenile Delinquency,* were published by Lexington Books in 1982.) The conferees, representing numerous disciplines and consisting of a mixture of academics and direct service people, attempted to do in three days what took us two years. We recommend that all who have a special interest in our project read *Early Childhood Intervention,* which includes easy-to-read essays, roundtable exchanges, and follow-up commentary.

The Racine Conference

A 1984 conference in Racine, Wisconsin, on the relationship between child abuse and delinquency was funded by the federal Office of Juvenile Justice and Delinquency Prevention and coordinated by the National Committee for the Prevention of Child Abuse. The thirty conferees included researchers, front-line workers in child protection and mental health, judges, and policymakers with expertise in child abuse and/or delinquency. The group was asked to consider all existing information on the relationship between child abuse and delinquency and then formulate recommendations. The conferees' recommendations included the following:

1. Interdisciplinary cooperation.
2. Specific and probing history taking at intake for delinquency.
3. Educational strategies aimed at implementing change within certain systems to recognize the youth as a victim as well as a perpetrator.
4. Therapeutic intervention for all abused children who come to the attention of the court exhibiting problem behavior, regardless of the disposition of the case.
5. Specific and different treatment, within the correctional system, of the young person who was abused.

6. Mobilization of citizens to help prevent child abuse and child victimization.
7. Early intervention.

Child Maltreatment Publications for Educators

A rapidly growing number of child abuse pamphlets, manuals, and workshop handouts have been specifically prepared for educators. In the main, these materials have focused primarily on teachers' legal obligations to report abuse, although it is interesting to note that the door has usually been left open for educator involvement beyond just reporting. Indeed, some of the more recent publications are quite emphatic that because of the large amount of time abused students are in school, educators must necessarily continue to be involved following a report. What the "extra" involvement is to consist of is only just now being examined, and our project is one of the first to do so.

The following are some of the educator materials we came across in the course of our project:

The Educator and Child Abuse, by Brian G. Fraser (National Committee for Prevention of Child Abuse, Chicago, 1977). Characteristic of the genre, this booklet identifies numerous symptoms of possible child abuse, including "nervous, hyperactive, aggressive, disruptive, or destructive" behaviors. Fraser makes an important point in acknowledging that although, legally speaking, the educator's role is generally limited to reporting suspected abuse, s/he has an essential part to play in helping investigatory personnel obtain a complete picture of the child. Fraser further acknowledges the presence of interagency communication problems involving schools and child protection units but urges educators to act "tenaciously" to overcome these problems.

Guidelines for Schools: To Help Protect Abused and Neglected Children (American Humane Association, Denver, 1984). This pamphlet, like several others, catalogues behavioral indicators associated with each type of abuse and neglect. Thus, delinquent behavior is symptomatic of possible emotional maltreatment, chronic running away of physical abuse, and so forth. Aside from these overly narrow linkages, acting-out behaviors are once again identified as warning signs for possible abuse.

Child Abuse and Neglect Curriculum in Schools (DHHS Pub. No. 81-30318, Education Commission of the States, Denver, 1981). Most significant about this pamphlet is the Commission's position that "it is important that teachers be trained to deal with the total child: intellectually, physically, and emotionally." Any schools that wish to implement a comprehensive teacher training program on abuse will find this pamphlet a useful reference.

The Educator's Role (National Center on Child Abuse and Neglect, DHHS, Washington, D.C., reprinted 1984). This government publication contains a chapter entitled "After the Report—What Schools Can Offer," signifying the growing awareness that reporting is not the end of educator involvement with abused students. It identifies several additional tasks, including providing child protection investigatory personnel with information, providing services to children and their parents, and participating in multidisciplinary teams.

How Schools and Educators Can Help Abused Adolescents, a Boys Town–sponsored pamphlet prepared by Barbara Lonnborg. Although very brief, this publication brings into clear focus the fact that many chronic acting-out adolescents suffer from underlying maltreatment. Also noted is that nearly half of all maltreated children are adolescents.

Child Abuse and Neglect: A Teacher's Handbook for Detection, Reporting and Classroom Management, by Cynthia Crosson Tower, prepared on behalf of the National Education Association. The title is further suggestive of the current trend of child abuse resource materials, pointing to greater educator involvement in abuse cases. Ms. Tower states:

Studies of learning patterns show that in order to learn, students must be sufficiently free from discomfort and conflict to channel their energies into comprehension. Yet the abused or neglected child may be expending this valuable energy on merely coping with the home situation. Only through treatment—the relief of this pressure—can the child be freed to take full advantage of the learning opportunities available. By detecting the abuse or neglect and facilitating such treatment, the teacher enhances the child's ability to learn.

Methodology

Numerous methodologies have been used in this Handbook to bring to the reader useful information about chronic acting-out children (CACs). For example, Chapter 6 is a summary of the formal research literature on numerous relationships that directly or indirectly relate to CACs; Chapter 7 relies on national statistics and project members' knowledge of other relevant factors; Chapter 9 utilizes standard legal research; Chapter 10 is a dialogue between project members; Chapter 11 is a survey of the educational and child abuse literatures; and Chapter 13 uses a team problem-solving approach.

The overall methodology is applied—a nonempirical process that attempts to draw together fragments of the best available information and arrange it in such a way that the subject can be seen more clearly.

Note

1. The project participants include David N. Sandberg, Henry Beyer, Judianne Densen-Gerber, Cynthia Mowles, Jaclyn Adams, Jeannette Gagnon, Rowen Hochstedler, Floyd Jozitis, Fred Nader, Jo-Ann Paveglio, Murray Straus, and Joanne Testaverde.

Acknowledgments

This Handbook is the result of a project that was greatly aided by a grant from the National Center on Child Abuse and Neglect (Washington, D.C.) and by the continuing support of the Boston University School of Law.

I would also like to thank my fellow project members: Jaclyn Adams, a special education coordinator with extensive experience in both the public and private sectors; Joanne Testaverde, also highly experienced in special education issues; Judianne Densen-Gerber and Rowen Hochstedler, psychiatric practitioners with years of experience in assessing child abuse and acting-out behaviors; Fred Nader, a long-time member of the juvenile justice community and former deputy director of the Office of Juvenile Justice and Delinquency Prevention (Washington, D.C.); Jeannette Gagnon, until recently a senior state administrator for child protection; Cynthia Mowles, a superintendent of schools with longstanding public concern about child abuse; Murray Straus, one of the world's pioneering authorities on family violence; Floyd Jozitis, former drug addict, therapist, and program director; Jo-Ann Paveglio, a public school speech and language therapist; and Henry Beyer, my colleague at Boston University School of Law and an unrelenting advocate for the rights of the developmentally disabled.

Our work was made easier by the contributions of four graduate students: Betsy Singer, Cindy Zelson, Debra Ludwig, and Peggy Daley. Recognition also goes to Cynthia Dunn—office manager, typist, and all-purpose assistant; to be successful, every project requires such a person.

All of these individuals made helpful suggestions, which found their way into the Handbook in one form or another. Jaclyn Adams provided invaluable advice on arranging and ordering of chapters, and project members who wrote chapters or parts of chapters have been duly identified. Jim Garbarino provided valuable guidance at the outset of the project. For better or worse, however, I lay claim to authoring most of the materials, including the project recommendations.

David N. Sandberg

Part I
Introduction

1
Introductory Questions and Answers

In anticipation of readers' concerns, the following questions and answers provide an overview of the subject matter and purpose of this Handbook.

Q: With which children is the Handbook primarily concerned?

A: We are concerned with children who self-identify by virtue of their chronic or repeated acting-out behavior. They are distinguishable from other problem children who do not misbehave in a pervasive manner and who therefore do not compel repeated disciplinary responses by educators. Many are apt to be child abuse victims; others are not. We refer to them as chronic acting-out children (CACs).

Q: Where are they found?

A: CACs are found at all educational levels—including elementary school, where the misbehavior is more likely to be perceived as symptomatic of developmental problems. It seems that for most of these children, their acting out commences in the elementary years and escalates over the years, often culminating in suspensions, expulsions, and/or involvement with the court system.

Q: How do you know that "many" CACs are child abuse victims?

A: This is based on direct service experience. Also, there is a small but persuasive body of empirical research indicating that delinquents have high rates of abuse and neglect. However, we know of no research that has attempted to determine maltreatment rates for so-called predelinquent CACs; therefore, we acknowledge a certain subjectivity to our use of the term *many*.

Q: Who are the perpetrators of the abuse?

A: There is a tendency to think in terms of parents only. However, CACs are also vulnerable to maltreatment, especially emotional/psychological abuse and neglect, by educators, court officials, and others.

Q: How many CACs are there?

A: This is not known, because not all dropouts, for example, are chronic behavioral problems in school. Also, many school systems do not gather suspension/expulsion data, which is probably a better indicator than dropout rates. In any event, educators know who these children are. Educators seem to be divided on whether there is an increasing number each year; however, almost all agree that the related problems are greater in number and more complex.

Q: What types of interventions do you have in mind, and what is the basis for the interventions?

A: Generally, we are proposing school-based interventions, which are necessitated by a student's persistent deviant behavior. These interventions are in contrast to, for example, testing all children upon entry into the public school system as part of a screening procedure to identify "predelinquent" or abused children. Interventions of the latter type are considered involuntary and are highly problematic, in that government intrusion is based on a statistical probability rather than on something a child has already done. Also, we favor nonpunitive interventions (e.g., special education assistance) rather than punitive interventions (e.g., corporal punishment, expulsion), with a particular eye out for the abuse/neglect factor. Chapter 18 presents a brief summary of several very positive intervention programs and concepts.

Q: Are you against punishment of any kind?

A: We are pretty much against punishment per se, which is different from setting limits and giving children meaningful consequences for unacceptable behavior. Punishment is also different from removing a child from the public school, provided that a more beneficial educational setting is offered the child. We discuss punishment and related issues in Chapters 10 and 23.

Q: Where in the school system are you advocating major intervention?

A: Responses have to be made at every educational level, because students are acting out in elementary, junior high, and senior high school. However, because many CACs self-identify during the elementary years, and because of the added difficulties of intervening during the adolescent years, we especially favor strengthened efforts at the elementary school level.

Q: Is acting-out behavior evidence of abuse/neglect?

A: Acting-out behavior, especially if chronic, is an indicator that abuse/neglect *may* be present. As the Handbook makes clear in several chapters, there is enough of a connection that evaluators should consider abuse/neglect as a very real possibility. This view is supported by research and by virtually all abuse/neglect materials prepared for educators.

Q: Does chronic acting-out behavior warrant or compel filing an abuse/neglect report?

A: Generally, it does not. Although there is a significant body of research linking such behavior and abuse/neglect, not all chronic acting-out children (e.g., delinquents) have histories of abuse and neglect. On the other hand, some very specific acting-out behaviors (e.g., extreme sexual provocation by a child) are suggestive of abuse/neglect to the point of probably compelling a report to child protection.

Q: Can educators ask a student if s/he is being abused or neglected without being sued?

A: Yes, if there is a reasonable basis for asking the question. The Phi Delta Kappan Educational Foundation has developed the "Suggested Interview Procedure for Students Suspected of Being Abused." This and other legal questions are addressed more fully by Attorney Beyer in Chapter 9.

Q: Should teachers be careful about their degree of involvement with abuse/neglect cases?

A: Yes. Dr. Densen-Gerber comments on this at length in Chapter 10.

Q: Can or should public schools do more in abuse/neglect cases than file reports with child protection?

A: Yes, they can and should. Abused/neglected children spend much of their lives in school; therefore, it does not make sense to assume that a school's only role in responding to their maltreated condition is to file an abuse/neglect report. This view is discussed throughout the Handbook. However, we also point out that it is the child protection system's role to investigate abuse/neglect once a report has been made.

Q: Is the Handbook a "how-to" instructional guide?

A: It is not a "how-to" guide in the sense of laying out in a simple one-two-three or formula fashion what to do when confronted with a maltreated child. An exception is the Summary Assessment Profile (Chapter 13). The Handbook's central purposes are to increase understanding of the maltreatment–acting out relationship and to promote more effective interventions, especially by the educational system. Along the way, we provide many pointers or general guidelines on how to proceed.

Q: Does the Handbook deal only with the maltreatment aspect of chronic acting-out students?

A: No. Although our principal concern is the maltreatment–acting out relationship, we take the position that many other important factors also need to be considered. Some of them (e.g., educational handicaps), in turn, have special linkages to maltreatment and chronic acting out. We again refer the reader to our Summary Assessment Profile (Chapter 13).

Q: How is this Handbook unique?

A: We know of no other publication that has attempted to draw together the constellation of issues that typically surround chronic acting-out children with maltreatment at the center.

Q: What stands out most after studying maltreated CACs nationally?

A: Many of the prominent issues are referenced in the conclusions and recommendations section (Part VI). At the top of the list, we would put the desirability of major intervention at the elementary school level. A close second is our feeling of bewilderment that the nation still does not have a comprehensive intervention system to serve failing, chronic acting-out children. On the positive side, it is also true that far more is available in the way of resources and know-how now than even ten years ago, principally because of the rise of the child protection and special education systems. Also, it was heartening to learn of the strong support of school-based interventions in abuse/neglect cases by the National PTA, the NEA, and other educator organizations.

Q: What do you want from educators and schools?

A: We seek five responses: (1) that they become more knowledgeable about behavioral problem children, especially their reality as frequent victims of child abuse and neglect; (2) when maltreatment is present, that they become more involved than just reporting a case to CPS; (3) that they recognize CACs as being handicapped, much as physically disabled children are, and avoid punishing them for their handicaps; (4) that they recognize that even the most destructive CACs can learn and usually want to, given an appropriate school environment; and (5) that they do an honest appraisal of their own contribution to the problem, just as members of other systems must do.

Q: What is your ultimate purpose?

A: Our ultimate purpose is to decrease the number and frequency of adverse developmental experiences for CACs and to increase their opportunity for a positive educational experience. Although reducing the incidence of later delinquency is a motivating factor for us, individual interventions (especially with elementary school students) are not well-grounded in delinquency prevention, as there is no certainty that a particular child will otherwise become delinquent. Seeking to improve a child's chances for educational success is a more defensible objective. The other primary motivating factor in our project is to protect children from child abuse and neglect through identification and intervention. Because not all chronic acting-out children are maltreated, it is sounder policy to base the intervention on a known factor (i.e., educational failure), keeping in mind that maltreatment may be a paramount underlying factor. An important corollary of all this is a shockingly high national dropout rate (see Chapter 22).

Q: Where can follow-up information be obtained?

A: Contact the Program on Law and Child Maltreatment, Boston University School of Law, 765 Commonwealth Avenue, Boston, MA 02215. Attn: David N. Sandberg, Director. (617)353-2904.

2
Definitions and Diagnoses

A number of terms, acronyms, and psychiatric/psychological diagnoses used throughout the Handbook are especially important. They are briefly discussed here.

Definitions

child abuse: Generally includes physical, sexual, and psychological or emotional abuse per state and federal statutes. Also includes neglect, except where otherwise noted, to eliminate repeated use of the more cumbersome "child abuse and neglect." In some parts of the Handbook, we use the abbreviation A/N to denote both.

delinquency: Generally includes status or CHINS offenses as well as delinquent (criminal) offenses. In some parts of the Handbook, the two are distinguished as separate juvenile categories.

CHINS: Acronym for Child in Need of Services. Common CHINS offenses include running away, truancy, being uncontrollable. Under the juvenile laws of most states, a CHINS (or PINS—Person in Need of Supervision) cannot be sentenced to reform school.

educators: Includes, broadly, teachers, administrators, and all school-based support personnel (e.g., school nurse, guidance counselor, school social worker, psychologist, special education staff).

chronic acting-out children (CACs): Children of all school ages who present serious and ongoing behavioral problems, often of an escalating nature. Behaviors include continual fighting with peers, ignoring teacher limit setting, drinking, using drugs, threatening educators, truancy, lying, and creating constant disruption in the classroom. CACs are readily distinguished from other children who exhibit a normal amount of "acting-up" behavior. The term as we use it excludes psychotic, autistic, and moderately and severely mentally retarded children. Delinquents and CHINS are two legally recognized types of CACs. The reader is also referred to the last section of this chapter for Dr. Densen-Gerber's analysis of acting-out behaviors.

child protection system (CPS): The designated state agency responsible for investigating reports of child abuse and neglect. Such agencies are also mandated to provide support services when a finding of abuse or neglect is made.

juvenile justice system: Primarily refers to each state's juvenile court system. Juvenile courts commonly deal with child abuse and neglect, CHINS, and delinquency cases.

interventions: Denotes, broadly, the myriad responses that educators and others make to chronic acting-out children. There are two main intervention categories: punitive (e.g., corporal punishment and expulsion) and nonpunitive (e.g., special education and filing an abuse report); some responses fall into gray areas (e.g., short-term suspensions).

children of alcoholics (COAs): A descriptive term for a large group of children, not all of whom act out, who are the subject of an increasing amount of attention within the mental health, juvenile justice, and child protection systems. Many acting-out children are COAs.

coded children: Children who are adjudged to be educationally handicapped under P.L. 94-142 (Education for All Handicapped Children Act). Common codings include learning disabled, seriously emotionally disturbed, and physically impaired. The central planning device for coded children is an individualized educational plan (IEP).

Psychiatric/Psychological Diagnoses

The following explanatory materials are derived from discussions with Dr. Rowen Hochstedler, a psychiatric consultant to our project; from the American Psychiatric Association's standard diagnostic manual (known as DSM III); and from several research literatures.

Dr. Hochstedler indicates that when he is asked to evaluate a chronic problem child, his initial task is to identify the child as belonging to one of the following categories:

1.   The psychotic
2.   The cognitively impaired (autism, retardation)
3.   The disordered or behaviorally disturbed

The psychotic and the retarded must be clearly identified. The chronic problem child who is psychotic can be differentiated by the presence of unusual or bizarre thought processes and affects. Although the child may not indicate these thoughts or affects in obvious ways, an experienced clinician, often with the help of psychological testing, can usually make this diagnosis. This diagnostic category is an important one, because the needs of a psychotic child are usually beyond the public school's ability to meet, and institutionalization is often necessary.

The chronic problem child who is cognitively impaired through mental retardation, autism, or organic brain dysfunction is usually readily identifiable. Psychological testing is frequently helpful to delineate the degree of impairment and to delineate areas of strength. The needs of these children are also specialized and may require special services or institutionalization.

Sometimes chronic problem children are assumed to be mentally retarded because they learn poorly and show poor judgment. It is extremely important to identify the presence of normal intelligence in some chronic problem children.

The psychotic and the retarded comprise a small percentage of all problem children. This leaves disordered children, who make up the great majority of problem children and are usually considered appropriate for placement in public schools, at least initially. Having ruled out psychosis and cognitive impairment, Dr. Hochstedler then considers several important subcategories of behaviorally disordered children, including attention deficit disorder, conduct disorder, and adjustment disorder. Overlapping can occur, and each disorder requires fundamentally different responses.

Attention Deficit Disorder (ADD)

The child with attention deficit disorder (ADD) has difficulty maintaining concentration on an assigned task to such an extent that effective learning does not take place. In years past, ADD went by such names as hyperkinetic, hyperactive, and worse (e.g., brain-damaged). Actually, ADD can exist with or without hyperactivity. However, whether or not they are hyperactive, all children with ADD share significant attentional difficulties and often suffer from impulsivity. These factors are clearly antithetical to learning, which requires at least a minimal ability to concentrate. These children are seen as problems in the classroom because they flit from one activity to another, disrupt classroom procedures, and fail to progress academically. They are unable to respond to "sit still" commands and are thus seen as oppositional.

Sometimes there is confusion about whether a child simply has a surplus of healthy energy or is hyperactive. DSM III indicates that "it is the quality of the motor behavior that distinguishes this disorder from ordinary overactivity in that hyperactivity tends to be haphazard, poorly organized, and not goal-directed."

Assuming that all other developmental factors are equal, common sense and DSM III tell us that an ADD child who also is hyperactive is in worse condition than a child who has ADD only. Whereas both hyperactive and nonhyperactive children often exhibit common features—such as negativism, low self-esteem, bullying, lack of response to discipline, and learning disabilities—the hyperactive child experiences them more intensely. Not surprisingly, the impairment and "at risk" status are also more severe.

Dr. Hochstedler comments that if a child has both ADD and hyperactivity, s/he is likely to be a classroom problem early on. Both conditions must be responded to. Medication (e.g., Ritalin) is appropriate for hyperactivity, nonchemical treatments (e.g., individual tutoring) for ADD. He makes several other points:

1. ADD is frequently a precursor of conduct disorders; early identification and remediation can prevent this progression.

2. ADD and conduct disorders can and do co-exist. Where they do, failure to respond effectively to the conduct disorder will negate efforts to remediate the ADD. This is akin to the alcoholic having to terminate his drinking before tackling any underlying causative conditions.

3. There is good evidence that ADD children do not mature out of their condition unassisted. Rather, the condition persists and forces these children to make related accom-

modations or adaptions. Some are fairly positive, though self-limiting (e.g., pursuit of careers that do not require reading and writing skills); others are destructive (e.g., substance abuse).

4. ADD is generally considered to be primarily linked to neurological/genetic factors. However, poor parenting (e.g., faulting, punishing, or beating a child for hyperactive behavior) greatly exacerbates the ADD condition.

5. Where an ADD condition gets worse, it becomes increasingly difficult to determine whether it is just an aggravated ADD case or also a conduct disorder. However, if the ADD and related acting out persist over several years, it becomes difficult not to make both diagnoses.

6. ADD is used as a description of an organic brain dysfunction primarily characterized by a short attention span. *Minimal brain damage* (MBD) is an older term used to describe an organic brain dysfunction primarily characterized by learning disability, short attention span, and the presence of "soft neurological signs" (e.g., clumsiness). MBD is not used in DSM III, as the term *brain damage* has pejorative connotations. Both terms imply organic etiology; both imply that treatment often including medication, is necessary. Both can exist with or without hyperactivity. Both imply a difficulty in learning. Both can exist with or without the soft neurological signs.

Dr. Hochstedler concludes:

> The pattern we see over and over with ADD children in the early years is their inability to pay attention and behave properly, followed by parents and teachers viewing the child as bad or unacceptable, which in turn strikes directly at the children's sense of self-worth, leading to ever more destructive behavior, greater disapproval, and so on. If this cycle goes on long enough, we then are likely to see the emergence of a conduct disorder. At this point, we now have a second and far more serious disorder to deal with.

DSM III identifies school failure as common to ADD children and indicates that ADD is ten times more common in boys than girls. In contrast to conduct-disordered children, children with ADD require residential treatment only "infrequently."

We note that research has documented an association between hyperactivity and disturbance of conduct (Cantwell, 1980) suggesting some if not many CACs suffer from both ADD/hyperactivity and a conduct disorder, and between hyperactivity and learning disabilities (Osman, 1979). Also, Dr. Henry Kempe refers to the "aggressive, 'hyperactive' children who represent so many of the abused children we see. . . . These children seem veritable demons who have responded to the experience of aggression with almost manic activity" (Kempe and Kempe, 1978).

Conduct Disorder (CD)

Conduct-disordered children are first and foremost rulebreakers and are calloused toward the needs and rights of others. Among other things, they are very much at risk for later adult personality disorders, including sociopathy. Not all conduct-disordered persons or adult sociopaths are violent; DSM III distinguishes among several types, including aggressive versus nonaggressive and socialized versus nonsocialized. The conduct-disordered children who have exhibited assaultive behaviors, arson, sexually aggressive behaviors, obscene phone calls, and the like, are categorized as "aggressive" and pose a greater threat to society; others are labeled "nonaggressive". Conduct-disordered children who are perceived as never having had the opportunity to learn moral and ethical behavior are categorized as "nonsocialized." Those who have grown up with families in which appropriate limits were set and at least some nurturance was given are categorized as "socialized."

To make the general diagnosis, Dr. Hochstedler looks for significant negative behaviors (e.g., stealing, lying, fighting, using/selling drugs) *over a long period of time,* although the diagnosis can be made as early as age 7 or 8. He also determines whether there are one or two events in a child's life (e.g., divorce) that are followed shortly thereafter by acting-out behavior; this phenomenon is characteristic of adjustment disorders but not conduct disorders.

After making a diagnosis of CD, Dr. Hochstedler next tries to identify school and family factors that fuel the disorder. These typically include child abuse, harsh discipline, spousal violence and alcoholism, adoption, multiple dislocations, divorce, and parents' criminal activity and antisocial lifestyle. Often, three, four, five, or even more such factors are present together, frequently reinforced by such cultural/environmental influences as racism.

DSM III identifies numerous "associated features" of CD, including unusually early smoking, drinking, and other substance abuse; temper outbursts and provocative recklessness; and academic achievement below the level expected on the basis of intelligence and age. It further cites such "complications" as school suspensions, legal difficulties, venereal disease, unwanted pregnancies, suicidal behavior, and high rates of physical injuries from accidents and fights.

Dr. Hochstedler estimates that at least 50 percent of all CACs are conduct-disordered. As their condition worsens in adolescence, their demeanor and behavior tend increasingly to provoke those in authority to punish them. As noted earlier in regard to ADD children, the result is a downward spiral.

What is required is a comprehensive intervention plan that first limits the acting-out behavior, then addresses, through counseling, the multiple factors that originally gave impetus to the behavior as well as any related trauma, such as ADD, which often includes a learning disability. Nonspecific interventions will not suffice with the conduct-disordered child.

As noted earlier, the greatest concern is that conduct disorders will develop into adult personality disorders. This alarming process is fueled by punishment approaches, when what is needed is to hold the child responsible for his/her destructive behavior without branding the child "bad."

Clinical studies have documented a high correlation between conduct disorders and overactivity or attentional deficits (Sandberg et al., 1978; Stewart et al., 1980, 1981). Studies have also shown that CD children are more likely than children with emotional disorders to show persisting psychiatric and social impairment (see, e.g., Robins, 1966; Graham and Rutter, 1973).

Adjustment Disorder (AD)

Children suffering from adjustment disorders often exhibit behavior as bad or worse than that of those who are conduct-disordered. Like CD children, AD children may also have an attention deficit disorder. However, the distinguishing feature of AD children has nothing to do with their behavior. Instead, it is the presence of a single traumatic event, or several events all occurring at about the same time, followed shortly thereafter by acting-out behavior.

Once again, the diagnostic distinction is critical in terms of correctly identifying some basic things a child needs in order to recover. If a child is conduct-disordered, the antisocial behavior is ingrained and, in a sense, has a life of its own separate from those multiple factors that originally gave rise to the behavior. This necessitates a major investment of intervention expertise in both the behavioral and the underlying causative conditions.

In contrast, AD children are much less committed to their acting out, which generally recedes in direct ratio to therapy that is able to successfully address the precipitating event(s). Once AD children are assisted in squarely facing a traumatic event, such as loss of a parent, and are further aided in expressing their anger and other feelings in a nondestructive manner, the prognosis for understanding the event and for resolution is good. And because their acting-out behavior does not have a life of its own, the behavior does not prevent resolution of core conflicts, as it does with conduct-disordered behavior. Thus, intervention for AD children requires less structure, is much more narrowly focused than that for CD children, is usually less costly, and generally carries higher hopes for positive outcomes

Dr. Hochstedler estimates that AD children make up between 20 and 25 percent of all disordered children.

Other Psychiatric Observations

Not all children fall neatly into the three subcategories of behaviorally disordered. For example, certain chronic acting-out children feature almost all characteristics of a diagnostic category, whereas other children feature only some characteristics or characteristics of more than one category.

Somewhat different are those children who are neither psychotic, retarded, nor behaviorally disordered. DSM III utilizes a "V-Code" for these children and identifies parent–child problems (e.g., child abuse) as one associated condition. Although these children are outside the scope of this Handbook because they do not chronically act out, brief mention is made of them here to further illustrate the limitations of psychiatric diagnoses and to emphasize that these children's need for intervention can be as great as the need of those who tip off their condition through acting out.

Other Research

A significant body of child abuse research suggests that child abuse precipitates disorders in children. Most noteworthy for present purposes is research linking child abuse and conduct disorders. As one commentator notes, it should not come as a surprise that many children who are abused in early childhood come to develop mental health problems such as anxiety, depression, and conduct disorders (Lindhold, 1985).

Acting-Out Behaviors[1]

First, it is important to understand that acting out is a coping mechanism for children who have a limited response repertoire. Acting out is a coping mechanism in the sense that when stress mounts, the acting out releases it. Other people react to stress through flight, withdrawal, and/or disassociating. Why one child reacts one way and another facing the same or similar psychosocial stressors reacts another way is unclear. However, the remedial task is the same: to enlarge the child's repertoire—with language development being a key—and to attack the sources of stress, including child abuse.

Acting-out behaviors also tell me a number of other things:

1. They are blocking a student from learning; s/he does not have enough remaining psychic energy to concentrate and therefore to learn.
2. They are symptomatic of a more serious condition, often intrapsychic (chemical origins, such as schizophrenia) or family/environmental.
3. They adversely effect others, resulting in negative feedback to the child and frequently reenforcing or forming a repetitive cycle.
4. They are indicative of major stress, pain, and anger.
5. They comprise a defense against vulnerability, fear of closeness, low self-esteem, insecurity, and even suicidal ideation.
6. They suggest a serious breakdown in the child's ability to communicate his/her needs in more accepted ways.
7. They are attention-getting or "flagging" acts, intended to alert us to a child in distress.

All of these are part of a vicious cycle; each feeds on the other, all too frequently creating self- and school-fulfilling prophecies of failure.

Note

1. This section was provided by Dr. Densen-Gerber.

3
The Effects of
Abuse and Neglect
on Children

This Handbook is concerned with two phenomena: acting out and child abuse/neglect. We refer the reader to Chapter 10 and to the case histories (Chapters 4, 8, and 24) for additional discussion by Dr. Densen-Gerber on the meaning of such behaviors. Child abuse/neglect is discussed throughout the Handbook; however, in view of its devastating effects on child development and its central role in this Handbook, we present here a summary of some of those effects.

Dr. Densen-Gerber and many other commentators have made the point that children respond differently to the same or similar experiences of maltreatment. Thus, one group of children may respond by acting out, a second group by withdrawing, and a third by over-achieving. She explains this in terms of differences in genetic makeup and coping mechanisms.

The third group of children—overachievers—raises the question of whether some youth survive maltreatment without experiencing long-term developmental harm. The answer from the research community is, "As yet, we don't know." It should be kept in mind that child abuse as a distinct phenomenon worthy of study and national public policy attention is still quite new, dating back to 1962, which is when Dr. Henry Kempe published his article on the battered child syndrome. The bulk of society's energy in the child abuse sector since that time has gone toward creating public awareness and implementing the reporting system. At this juncture, we still know little about treating abuse victims, perhaps because research has not had time to precisely assess the long-term effects of abuse.

We are not, however, totally bereft of such data. First, we have a body of anecdotal information provided by professionals who have had ongoing contact with abuse victims. One of the most influential conveyers of this type of information was Dr. Kempe, who based his data on his clinical work with abused children and abusive parents in Denver. He believed that abuse has a "profound and scarring effect on a child's personal development and educational success." He cites delays in motor, social, cognitive, and speech development as common to abused children, such that many of these children enter school with "distinct disadvantages."

These and similar observations have been made by other frontline personnel and are mirrored by the research that has been done. Elizabeth Elmer is generally considered to be the first researcher to do a long-term follow-up analysis of child victims. Her 1967 study of thirty-three cases found 88 percent to be seriously affected, including mental retardation, speech defects, physical handicaps, and significant emotional disorders (Elmer and Gregg, 1967). In a later (1977) study of seventeen abused children eight years after maltreatment, the victims revealed impulsivity, poor school performance and social adjustment, speech difficulties, and behavioral disorders.

Some observers have pointed out that Elmer found similar deficits among members of her control group, who all came from lower SES backgrounds. This has prompted people such as Dr. Eli Newberger and even Elmer herself to caution against an assumption that abuse is the sole source of these children's problems; poverty and other socioeconomic factors may also be powerful causative agents. Kempe, however, theorized that Elmer's controls, although not known to have been maltreated, may well have been, thus accounting for the similarity in outcomes and confirming his belief that abuse/neglect is the most powerful agent.

Dr. Harold Martin (1976) has also conducted follow-up research on abuse victims, and found similarly disturbing effects. He and his colleagues assessed fifty-eight children five years after treatment. Some neurological abnormality was found in all but five cases. Noteworthy is that the fifty-eight cases were not especially severe in terms of their maltreatment.

Other findings of long-term follow-up studies include significant intellectual or emotional deficits (Morse et al., 1970) and developmental delays in language (Kent, 1976). Additional studies, though not longitudinal, have noted other effects of child maltreatment on some victims: suicide attempts (Maisch, 1976; Molnar and Cameron, 1976); conduct disorder (Brown et al., 1985); poor self-image (Conte, 1985); and psychiatric illness in adulthood (Carmên et al., 1984).

In a study of 500 students in San Diego, half with records of alleged maltreatment and half without, school personnel were asked to rate both groups of children. The researchers, Smith and Bohnstedt (1984), report:

> As hypothesized, both nurses and counselors more frequently rated victims below average in academic achievement, social adjustment and peer relations, as contrasted to comparison subjects. School nurses rated 37% of victims as having a serious problem on one or more dimensions, contrasted to 15% of comparison subjects. District counselors rated 44% of the victims as having a serious problem on one or more dimensions, and 56% were rated below average on at least one criterion. This contrasts with 10% and 12% respectively for comparison subjects. . . . Since low school achievement and school behavior problems are strongly correlated with child victimization, we are currently exploring the implications of these findings for intervention strategies and for improved inter-agency cooperation.

Recently, Dr. Margaret Lynch (1984), senior lecturer in community pediatrics at Guy's Hospital in London, has reported on her follow-up study of forty physically abused children who, along with their families, had undergone residential treatment at Park Hospital in London. Notwithstanding this specialized therapeutic care and some very substantial gains, four years later, 63 percent of the abused children continued to experience significant problems of a neurological, developmental, intellectual, and behavioral nature.

Dr. David Finkelhor has surveyed the various short- and long-term effects of child sexual abuse as reported in many different studies. Notwithstanding the contention of some researchers that the effects have been greatly overstated, he concludes that the best evidence to date suggests that sexual abuse is a "serious mental health problem, consistently associated with very disturbing subsequent problems in a significant portion of its victims" (Finkelhor, 1986).

Additional research, discussed in Chapter 6, has found links between child abuse and such problems as learning disabilities, truancy, running away, and juvenile delinquency. The research evidence would therefore seem to make a convincing case that child maltreatment leads to all manner of developmental retardants. The problem, as numerous commentators (e.g., Newberger) have pointed out, is that nearly all research that has been done suffers from one or more methodological flaws, which make it impossible to conclude that abuse alone causes specific outcomes. Given the multiproblem nature of most abusive families, it is difficult to control for other individual, family, and socioenvironmental factors that adversely affect a child's development.

And, as Garbarino (1984) has noted, the sequence of events is crucial; for example, does a child become hyperactive and aggressive after the onset of abuse or do hyperactivity and aggression occur first and then provoke abusive responses? Still another problem is that abuse researchers are usually in the position of using victim subjects whose condition is so bad that they have come to the attention of authorities. We know very little about abuse victims who never come to the attention of the courts, schools, or mental health agencies. Presumably, some of these victims are able to withstand abusive treatment without major harm.

However, the children who are the subject of this Handbook have the shared characteristic of being known to a system—not necessarily for child abuse but for chronic acting out and school failure. It is therefore informative for educators to note the "effects" data in this and following chapters, which, as a whole, suggest a pattern of developmental delays (especially in the critical area of language facility), inability to concentrate, repeated acting out, and school failure. The presence of these factors does not prove that child abuse is involved, but the anecdotal and research data suggest that it is a *probable* attendant factor. At the least, evaluating personnel should be mindful that abuse or neglect may underlie the manifest problems in school.

Making these connections is essential if the children involved are to be properly assessed and treated. Otherwise, the prevailing tendency is for educators to make increasingly punitive responses, so that by the time these children reach junior high school, they are often viewed almost exclusively as disciplinary problems. We would add that notwithstanding many unanswered research questions concerning the effects of maltreatment, including causative issues, sufficient data exist for educators to conclude that when child abuse/neglect is present, it is a major impediment to chronic acting-out children in getting themselves sufficiently under control to succeed academically.

4
Case 1:
George, Age 16

Summary Assessment Profile

A. CHILD FACTORS
1. **Academic Performance**

Public school history: George's mother says that he was described by his kindergarten teacher as "dumb and stupid." George repeated kindergarten and second grade because of learning difficulties and delays. These problems are likely related to a significant hearing loss during his formative years. Also, George's language development was hindered because of his deafness.

It appears that he was never fully promoted from one grade to the next but was promoted for social reasons. During midyear of fifth grade, he was moved to grade six because of his large size and social awareness. The last grade he completed was grade seven. Although he failed most subjects, he was placed in grade eight.

His available report cards, going back to 1980–81, reveal poor school performance, with mostly Ds and Fs in major subjects.

a. *Language competency:* Recent school testing done by residential staff indicates reading and math achievement to be fifth-year level, about two years behind his grade placement and four to five years behind his chronological age achievement expectancy. George exhibits deficits in basic language skills such as reading and spelling.

b. *Areas of success:* He usually receives Cs and Bs in home economics. George states he always worked in this class because "you ate what you made."

2. **Acting-Out Behaviors**
a. *Age of onset:* 10.
b. *Types and places:*
  (1) *School:* Threatening and bullying classmates, beginning in third grade. George claims this was in retaliation for their making fun of him. A 1980 school report describes George as "having a short fuse . . . easily frustrated, a disrupter in class." At onset of adolescence, he began to truant. When he did attend school, he was frequently cited for rule infractions. In one two-month period, the school took fourteen separate disciplinary actions for a variety of behavioral offenses.

(2) *Home:* George also began to lose control in the home at age 10. He punched walls and generally was oppositional. He also was violent (see *sibling violence*). At 12, he began to drink at home.

(3) *Community:* At age 14, George's delinquent conduct in the community led to frequent involvement with the juvenile court. Offenses included fire setting, malicious damage to property, and shooting out building windows with a gun. He also appeared before the court on CHINS offenses.

3. **Medical/Psychiatric Status**

   a. *Size/appearance:* George is about 5'11", 140 lb., and very lean. He has poor posture and a distinctive gait.

   b. *History of injuries, illnesses, handicaps:* George missed many activities that normal children experience because he was born with a hearing impediment. He was also in a wheelchair as a toddler because of a disability caused by the ball and socket of his hips growing incorrectly, turning his feet inward. He underwent corrective surgery at age 5 and was bedridden for six months. George wore corrective shoes until age 9.

   To correct the hearing deficit which was not discovered until approximately age 6, he underwent ear surgery. Until age 13, he continually needed medical treatment for ear fluid and hearing problems.

   c. *Neurological impairment:* George has a sensorineural hearing loss in both ears.

   d. *Psychiatric diagnosis:*

   Axis I—conduct disorder in adolescence with mixed behavioral and emotional features.

   Axis II—none.

   Axis III—by history: bilateral hearing loss, partially corrected surgically.

4. **IQ**

   a. *Full scale:* 89

   b. *Verbal:* 82

   c. *Performance:* 98

5. **Child Maltreatment History**

   a. *Source:* Intrafamily, peer, institutional.

   b. *Type:* Physical, emotional/psychological, neglect.

   George reports that his adoptive father began to physically abuse him when he was 10. Usually he was beaten with a belt or punched. George also indicates that his mother would occasionally use a belt on him. Other children in the home have also been abused by both parents. In addition, George was taunted by peers at an early age because of his physical handicaps. He was also the victim of institutional (school) abuse on at least one occasion, when his teacher called him "stupid."

   Neglect is present as evidenced by the mother's history of frequenting bars. Also, visitors to the home describe the living conditions as filthy.

   c. *Severity:* The physical abuse was quite severe, as was the neglect.

   d. *Frequency:* The physical abuse occurred regularly, and the mother's neglect has been pervasive.

   e. *Duration:* Physical abuse since age 10; neglect predating age 10.

6. **Substance Abuse:** George admits to being alcoholic and has attended A.A. as part of his treatment. He also acknowledges prior heavy marijuana use, beginning at age 14.

7. **Suicide Attempts:** None that were obvious. However, George would often respond with anger toward his parents by acting recklessly—for example, going as fast as he could downhill on his bike without using the brakes.

8. **Educational Handicap:** George has been coded "learning disabled" since grade one.

9. **Cultural Factors:** Caucasian, French/Irish, Catholic.

10. **Peer Relationships:** George was a loner for the most part, partially because of his hearing deficit. His companionship was more with his stepfather, uncle, and grandfather than with peers. His tendency was to hang out with adults, telling yarns and drinking.

11. **Strengths:** George still has such a beaten-down sense that strengths are not readily apparent. However, he demonstrated a desire to learn at the special school he now attends and an ability to attain some academic success.

12. **Other**
    a.   George's mother has historically assigned him the role of caretaker for the younger children in the family. When he talks about his mother, he sounds like a disgruntled but protective father.
    b.   George's mother often "entertained" male friends at home in her doorless bedroom.

B.   FAMILY FACTORS
1.   **Changing Parental Figures**
    a.   *Divorce/remarriage/equivalent:* George's biological parents were married in 1965. They separated several months after George's birth and divorced in 1970.

    His mother remarried in 1972. She and her second husband had three children (all girls). Prior to this marriage, her second husband had four sons and a daughter. In 1982, they were divorced. George was sent to live with his stepfather because his mother felt he was too difficult a child. However, the stepfather and his live-in girlfriend claim they could not handle George's behavior and returned him to his mother. George's mother subsequently married a third time. They had no children and were recently divorced.
    b.   *Adoption:* The mother's second husband adopted George and George's biological sister in 1982.
    c.   *Foster parents:* none.
    d.   *Deaths/disappearance/abandonment:* George has not seen his biological father since the divorce in 1970.

2.   **Siblings:** George is the fourth of ten children. His siblings include one biological sister, four stepbrothers, one stepsister, and three half-sisters. Not surprisingly, George expresses confusion over family relationships.

3.   **Economic Status:** George's mother is on welfare, and his stepfather is only periodically employed.

4.   **Spousal/Sibling Violence:** George's biological father beat George's mother throughout the marriage, including during pregnancies. The abuse was the grounds for their divorce. The second husband was not physically abusive to

George's mother, but her third husband was. George himself has attacked family members, including breaking his sister's nose and throwing his mother across the room. George claims these attacks were provoked by family disagreements, sibling teasing, and criticism or discipline by a parent.

5. **Parental/Sibling Substance Abuse:** George's mother is an alcoholic, with a history of frequenting local bars as well as drinking at home with her children, including George starting at age 12. On at least one occasion, George threatened his mother with a baseball bat to prevent her from going out to drink. George's older sisters abuse alcohol and drugs.

6. **Parental/Sibling Perpetration of Child Maltreatment:** The physical abuse was primarily by George's step/adoptive father, who is no longer in the home. There was secondary physical abuse by George's mother. The neglect was primarily by George's mother, abandonment by the biological father.

7. **Relocations:** George has resided all his life in the same community. However, his family lived in eleven different apartments, resulting in George's changing schools on two occasions.

8. **Psychiatric/Medical Status of Parent(s):** George's mother has twice tried to commit suicide. Little is known about the specifics concerning these attempts.

9. **Integration/Isolation:** George's isolation has been caused in part by his mother's assigning him a major child care role at home since George was about 10.
   a. *Family:* There is a lot of discord within the extended family, but there is a sense of family.
   b. *Community:* George's family was/is perceived as a poor, neglected family. They have no real integration within the community.

10. **Advocacy Capability:** None of the three father figures has taken an active interest in George. Neither has his mother. None of the parents appears to have advocacy capability.

11. **Other:** None.

C. PRIOR SYSTEM INTERVENTIONS
   1. **Public Schools:** George was identified as a "special needs" child in grade one for specific learning disabilities, although he was not coded for his hearing deficit. He received special educational services throughout his public school experience. Services have included speech/language therapy and tutorial instruction for reading and language-related skills. However, no program of therapeutic counseling was ever implemented by the schools.

   2. **Child Protection:** No CPS interventions were made prior to George's placement at a residential program, where the professional staff filed neglect and abuse reports with CPS. The reports were based on other children still being in the home. George's mother subsequently stated that a "mentally retarded neighbor" filed the reports.

   3. **Judicial:** The first court intervention was at age 14 on a CHINS complaint filed by the school for truancy. George and his family were referred to counseling. At the end of this period, George was back in court on new charges involving damage to property and criminal mischief. He received one year of probation and was required to make restitution. A month later, a second CHINS petition was filed for truancy, resulting in a second order of probation and a condition of good behavior. When George continued to act out, the court modified the order to placement at a residential program.

4. **Mental Health:** Prior to his present placement, George attended outpatient counseling for six months per the aforenoted court order.

Interview with Dr. Densen-Gerber

David Sandberg (DS): What is the ethos of this case based on your review of the reports?

Dr. D-G: Chaos, drinking together, loose sexual boundaries, constant changes, disruption, no roots, physical abuse and neglect, changing figures, physical handicaps, and the absence of credible role models. Foremost, the case illustrates institutional abuse and neglect.

DS: What is the institutional maltreatment?

Dr. D-G: For one thing, there is no reason why the system waited to age 13 to rectify his hearing deficiency. Furthermore, he was never specifically coded for the hearing loss, being called "dumb and stupid" does not help, and neither does the lack of the school system ever notifying the child protection system when it must have been apparent to everyone that this was likely an abused or at the least a neglected child.

DS: In addition to the institutional maltreatment, what initially strikes you?

Dr. D-G: First, I note that he is white and, although a little on the tall side, really of average size. Both of these put him in the mainstream. Children do not wish to feel different, and the presence of mainstream factors offers some encouragement regarding outcome in these cases.

Second he is the fourth of ten children, and in so large a family—even if his mother was very strong, which she is not—it would be difficult for George to receive sufficient nurturance. This is especially so given the chaotic father figure situation in this family.

Third, why does his step/adoptive father have his children living with him? It may be indicative of the first wife being totally unable to nurture her children. If so, we can assume these children came into George's home with significant nurturing deficits. This view is further supported by the step/adoptive father hardly being a caring figure himself. A related concern here is George having been the oldest among his biological family, then being replaced by the older step-siblings. This meant to George that he had to redefine his role within this suddenly enlarged family, and it is unlikely these parents assisted him in doing this. The introduction of older siblings into a family is very traumatic.

Fourth, George was also confronted with the new men his mother kept bringing into the house, forcing yet another role adjustment on George, who is his mother's oldest male child. It is very likely that George expended a lot of energy trying to adapt and adjust to these constant changes in his family constellation, energy other children had available to devote to learning. And keep in mind, we haven't even considered the violence, abuse, and handicaps, which are major factors here.

DS: What does George's diagnosis of "conduct disorder" mean, and how serious is the underlying condition?

Dr. D-G: His diagnosis of CD means that he has crossed the line from episodic acting out to being clearly antisocial, with CD often being the forerunner of adult sociopathy. It's a very serious disorder and, if unchecked, will likely evolve into sociopathy. It's a disease with a natural course.

DS: What is the effects of George's mother carrying on sexually in the home with the bedroom door open?

Dr. D-G: It is an "incest equivalent," meaning that he is allowed to indirectly share sexual intimacy with his mother. This has very significant implications, especially for schools—for example, whether he can "hear" better from a male or female teacher. If he is enraged at his mother for her extraordinary sexual conduct, which he may well be, there will be a lot of negative female or mother transference. This means he will tend to project his hostile feelings about his own mother onto female teachers. This will result in his being "blocked" from hearing female teachers; consequently, a male teacher would be better. However, if he is singularly focused on her as the one constant in his life, he may be receptive only to a female teacher. This prospect is made more plausible by the presence of abusive father figures. I need more information to make this determination, but what I can say with confidence is that transferential issues are extremely important factors in George's being able to learn and that he very likely can learn significantly better from one sex than from the other.

Aside from transference and the incest equivalent, the mother's continuing sexual activity with her husbands and other men who she did not marry has to cause George much shame. Such shame is devastating to a child and usually results in lowered self-esteem and embarrassment at bringing a friend to the home. Absent treatment, we should not expect George to gain sufficient cognitive distance to understand these feelings, which add further emotional turmoil.

Moreover, despite all the abuse, neglect, and shame, he will be compelled to defend his mother in particular. The mother engaging in sexual activity in a bedroom with no door is also clearly indicative of a person whose sense of propriety and boundaries falls way outside the norm and may evidence severe psychiatric disturbance. Lastly, I am not sure we have the total incest picture. George as the oldest biological male of this mother may well have been exposed to more than we know about. In any event, we have the equivalent.

DS: Any comments about divorce in this case?

Dr. D-G: His biological parents' divorce is more than a divorce; it's abandonment by the father. Thus, we can assume that abandonment is an ever-present trauma to George, and educators need to know this. It should tell them that he is very sensitive about abandonment issues and may perceive abandonment when you and I do not.

DS: What is your explanation for George's liking and doing well in home economics?

Dr. D-G: Home economics was the one place where George could gain gratification. It was the one place in school where well-developed language skills were not needed. Also, doing well in this class signals that George wanted to do well in school. I understand he is experiencing success at the special school he now attends.

DS: What other significance does all the coming and going of people in his home, especially father figures, have for his educators?

Dr. D-G: All of the "coming-and-going" makes it especially important that George have a primary teacher with whom he spends most of the day. Unfortunately, middle and senior high schools are not structured this way, thereby recreating the lack of stability that characterizes the primary home. This boy, for one, will not learn until the "coming-and-going" stops, and this explains in part why he is well-placed at the present school, where he learns many subjects from the same teacher. Other children from reasonably stable homes can tolerate such "coming-and-going." People like George usually cannot.

I want to emphasize again how much all children—K–6 kids in particular—need constancy of place and constancy of face. Even so-called normal children need this at school. A child like George needs it even more, and he will need it right through high school because of his deficits. Unfortunately, once he gets to junior and senior high, he will be made to feel different and inadequate if he is kept in a single room or with a primary teacher, because all the other students are moving from class to class. However, changes in the educational system should be made to accommodate the many youngsters like George from chaotic primary-nurturing settings.

DS: At this juncture, let me ask you your opinion about George's ability to do well in school with all this going on.

Dr. D-G: It borders on the unbelievable to think that George could go to school each day, concentrate, and have sufficient stability to learn. If he had gone to school and done well, I would have to postulate that he was in some type of disassociative state. But once he was in an environment that understood him, he revealed a desire and an ability to learn.

DS: How bad is George's case, at least based on as much as we've discussed so far?

Dr. D-G: As bad as George's situation is, there are much worse home environments. At least he had constancy in the same mother figure and the continuing presence of the biological siblings, and his family did not continually move from one community to another, unlike some other cases. How beneficial these "constants" have been is difficult to say, but at least his world has not been totally unpredictable and rootless.

DS: What about the other forms of maltreatment in this case?

Dr. D-G: George has been physically abused by both his mother and father figures. So, in addition to her very damaging open sexual conduct, she beats George and threatens him with her own suicide. This adds enormous additional stress and anxiety, further blocking him from learning. We must remember that (1) she is his mother and (2) she is the only constant adult figure he has known.

I suppose for us adults to really understand, we would have to imagine ourselves as teachers being continuously subjected to violence, rampant sexual conduct, and death threats and then expected to come to class with the patience and understanding needed to teach. Add to this a threat of being fired if we responded emotionally or behaviorally, and you begin to get a sense of the double bind these children are in. The double bind is, of course, that these children, through no fault of their own, are being filled with anxiety at home, then placed in a frustrating situation at school where they are emotionally blocked from learning. This leads to acting out to release the enormous stress, which in turn leads to further punishments and sometimes even more abuse at home for getting in trouble in school.

Before continuing, I want to point out how particularly devastating it is for mothers who are the primary nurturing figure, such as George's mother, to abuse their young. It places the child in the intolerable position of having to fear the very person s/he looks to for nurturance.

Also, regardless of who does the abusing, physical abuse victims, as Dr. Hochstedler pointed out in our first NCCAN project, exhibit significant difficulty in distinguishing between nurturance and violence, because in their experience the two often come in the same package. Dr. Hochstedler also indicated that for some sexual abuse victims, nurturance and sexual exploitation become jumbled, thus offering some explanation of why child victims often get themselves into terribly exploitative, abusive situations as adolescents and in adulthood. Unlike you and me, victims often have a great deal of difficulty keeping these things clearly separated. Many feel it is better to be beaten than ignored, and they interpret violence as caring.

DS: Let's stop once again and ask about the effect of all this on George.

Dr. D-G: The sum of all this to George is an overwhelming feeling of powerlessness. He can't stop his mother from carrying on sexually with men; he can't stop the violence; he can't stop the threat of suicide.

In addition, he is further different from his peers because of a hearing deficit that his mother never responded to. He also had to be in a wheelchair during the preschool years, adding an even greater feeling of powerlessness. I cannot emphasize enough how devastating it is for children to feel different. We can fully expect that his handicapping conditions gave rise to additional feelings of anger. Even in a highly supportive nurturing home environment, this boy would need special attention.

DS: How do you interpret George's substance abuse?

Dr. D-G: For him, he used substances mainly to alleviate emotional pain, to escape failure in the home and school, which were the totality of his world.

DS: Your thoughts on his language deficiencies?

Dr. D-G: Not surprisingly, psychological testing reveals low vocabulary scores. The tragedy is that a child such as this is desperately in need of good language skills to articulate his anger, pain, and needs. Yet his language skills are very poorly developed, greatly reducing his response repertoire and thereby increasing the likelihood of acting-out behaviors being the primary means of expression.

Also, the significant discrepancy between performance and verbal scores on the WISC IQ testing is very common with chronic acting-out people. It indicates that they have good basic intelligence but are thwarted in utilizing it productively because of poor language skills, resulting in feelings of frustration and anger. This directly relates to "blocking" and their requiring maximum language development inputs. But in the interim, a child like George needs additional ways of releasing his extreme anger and frustration. Running, hiking, punching bags, and similar athletic activities are useful outlets.

DS: What are your thoughts about George's acting out in school?

Dr. D-G: Some of it makes perfect sense. For example, he retaliates against classmates who torment him about his handicap. An appropriate educator response would be to have the entire school learn that sadistic behaviors toward peers are unsocialized and unacceptable. It is the school's job to help socialize the young. If one wants to compare misbehaviors, the tormenting is an affront to the school environment, whereas George's retaliation is at least understandable.

George's truancy is also logical when interpreted as removing himself from continuing failure and escalating feelings of negative self-worth. The adult counterpart is to resign from a bad job situation. So, is this behavior maladaptive? It depends on how you view it. And certainly the fourteen disciplinary actions, which I presume were punitive in nature, will not do anything positive for a youth like George, who has been severely punished by both parents for years. For a 14-year-old from a stable home and without handicaps who is just into adolescent rebellion, these responses might do some good. For George, they will do no good. Worse, they reinforce his feelings of being valueless and not belonging in school.

DS: As George's acting out escalated within the schools, what would have been a better response for educators to have made?

Dr. D-G: He needed one-to-one counseling, bonding with a responsible adult, consistency, small classrooms, play therapy, home visits, and family therapy to enable him to ventilate his feelings of rage and deprivation. He also needed prompt correction of his hearing deficiencies. He was not an oppositional child. As previously noted, he wanted to do well in school. Also, he will not respond well to punishment; he needs positive reinforcement. It is not that some of the educators involved with George in the public schools didn't care. They probably did, but it required more than caring to make the needed decisions on his behalf.

DS: Although the school acting out seems to have been relatively benign, his acting out elsewhere became increasingly serious. What do you make of it?

Dr. D-G: Breaking his sister's nose and shooting out windows are more recent behaviors that are indeed disturbing. They mean, "I am enraged and I am out of control." He was prehomicidal, and the court was correct in sending him to a residential treatment center with close supervision. Once he reached adolescence without the interventions he needed, he quickly became too much for the school system.

DS: But I take it you are still convinced that prior to the escalation of behavior in adolescence, the public schools could have handled him?

Dr. D-G: There is no question in my mind that he was a proper candidate for mainstreaming in the public schools, especially in K–6. Notwithstanding all his deficits when he first arrived at school, he could have made it. He was not so disturbed then that he needed residential treatment. He needed a nongraded system with much "stroking" and encouragement and a school advocate who could follow him year after year.

If all the work that is being done now had been started in grade K, when it should have been very clear that he was in great need, there's a good chance he could have succeeded in public schools. The schools lost this one. I do not say that to blame them, but simply to point out what can be done in these cases. I also want to reiterate that if schools want to improve interventions with acting-out children, especially those who are maltreated, they will have to face their own contribution to a child's failure. It is not just the children and the parents who have contributed to the problems. We can say that George's mother didn't know any better because she was too ill. She is a person experiencing a great deal of inner turmoil who can't protect herself and might well respond favorably to a system person's reaching out to her.

But educators, being in the child development business, should have known that George was in major need of help as early as grade K. All he received was limited help and then increasing punishment for his school misbehaviors. Even with the family chaos, the public school has to accept responsibility for this failure.

DS: Lastly, what is your sense of the impact on George of not having made it in the public schools?

Dr. D-G: It reinforced all the failure he was experiencing in the home and his personal feelings of powerlessness.

Part II
Description of Chronic Acting-Out Children

5
A Broad View

Factors Involved in Chronic Acting-Out Behavior

A composite picture of chronic acting-out children includes the following factors:

Child abuse and neglect

Learning disabilities and other special education handicaps

Substance abuse

Multiple parental figures, divorce, death, abandonment

Multiple relocations

School failure, suspensions, expulsion, dropout

Conduct disorder

Foster home placement

Victimization/self-mutilation

Victimizing

Attention deficit disorder

Lack of trust

Confusion over sex, violence, and nurturance

History of physical injuries, illnesses, and hospitalization

Neurological impairment, CNS damage (MBD), impulse disorder

Anger, rage, frustration, depression

As a case in point, we refer to a recent special education hearing that considered the adequacy of an IEP for a 10-year-old boy named Thomas who is coded seriously emotionally disturbed. The hearing officer's written decision references the following: emotional and behavioral problems; severe punishment by his father, resulting in two child abuse reports filed by the school; difficulty with impulse control; periodic suicidal behaviors (e.g., running in front of cars); above-average IQ; attention deficit disorder; presence of "many problems" every school year, including disruption in class; suspension for hitting a teacher aide; potential conduct disorder; depression and anger.

One might ask, "What can we do when confronted with such multiproblem children?" First and foremost, we suggest stopping the abuse, which apparently the school was able to do after filing two reports with child protection. Significantly, special education personnel and the hearing officer openly acknowledged Thomas as an abused child, including the statement of a psychiatric social worker that "Tommy was typical of many abused children who provoke others into abusing them." A report by a clinical psychologist noted that "Tommy's thematic stories were replete with themes of children being punished, often unfairly. He has a lot of fear, anger and resentment associated with punishment."

Recognition of Tommy's abuse, his educationally handicapped status, and his corresponding special needs are cornerstones of hope. It is difficult to imagine a positive outcome in this case without awareness of these issues. Yet much more is involved. For example, his ADD condition was an obvious complicating factor that required expert evaluation. In Tommy's case, Ritalin was found to be a useful agent, but, appropriately, its calming effects were not allowed to be used as evidence that Tommy's emotional and behavioral problems had vanished.

All in all, it is a grim prospect to face up to all the conditions that obstruct the normal development of children such as Tommy. This very grimness is no doubt responsible, in part, for the historical tendency to view these children in an overly simplistic and often negative manner. Respected professional leaders from the child abuse community have been instrumental in beginning the process of broadening our understanding of disruptive, often unlikeable children. Dr. Vincent Fontana, a pioneering physician in the child abuse field, has observed that most teenage delinquents, alcoholics, drug addicts, and prostitutes are products of multi problem homes where they suffered abuse and neglect. The Kempes note that:

> Not all children who have been abused are compliant and anxious to please. At least one fourth of the young children (and more, we suspect, of the older ones) are negative, aggressive, and often hyperactive as well. These children seem veritable demons, who have responded to the experience of aggression with almost manic activity. They move constantly, unable to sit still or attend more than briefly, and are almost completely incapable of playing acceptably with other children. (Kempe and Kempe, 1978)

Boys Town, which has observed and cared for many troubled and maltreated children over the years, has also attempted to educate the public about multiple linking factors. In its publication *Clues of Learning Disabilities,* mention is made of such related factors as short attention span, extreme overactivity (or underactivity), a quick temper, and a tendency to be impulsive. Such clues are also associated with child maltreatment.

The links between child maltreatment and other disruptive phenomenon are discussed in detail in Chapter 6. Beyond maltreatment linkages, research has also established connections among a number of our other composite factors, further drawing together this complex mosaic that makes up many CACs. For example, conduct disorder has been linked with attentional deficits (Stewart et al., 1981). In fact, one of the major findings of our project is the striking number of interrelationships involving the factors cited at the beginning of this chapter.

Our intent in identifying these factors and their relationships is to increase the understanding of people in the educational, child protection, and juvenile justice systems about what is meant by labeling children "multiproblem" children. We are also interested in getting these people to appreciate fully the extent of these children's difficulties, which make productive learning and acceptable behavior so hard.

We pause here to caution against an assumption that the presence of some composite factors implies the presence of others. We use the term *composite* advisedly, noting that not all factors are present in all cases. To further make this important point, the aforenoted Boys Town publication indicates that "children with learning disabilities do not usually show all these signs, and children who do not have learning disabilities may show some of them . . . a pattern of these characteristics, when they are persistent, may indicate that the youngster has a learning disability." Also, adolescent CACs are apt to exhibit more of these factors than preadolescent CACs are.

Nevertheless, all CACs are multiproblem children. Moreover, intervenors have to guard against drowning in a sea of professional depression. There are hopeful signs. First, as wounded as many of these children are, they often have strengths. For example, Tommy has good intellectual resources, as evidenced by his IQ score and above-average language scores. Susan, whose case history is given in Chapter 8, has superior intelligence and good survival instincts and has avoided major substance abuse. Larry (Chapter 24) is good with his hands (e.g., carpentry). Rather than construing these pluses as evidence that there is nothing really wrong with these children (in fact, a lot is wrong), they can be seen as reasons to be hopeful, provided that a comprehensive assessment is done and that remediation efforts target the more handicapping deficits. Appropriate remediation includes involvement of persons with the needed expertise whenever possible. Thus, for example, the hearing officer in Tommy's case correctly concluded that the public school's special education personnel, notwithstanding "many good faith efforts," were simply not equipped to provide him with the combination educational and therapeutic milieu he needs. In turn, this was the basis for the officer's ordering a residential placement.

We would like to make one additional point in encouraging a broad view of chronic acting-out children. Some distinction needs to be made between what we call secondary or backdrop issues and primary issues. For example, being a COA or a child of divorce is unquestionably a very significant life experience. For some children, such factors can even reach the level of a foremost inhibitor of healthy development. Because these experiences are so common to chronic acting-out children, we have developed materials on them for inclusion in this Handbook. However, maltreatment, substance addiction, or serious learning disabilities quickly rise to the top as priority concerns that must be identified and remediated if chronic acting-out students are to avoid major disasters such as expulsion.

Utilizing this major versus secondary issue assessment approach is admittedly risky. For one thing, it can blind people to important connections between factors. For another, it can suggest that factors given secondary status are not important. However, it is our opinion that widespread acceptance of a broad view approach to chronic acting-out children is contingent on prioritizing the numerous issues that adversely impact them. Absent this framework, most professionals, including educators, are apt to feel overwhelmed and paralyzed.

One must begin somewhere. We leave it to each assessor group to determine priority issues requiring initial attention, except for child maltreatment, which we and current laws accord top priority status in all cases.

Theories Regarding Origins of Acting-Out Behavior

As one might imagine when examining something as complex as acting-out behaviors, researchers have come upon many different theories to explain the "whys" behind the behaviors. The many theories about the origins of delinquency, for example, can be consolidated within three main categories:

Individual factors: Researchers favoring this theory argue that individual or personal factors, such as learning disabilities and neurological impairment, best explain the delinquent behavior of many youth.

Parental or family factors: This theory holds that the parents and the parent–child relationship are the keys to understanding delinquency. Thus, such things as parental discipline, maltreatment of offspring, spousal violence, and parental alcoholism are considered of foremost significance.

Sociological or environmental factors: Researchers adhering to this theory believe that factors external to the individual or the family, such as racism, classicism, and peer and gang influences, best explain why children engage in delinquency.

Other researchers believe that the three theories must be individually considered and in relationship with one another if the origins of delinquency are to be properly understood. We take a similar view of CACs, whether delinquent or not, although once again we give priority attention to child abuse. This is not because researchers have established that child maltreatment is the chief cause of acting out; they have not. Rather, we know that chronic acting out is often a symptom of maltreatment, which poses a major and often an immediate threat to a child's individual, family, and educational well-being.

Cause and Effect: Linkages and Nonlinkages

As the foregoing discussion indicates, no single factor has ever been shown to be the primary explanation for delinquent conduct, nor is it likely that one ever will be. However, many years of delinquency research have pointed to a number of factors that show up in study after study: race, low socioeconomic status, large families, severe parental discipline, and poor educational experiences. In more recent years, studies have demonstrated an unusually high prevalence of child abuse and learning disabilities among delinquent children. In addition, we know from direct service experience that numerous other factors, such as substance abuse, are commonly seen in acting-out students.

In the effort to organize all of these factors in a useful way, it is helpful to consider causation. Very likely, each of these factors contributes to a child's acting out. But researchers have not been able to isolate one from the other, assigning causative weight to each. On the other hand, researchers have shown that some of these factors, including maltreatment, are present among chronic acting-out youth at a much higher statistical rate than among similarly situated youth.

From a lay perspective the terms *cause* and *effect*, used informally, can be helpful in better understanding the role of each factor. For example, child maltreatment can be seen as a cause, and the myriad difficulties that thereafter befall the child victim (e.g., being violent or truant, failing in school) can be seen as effects. In a similar manner, spousal violence, parental alcoholism, divorce, relocations, and other family trauma are frequently significant precursors of difficulties in school. Viewed in this manner, certain student behaviors can be seen as effects (or symptoms), thereby warranting an examination of causes.

Another consideration when examining the assorted factors associated with chronic acting out is that some factors have a demonstrated link with one another, whereas others do not—or the link has not been clearly established by researchers. For example, both learning disabilities and child abuse have been empirically linked to delinquency, which can be seen as a certain type of CAC behavior. In addition, there is evidence that child abuse is linked to educational handicaps. On the other hand, divorce and parental alcoholism is at such a high rate nationally that it can no longer be said that delinquent children experience these family conditions at a higher rate than nondelinquent children. However, because divorce and multiple relocations are increasingly understood as potentially traumatic experiences, any intervention with chronic acting-out students must consider them.

The factors we discuss in Chapter 6 have empirically based linkages, whereas the ones in Chapter 7 do not. Yet all are significant in the lives of many of these children.

6
A Closer Look

Some of the sections in this chapter draw heavily upon research data related to delinquents. The question arises of how delinquents are relevant to younger children who act in nondelinquent ways? The answer is that they share the important trait of chronic acting-out behavior; therefore, reliable information about one group can be helpful in understanding the other.

For example, if delinquent CACs have high rates of learning disabilities (LDs), it is not unreasonable to conclude that nondelinquent CACs *may* have similarly high rates, thereby warranting an inquiry about LD in individual cases. It is quite another matter to conclude that a nondelinquent CAC with LD *will* become delinquent when there is no data to support such a forecast. Yet it would be unrealistic to think that such a child is not more susceptible to later delinquency than non-CACs are.

It also strikes us as unhelpful to ignore a valuable body of delinquency research on the basis that it has no relevancy until a child actually becomes a delinquent, especially when delinquency is viewed as simply one type of chronic acting-out behavior. Until researchers are able to develop data on younger nondelinquent CACs, we are necessarily in the position of looking to delinquency research as an important way of better understanding these children.

The Relationship between Child Abuse and Delinquency

In the past several years, considerable public attention has been paid to the frequency with which child abuse is present in the backgrounds of delinquent children. Prominent examples include hearings conducted by the U.S. Senate Subcommittee on Juvenile Justice (1983) and workshops sponsored by the Denver-based National Conference of State Legislatures at regional (Washington, D.C., 1983) and annual (Boston, 1984) meetings for members of the nation's fifty state legislatures. Also, federal government agencies with jurisdiction over child abuse (National Center on Child Abuse and Neglect) and delinquency (Office of Juvenile Justice and Delinquency Prevention) have funded research-related activities.

In addition, most major child abuse conferences in the past several years have included seminars on the abuse–delinquency connection. Examples include the Sixth National Conference on Child Abuse and Neglect (Baltimore, 1983), the Fifth International Congress on

Child Abuse and Neglect (Montreal, 1984), and the Seventh National Conference on Child Abuse and Neglect (Chicago, 1985).

The primary impetus for all this attention has been a relatively small but harmonious body of research indicating that child abuse is present in from 50 to 100 percent of delinquent populations. For example, in our 1982–83 NCCAN-funded study of 150 delinquents, we found an abuse rate of 65 percent, with over half of the abuse victims having experienced more than one kind of abuse or the same kind of abuse by more than one parent. Such a high prevalency rate, much higher than that for nondelinquent youth in the general population, is what leads researchers to conclude that a significant relationship exists between child abuse and delinquency.

Thus, there is not much question that anyone dealing regularly with chronic acting-out children who become delinquent needs to know that in any given case there is at least a 50–50 chance that these youth have an abuse history. The importance of knowing this lies with developing relevant intervention strategies that target the abuse, in terms of both stopping it and providing a program of therapy to deal with its aftermath. To illustrate, juvenile courts are increasingly inquiring about abuse histories as part of preparing the social history that judges commonly rely upon in making postadjudicatory dispositions.

Beyond this all-important initial awareness of a significant connection between abuse and delinquency, a question arises regarding the nature of the relationship—for example, does abuse cause delinquency? Most research has not considered much more than prevalency rates, although, clearly, a simple cause–effect relationship is not what is going on, as not all abused children become delinquent. Moreover, virtually all researchers in child abuse and delinquency issues are convinced that both child abuse and delinquency have multiple origins.

The most thorough analysis of the child abuse–delinquency research is contained in an unpublished paper by James Garbarino, "Child Maltreatment and Juvenile Delinquency: What Are The Links?" Garbarino prepared his analysis under contract with OJJDP as resource material for a 1984 conference in Racine, Wisconsin.

At the beginning of his analysis, Garbarino notes some of the difficulties in comparing child abuse–delinquency studies, such as researchers using different definitions of *child abuse* and *delinquency* (particularly, some researchers including CHINS, others excluding them). He also discusses studies that have attempted to examine the abuse–delinquency connection beyond simple prevalency rates. These include studies that have looked to see whether specific kinds of abuse experienced as a child (e.g., physical abuse) consistently lead to later kinds of specific delinquency (e.g., assault). Thus far, the answer is no, except that several researchers have found very high rates of sexual abuse among teen prostitutes, suggesting some type of causal connection between being sexually abused as a young child and later involvement with prostitution.

A related question is whether violent delinquents have unusually high rates of physical abuse experienced in earlier years. The individual who has done the most research on this is Dorothy Otnow Lewis, a psychiatrist at New York University School of Medicine. In studying several groups of violent and nonviolent delinquents, as well as nondelinquent "controls," she and her colleagues have consistently found much higher rates of physical abuse among violent delinquents. They have also found higher rates of physical injuries sustained as young children, higher rates of hospitalization for those injuries, and higher rates of neurological damage.

José Alfaro is generally considered to have conducted the most comprehensive abuse–delinquency study. He also found an unusually high rate of physical abuse among members of his delinquency sample reported for violent crimes. It should be noted that the Alfaro study, carried out in New York in the 1970s under mandate from the New York State Assembly Select Committee on Child Abuse, is unique in that it explored the relationship between child abuse and delinquency in two directions. Children reported to New York child protection agencies in the late 1950s were traced ahead to learn of subsequent involvement with delinquency courts, and an early-1970s group of delinquents was traced backward to learn of earlier contact with child protection agencies. Both groups were found to have high contact rates.

The Alfaro and Lewis findings on links between physical abuse and later violent delinquency should not be construed to mean that physical abuse victims who respond to their condition by acting out always do so in a violent manner. It is significant that both researchers began with a group of violent delinquents and traced backward to find the physical abuse. In contrast, when one begins with a group of physically abused children and follows their development, it is clear that some will act out violently, some nonviolently (e.g., truancy, running away), and others not at all.

Tangentially related to the Alfaro and Lewis findings is research by Dr. Ralph Welsh (1976), a Bridgeport, Connecticut, psychologist who is both a researcher and practicing psychologist. Rather than looking for a relationship between physical abuse and violent delinquency, his thesis, confirmed by all of his studies, is that "severe parental punishment" is the only delinquency variable to be found in the background of every recidivist delinquent. He is sufficiently convinced of this finding to have made a public offer of $100 to anyone who can produce a recidivist delinquent who has not been hit with a belt, board, extension cord, fist, or similar object. Most important about Welsh's work is his empirical debunking of the notion that delinquency is a product of parental permissiveness.

After reviewing the studies by Lewis, Alfaro, Welsh, and others, Garbarino concludes that there is persuasive evidence of an important, yet vexing, relationship between child abuse and delinquency. He reminds us that notwithstanding our tendency to think only of very young abuse victims, national reporting data reveal that approximately 40 percent of all reported subjects are adolescents. This, in turn, raises a question about how much a youth's acting-out behavior, including delinquency, leads to abusive treatment by parents and institutional caregivers, further complicating the overall cause–effect analysis. He concludes:

> There undoubtedly is no simple cause–effect mechanism operating here. Many intervening and confounding factors probably are present. Unraveling the connections is complicated by the possibility that the links are different for different types of maltreatment and different types of proscribed adolescent behavior. One might suspect that family and other social network variables, as well as economic and perhaps cultural ones, shape the relationship. Finally, of course, are basic individual differences such as temperament and sex, even height and weight, that personalize any general equations describing the situation. (Garbarino, 1984)

Although Garbarino is correct in his conclusions about the many uncertainties of the abuse–delinquency relationship, we need to keep sight of what researchers have confirmed—namely, that delinquent children have uncommonly high rates of child abuse. This, in itself, is sufficiently compelling to warrant significant policy changes in how judicial, mental health, and educational personnel handle these youth. And such policy changes are occurring, as evidenced, for example, by the State of Wyoming amending its delinquency statute to require that abuse/neglect information be made part of the court's predispositional social history. Similarly, the Santa Clara, California, Probation Department has developed a Child Abuse Screening and Treatment System for every juvenile who enters the court system. Such developments speak to greater judicial precision in identifying delinquent maladies prior to making a dispositional decision.

The Link between Learning Disabilities and Delinquency

The connection between learning disabilities and delinquency not only has been empirically documented but has received more attention at the policy level than any other individual factor associated with delinquency, including child abuse. For example, in 1983, the American Bar Association's House of Delegates formally adopted a resolution calling upon all members of the legal profession to improve their handling of juvenile cases through recognition of the important role of learning disabilities in many of these cases. This would include identifying LD conditions and making appropriate referrals.

Another prominent example is Canada's Young Offender Act, enacted in 1982, which recognizes the LD–JD connection. Other recognition can be found in Wyoming's juvenile code and in West Virginia Supreme Court case law. For example in a 1982 case, the court instructed the state's juvenile courts to make inquiries about the possible presence of learning disabilities prior to sentencing certain youth. In addition, with the passage of local special education laws prompted by P.L. 94-142 (Education For All Handicapped Children Act), states such as New Hampshire have amended their delinquency and CHINS statutes to include a section empowering juvenile courts to direct school units to evaluate young offenders for possible learning disabilities. Thus, learning disabilities have forced their way into the delinquency court scene in a way that child abuse has not yet been able to do.

Within the learning disability community, the Association for Children with Learning Disabilities (ACLD), located in Pittsburgh, has widely advertised that "labeling youngsters as 'uneducable, behavior problems, underachievers, etc.' continues to plague the development of children with learning disabilities." Their all-important point is that these children are doubly at risk: first, because of their handicapping condition and, second, because of their related behavior, which begins to attract the lion's share of people's attention, resulting in increasingly punitive responses. Fortunate is the LD child who does not respond to his/her condition by acting out.

Boys Town, in conjunction with the ACLD, has also advertised the LD–JD link, citing a recent review of an ACLD remediation program for delinquent youth, which focuses on academic achievement versus psychotherapy, for example. The LD youths received individual instruction in the area of their greatest academic deficiency. The review showed that after fifty-five hours of remediation, academic achievement improved "dramatically," and delinquent activity fell "abruptly" after only thirty-five hours of instruction. We came across other people in the United States and Canada who reported similar dramatic results when delinquent children were enrolled in highly individualized educational programs. All stressed the need for the earliest possible intervention "before they get into the viciously escalating cycle of school failure and peer ridicule."

The lead research was conducted several years ago by the National Center for State Courts (Williamsburg, Va.), under a grant from the National Institute for Juvenile Justice and Delinquency Prevention (NIJJDP) in Washington, D.C. The NIJJDP had previously funded a survey of the LD–JD literature, which, as of the mid-1970s, was deemed by the investigator (Charles Murray of the American Institutes for Research) to be deficient and unable to establish any link between the two. Murray recommended to the NIJJDDP that it fund a better designed research project as well as a demonstration remediation program. The National Center for State Courts received the research award and the ACLD the demonstration project.

Interested readers can contact the National Center for State Courts for an excellent summary of their ultimate research findings based on a cross-sectional and longitudinal study of almost 2,000 youths. The following are some of the findings:

1. A significant relationship exists between LD and JD; that is, adolescents handicapped by LD are "at high risk for delinquency."
2. LD youth reported significantly greater delinquent activity than their non-LD peers.
3. Boys with LD engaged in more violence and experienced more school discipline problems than their non-LD peers.
4. Extrapolation data indicate that on a national basis, 9 of every 100 young males with LD have been officially adjudicated as delinquent, versus 4 of every 100 non-LD young males.
5. Between 30 and 50 percent of all officially adjudicated JDs nationally are learning disabled.

The researchers for the National Center for State Courts commented:

> Most practitioners and researchers believe that it is important to identify and offer special services to learning-disabled children before they become official delinquents; that is while they are still at an early age. . . . In order to be optimally effective, special delinquency control and prevention programs for learning-disabled children and youths will require the close cooperation and coordination of juvenile justice, educational, and youth service agencies. (Dunivant, 1982)

In reviewing the National Center's evaluation of the ACLD's demonstration remediation program, it is interesting to note the finding that changes in delinquency were not significantly related to changes in academic achievement. Instead, it was the youths' change in attitude about school that corresponded very strongly with delinquency reduction.

Noel Dunivant of the National Center indicates that the ACLD has developed curriculum guides and training packages for interested communities. He also notes the essential need for—but extreme difficulty in bringing about—interagency cooperation.

In reflecting upon both the National Center's landmark research and its positive findings concerning the ACLD demonstration project, Dunivant (1982) concludes that the two

> . . . clearly show that children and youth handicapped by learning disabilities are at relatively higher risk of becoming delinquent than their non-learning-disabled peers. Furthermore, the risk of delinquency is reduced by participation in a rehabilitation program designed to provide appropriate remedial instruction. It is recommended that such prevention and rehabilitation services be made widely available to youth with LD.

Although P.L. 94-142 has spawned some assistance for early intervention with LD children, it can accord no better relief than the training of special education personnel allows for. The ACLD model and those like it require a specific expertise that understands both the LD and the acting-out components of a youth's life. Also, it should be remembered that not all chronic acting-out children have LDs or are codable under the "seriously emotionally disturbed" criteria, thereby leaving significant numbers beyond the current reach of special education resources. The strengths and limitations of P.L. 94-142 will be considered more thoroughly in Chapter 19.

Neuropsychiatric Links to Delinquency

Dr. Dorothy Otnow Lewis, as much as anyone, has made us aware that social and psycho-dynamic factors alone do not explain chronic behavioral problems and especially violent delinquency. She and her colleagues have conducted several studies since the mid-1970s on violent youth. Their findings on causes of these young people's violence consistently point to the combination of neuropsychiatric vulnerabilities and a history of child abuse and/or family violence. More specifically, these researchers stress that brain damage alone, psychosis alone, and even child abuse alone do not cause violence. Together, these conditions seem to create violent individuals. Some of their other research findings include the following:

1. Compared to nondelinquent youth, delinquents suffer a disproportionate number of head and face injuries as young children. The more violent the youth is, the more apt s/he is to have experienced such trauma.

2. Delinquents have significantly more hospitalizations than nondelinquents over the course of childhood. Hospital contacts were highest when these children were 0–4 and 14+, which is suggestive of the ameliorative role of schools.

3. Major neurological problems, such as seizures, electroencephalographic abnormalities, and abnormal Babinski sign, were present in nearly 50 percent of the most aggressive boys studied.

4. Epilepsy (specifically, psychomotor epilepsy) was more prevalent in the group of violent incarcerated youth than in the general population of delinquents studied. Although occasionally the psychomotor epilepsy in the adolescents studied was associated with violence, all of the psychomotor epileptic subjects had been violent at times other than during seizures.

5. The psychomotor epileptic symptomatology was strongly correlated with several psychotic symptoms, including auditory and visual hallucinations, paranoid ideation, and loose, rambling, illogical thought processes.

6. Seventy-five percent of the violent youth had been brutally physically abused, versus 33 percent of the nonviolent delinquents studied. Moreover, 78 percent of the former group versus only 20 percent of the latter had witnessed extreme acts of violence against other people, usually in their own homes.

7. Among incarcerated juveniles, equal proportions of males and females evidence serious neuropsychiatric symptoms or signs.

8. A significantly greater number of the violent youth studied than nonviolent offenders had definite histories of paranoid symptomatology.

9. Members of the violent group had especially severe verbal deficiencies. *Note:* Apart from questions of cause–effect and conflicting findings by other researchers, Dr. Lewis is on firm ground when she points out the frequency with which damage to the central nervous system and related sequelae—such as learning disabilities, attention deficit disorders, and impulsivity—are present among delinquent youth, especially those who are violent.

10. WISC results indicated minimal differences in IQ between violent and nonviolent delinquents.

11. The violent delinquents rarely perceived themselves as provocateurs. Instead, they interpreted personal encounters as threats leading to their having to defend themselves. *Note*: This brings to mind the well-known Wyoming case of Richard Jahnke, a 16-year-old battered child who assassinated his violent, abusive father. Child abuse experts were prepared to testify that a person such as Richard Jahnke, who has been assaulted for years, comes to have a "distorted" sense of danger, such that the experts viewed the assassination as self-defense rather than murder.

These findings have led Dr. Lewis to recommend that all medical personnel evaluating recidivist delinquents should look for a history of prenatal problems, major accidents or injuries, severe head injuries, neurological abnormalities, epilepsy/blackouts/fainting, family psychiatric problems, and child abuse. Her experience is that medical people often fail to consider or properly assess these factors that may contribute to the aggressive behaviors. She also perceives an essential need to interview family members to obtain this much-needed medical history.

Even if they are less prevalent than Dr. Lewis has found them to be in the delinquents she studied, there would still be ample reason for professionals always to consider neuropsychiatric factors and histories of violence when evaluating very aggressive, hostile children. Perhaps most significant is her belief that, notwithstanding the presence of serious neurological and/or psychiatric disorders, these children are capable of remediation. One of her fears is that absent a careful assessment, these adolescents will be dismissed with the "dead-end diagnosis" of conduct disorder.

Dr. Lewis is not alone in finding a disturbingly high rate of neurological impairment and related CNS damage among delinquents. For example, in the Boston area, Dr. Melvin Levine and several others recently identified significant differences between delinquents and nondelinquents in visual processing and auditory-language function. Almost half of the delinquents studied had at least one area of development lag. Moreover, as Dr. Lewis points out, severe CNS trauma has long been recognized as being associated with behavioral abnormalities.

Taking a step back from this discussion, a question arises regarding how such data on violent delinquents is relevant to young children. After all, violent delinquents are a long way from elementary school children, even those who present serious behavioral problems.

First, although there are no linear connections between being a chronic acting-out third-grader, for example, and a mid-adolescent delinquent, both of these children are noteworthy for their behavior. And if a third-grader's behavior is violent, we would do well to have the work of professionals such as Dr. Lewis in mind.

Second, it is to be remembered that much of the trauma Dr. Lewis identified in the delinquents she studied was experienced years before these youth became delinquents. Indeed, it is very likely that most of them resembled the "predelinquent" children who are the subject of this Handbook. Fortunately, only a small number of delinquents are truly violent, just as relatively few behavioral problem students are violent, particularly at the elementary school level. Yet violent youngsters are the most troublesome of all students, and educators need to be mindful that violent individuals, as Dr. Lewis indicates, have often experienced major trauma, including severe physical abuse, and/or exposure to family violence, even before they get to elementary school.

Third, it is not just the delinquent who has significant neurological impairment. Many child abuse victims are similarly affected, including some who are not aggressive.

It is beyond the scope of this Handbook to attempt to detail the intricate relationships between damage to the central nervous system and such apparently related phenomena as attention disorders, impulse disorders, hyperactivity, learning disabilities, behavioral problems, and child abuse. Therefore, we simply make the point that every school intervention team—whether the prevention focus is delinquency, educational handicaps, child abuse, or school failure—should have someone on the team who has an understanding of neuropsychiatric factors. At the very least, the team needs to be aware that especially aggressive or violent children may well be abuse victims and may have central nervous system damage that directly affects their ability to learn.

In concluding this section, we would like to share with the reader some other observations by Dr. Lewis:

1. Neglect, through parental failure to protect young children, also contributes to CNS damage caused by injuries and accidents.

2. ADDs and LDs (especially reading disabilities) are very prevalent among delinquent children. Although the cause of ADD is not clear, ADDs and related behavioral problems do respond to "multifaceted treatment programs that include special education intervention, appropriate medication, and family interventions to reduce excessive stimulation and provide supportive structure."

3. ADD, hyperactivity, and LD are disorders that may reflect pervasive rather than minor CNS injury.

4. Reading disorders among delinquents probably have many different causes.

5. A central concern with CNS damage is a child's diminished control over impulses.

6. ADD and epilepsy are serious neuropsychiatric disorders.

7. Child abuse often leads to CNS dysfunction and poor impulse control.

8. Historically, delinquency theorists have focused on personality factors (e.g., characterological defects such as conduct disorder) and parental factors (e.g., disciplinary techniques, socioeconomic status) to the exclusion of neuropsychiatric factors. However, in recent years, increasing attention is being given (and rightfully so, according to Dr. Lewis) to relationships between such childhood conditions as MBD, ADD, specific learning disabilities (e.g., sequencing problems, visual and auditory discrimination problems), and antisocial behaviors.

9. There are multiple causes of violent and nonviolent delinquency. Clearly, such factors as psychiatric disturbance in parents and violent fathers are very significant. These, as

well as neuropsychiatric and other factors associated with chronic delinquents, need to be considered when conducting assessments.

10. The origins of the various neuropsychiatric-related factors associated with delinquency are increasingly known, and include such things as prenatal difficulties, accidents, and injuries as well as such inherited vulnerabilities as ADD, psychosis, depression, and epilepsy.

The Relationship between Child Abuse and Developmental Disabilities

The preceding sections discussed the documented connections between learning disabilities and delinquency and the neuropsychiatric links to delinquency. This section is concerned with connections between child maltreatment and developmental disabilities in the broadest sense—meaning learning disabilities, neuropsychiatric links, and other psychological and physical handicaps.

In our search for linkages between child abuse and developmental disabilities, we came across the following:

1. In a presentation at the 1983 National Conference On Child Abuse and Neglect in Baltimore, entitled "Potential Prevention: Screening for Developmental Disabilities at Intake and Improved Service Delivery to Abused and Neglected Children," the presenters (M. Souther et al.) cited NCCAN-funded research in West Virginia that found that as many as six out of ten abused/neglected children receiving protective services are also developmentally disabled. Specifically, 86 of 125 children receiving protective services in two West Virginia counties were found to have one or more disabilities, including emotional disorders, specific learning disabilities, speech/language impairments, and mental retardation. Because the developmentally disabled are so at-risk for abuse, and vice versa, the presenters recommended that service providers with expertise in one of these phenomena receive training in the other.

2. Thirty-six abused children admitted to an inpatient psychiatric ward were compared with a matched nonabused control group concerning intelligence and learning disabilities. The frequency of abuse was 40 percent higher in the mentally retarded children and in children of normal intelligence but with learning disabilities as compared with children of normal intelligence and no learning disabilities (McDanal and Bolman, 1979).

3. According to one researcher (Kline, 1977): "Teachers should be aware that high incidence of retardation, growth and neurological problems, and impaired emotional functioning are found among physically abused children. . . . Children adjudged abused or neglected are disproportionately represented in special education classes."

4. A five-year study of fifty-eight moderately abused children found 53 percent with some neurological abnormalities, of which 31 percent were moderate to severe (Martin, 1976). Martin has also conducted studies in which 80 to 100 percent of all students receiving special education were found to have related histories of abuse and neglect (Martin, 1976).

5. Nearly 10 percent of the total child abuse cases in England each year result in some level of brain damage. Many of these children experience academic learning difficulties, stemming primarily from deficits in perceptual abilities and perceptual motor skills.

6. Boys Town recently opened a new center for the prevention and treatment of abuse and neglect of handicapped children. Boys Town executive director Reverend Robert Hupp commented: "For 67 years Boys Town has been taking care of abused and neglected children. . . . This new program is an extension of that concern."

7. A follow-up study of forty physically abused children in Oxford, England, showed 63 percent suffering from significant problems four years after an initial intervention and treatment. Problems included neurological, developmental, intellectual, and behavioral difficulties, many of them requiring very long-term intervention (Lynch, 1984).

8. In a well-known 1962 study, C. Henry Kempe et al. found that 85 of 302 abused children in seventy-one hospitals had suffered neurological damage. Thirty-three of these children subsequently died as a result of their injuries.

9. Over 30 percent of the children in a follow-up study of abused children evidence central nervous system damages and 57 percent had IQ scores of 80 or less (Elmer, 1977).

10. In a recent study, child abuse was a significant factor in thirty-six out of eighty-six cerebral-palsied children ranging in age from six months to 18 years. Nearly half of the thirty-six children were sufficiently abused to result in state assumption of custody. The researchers were able to determine that for eight of the thirty-six children, the abuse caused the cerebral palsy (Diamond and Jaudes, 1983).

A particularly useful publication on the subject is Dr. Donald Kline's (1982) *The Disabled Child and Child Abuse,* a pamphlet published by the National Committee for Prevention of Child Abuse in Chicago. Dr. Kline points out that no research has established a definite cause-and-effect relationship between some disabling conditions and abuse. However, studies have shown a correlation, leading professionals to believe that disabled children do constitute a high-risk group for abuse. He concludes:

> Failure to recognize that abuse and neglect may cause irreparable handicapping conditions in children or that "different" children often invite abuse and neglect is not only costly to the child and his family but also costly to society. The abused or neglected child may suffer irreparable neurological damage, severe physical handicaps, delayed language or speech impairment, and there is a strong possibility of lowered intellect. An abused or neglected child may experience academic failure, requiring additional costs in providing an appropriate education as required by the Education for All Handicapped Children Act. Abuse and neglect often leads to delinquency and in many cases to adult criminal acts, for which society demands retribution. Again, the costs to society are enormous.

We also refer the reader to "Child Abuse and Developmental Disabilities: Essays," which can be obtained from the National Center on Child Abuse and Neglect (Publication No. OHDS 79-30226). The NCCAN publication is an output of an HEW Region I (Boston) conference, which brought together professionals from both the developmental disabilities and child abuse professions to examine links between the two phenomena. Although expert presenters indicated that additional research is necessary, it is interesting to note three studies that found that a developmental disability frequently *precedes* child abuse. Most well known is a 1970 study by David Gill of 6,000 cases of confirmed child abuse in which 29 percent evidence some form of developmental disability prior to abuse. The other studies found rates of 58 percent and 70 percent.

The authors of the NCCAN publication conclude:

> The fact that we cannot adequately demonstrate how large the association between developmental disabilities and child abuse is, how consistent such an association might be, or in what order the phenomena occur, indicates the need for research on this issue. Such research is more than an academic exercise designed to satisfy our curiosity or confirm our assumption. Research on this topic is important because of the many important policy issues that are part of the proposed relationship between child abuse and developmental disabilities. Clearly, if abuse (pre-natal or post-natal) is found to produce many developmental disabilities, then we may well be identifying an important variable for spotting abuse. If, on the other hand, the disability produces a vulnerability for being abused, then such information is critical for those in the field of providing primary care and services to children with developmental disabilities as important *predictor* variables for predicting future abuse and would also provide an important intervention point for alleviating the risk of abuse.

The Link between Child Abuse and Running Away

For centuries, children who ran away were considered bad. This particular type of behavior was viewed as blatant evidence of the child's need to be dealt with firmly, including incarceration in reform schools and jail. This was the case even after millions of Americans fondly read *The Adventures of Huckleberry Finn,* in which Huck ran away from home because he could not take Pap's beatings anymore.

The convergence in the mid-1970s of mounting public awareness about child abuse and a renaissance in juvenile justice, led by Senator Birch Bayh, resulted in a dramatic change in attitude toward runaways. Federal legislation created the National Center on Child Abuse and Neglect (NCCAN), the Office of Juvenile Justice and Delinquency Prevention (OJJDP), the Runaway and Homeless Youth Act, and, as part of the OJJDP Act, legislation decriminalizing so-called status offenses, such as running away, truancy, and incorrigibility. Today, many states have PINS (Persons in Need of Supervision) or CHINS (Children in Need of Supervision) statutes barring incarceration of children for status offenses. The underpinning for these laws is a recognition that the child has committed no criminal wrongdoing and is in need of mental health and child protection services, not punishment.

Research conducted over the past fifteen years consistently indicates that more than half of the nation's one million annual runaways leave home because of physical abuse or neglect. One-third leave because of sexual abuse (some studies suggest the rate may be as high as 60 to 80 percent). For example, in a recent study of runaways in Toronto, 38 percent of the male runaways and 73 percent of the female runaways had histories of childhood sexual abuse (Burgess, 1986). Other runaways are actually "throwaways"—offspring who have been pushed out of the home or abandoned. Recent federal government statistics reveal that the median age for runaways is 15; 70 percent are white, 20 percent black, and 10 percent of other racial/ethnic origin. The government estimates that one-third to one-half of all runaways are victims of maltreatment.

Dr. Henry Kempe was aware of the child abuse–running away connection, as was his pediatrician colleague, Dr. Brandt Steele. Dr. Kempe reported in *Child Abuse* (1978) that over half the runaway adolescent girls they saw at Denver General Hospital were sexual abuse victims. Many had experienced physical abuse as well.

Thus, there is no question that runaways have a high incidence of family maltreatment. Perhaps more so than with other behaviors or conditions that link to child abuse, it is reasonable to postulate that the child abuse–runaway relationship has strong causal features; that is, many children run away for the specific purpose of escaping further child abuse, precisely as Huck did over one hundred years ago.

Overall, the U.S. Department of Health and Human Services estimates more than one million runaway and homeless youths. In a recent *Federal Register* announcement, the DHHS stated:

> Reports by runaway youth centers indicate a growing proportion of youth arriving at the centers with multiple and complex problems. Substance abuse by youth, sexual abuse or physical abuse by the adults, conflicts in school or with peers, and problems of teen pregnancy, prostitution and suicide all seem to be on the increase in youth appearing at centers.

Are we suggesting that runaways come solely from the ranks of the multiproblem chronic acting-out students? No. Federal government statistics tell a different story—that most runaways are from "middle and upper class" backgrounds. In this sense, runaway behavior may resemble substance abuse. On the other hand, these statistics include only "official" cases—those that get reported to the police or to a runaway hotline. In our experience, chronic acting-out students, who for the most part do not come from the upper or middle classes, commonly have had at least one episode of running away by the time they are of junior high school age. Often, the running away is very brief or involves relocating temporarily with a nearby relative or at a friend's home. Most significantly, the running away often goes unreported by the parents, who, unlike their more affluent counterparts, are apt to downplay the running away. At the least, running away is *always* symptomatic of a serious problem, regardless of the type of child involved. Runaway experiences invariably leave children disoriented and behind in their schooling. For CACs this is apt to be doubly so.

School Failure and Delinquency

Whereas child abuse and LD are more apt to be *causes* of such problems as school failure and delinquency, school failure can be seen as both a cause (e.g., of delinquency) and a behavioral symptom or effect (e.g., of LD and child abuse). The school failure dimension of CAC lives is probably best understood as a daily reality rather than as a single climactic event.

Furthermore, although our relatively recent knowledge of LD and other educational handicaps has replaced some of the older references to school failure, in the research literature and elsewhere, it encompasses much more than these handicaps. It includes numerous causes and effects, such as truancy, dropping out, teenage pregnancy, suspension and expulsion, school violence, and corporal punishment—all of which are increasingly viewed as subjects unto themselves. This is both good, in that each is accumulating a valuable knowledge base, and bad, in that compartmentalizing such issues works against our seeing their essential interconnectedness.

For the sake of maintaining a simple focus in this section, the discussion of school failure and its relationship to delinquency will exclude any underlying consideration of causes of school failure or consequences, which are treated later in the Handbook. Instead, the term will be used much as it was in the early days of delinquency research, simply connoting the very important fact of not succeeding educationally.

Although an isolated study or two have shown that acting-out behavior actually lessens following a youth's termination of school participation, most delinquency researchers have found that school failure is commonly found in the backgrounds of delinquents. Among the first researchers to comment on this were the Gluecks (1968), who noted extreme differences in (1) levels of educational success and (2) attitudes toward school between groups of delinquents and nondelinquent controls.

In another well-known study of 500 antisocial youth who were traced thirty years after their involvement as adolescents with a treatment program, the researchers concluded that "without early intervention, anti-social children [known today as conduct-disordered] amass a severe educational handicap. If anti-social behavior were controlled earlier, children who now become severely retarded in school and drop out before they even reach high school, would be able to remain in school and progress along with their classmates" (Robins, 1974).

In a study by Marge Csapo of British Columbia (Csapo and Aag, 1974), she found that school failure was a major causative factor of delinquency in youth participating in a tutorial demonstration project named *Operation: Step Up*. Rather than associating school failure with the delinquent youth, Csapo views the schools as failures in their mishandling of many acting-out youth. Thus, like the ACLD project in the United States, noted earlier, she concluded that changing the educational approach to predelinquent or delinquent youth is a key to delinquency reduction.

Hirschi (1969) has illustrated the school failure–delinquency relationship as follows:

Academic Impairment	→	Poor School Performance	→	Dislike of School	→	Rejection of Authority	→	Delinquent Behavior

Such a model, although excluding all other possible causes of delinquency, is striking in its suggestion that removing the negative effects of an LD condition or changing a poor school performance into a good one may be so influential as to eliminate later delinquency altogether. The ACLD and Ms. Csapo would concur.

As with any two complex human phenomena, researchers differ regarding how school failure relates to delinquency. Yet, as with the learning disability–delinquency and child abuse–delinquency connections, research has convincingly established a positive link between the two; that is, school failure is a significant factor in delinquency. Judges have taken note of this. For example:

Judge Jack Newman, participating in a 1981 seminar at the Center for the Study of Democratic Institutions, "Violence in American Life," shared what he has observed about the delinquents that came before his court: "Almost universally, they are having trouble in school. Typically, they first perform poorly in school, and then they become truant."

An anonymous Denver judge commented: "As I looked back over the seven hundred or more cases I had heard in a ten month period while serving as juvenile court judge, I had a gut reaction that made me almost physically ill. I cannot remember them by name, but about eighty percent of the boys and fifty percent of the girls were experiencing difficulties at school. There is such an obvious pattern, once you are alerted and have some idea of what to look for, that I could not understand why people who have worked for years with disturbed youngsters have not tried to do something about it."

Similarly, Marge Csapo writes:

So far [up to 1974], our traditional methods in corrections seem to be "hit or miss" affairs—indeed, it is difficult to define precisely what those traditional methods actually are. With the present state of knowledge we should be learning how to apply to corrections the techniques which have been developed in other sciences. (Csapo and Aag, 1974)

Public Law 94-142 makes this statement a little less true today—at least in the United States, where special education programming has eliminated some school failure. Nonetheless, school failure will continue to be experienced at a high rate by CACs until child development people nationally come to find this unacceptable.

Once the school failure–delinquency problem is properly understood, then training can capitalize on the substantial knowledge base that Marge Csapo and others talk about. This would include educationally based service models, such as hers and ACLD's, plus an awareness on the part of intervening personnel of the role of specific elements of school failure, such as LD and child abuse. Most heartening are wholesale legislative initiatives targeting the school failure problem, which are discussed in Chapter 18.

The Relationship between Child Abuse and School Failure

In *The Human Factor: A Key to Excellence in Education* (Mintzies and Hare, 1985), published by the National Association of Social Workers (see Chapter 16), it is stated that "research evidence is mounting to indicate a connection between abuse and neglect and school problems." *Human Factor* cites a 1976 study in California involving 378 children who had been removed from their homes by child protection authorities. The researcher (Kent) found that these children had significant academic, behavior and peer-relationship problems in school. More specifically:

Fifty-three percent of the abused children and 82 percent of the neglected children were rated "below average" or "failing," versus 28 percent of the control group.

Concerning peer relations, 67 percent of the abused children and 60 percent of the neglected children were rated "unsatisfactory," versus 23 percent of the control group.

The abused children were rated as more aggressive and disobedient than either the neglected children or the controls.

In a 1975 Utah study of 138 children referred to the courts for abuse and neglect, the researchers (Kline and Christiansen) found that the academic achievement of maltreated children was generally below average. The majority of the children were below grade level in reading, spelling, and mathematics.

These findings should not surprise us, as even a mature adult would have great difficulty remaining on an even keel while experiencing major turmoil in the home. Henry Kempe was convinced that all abused children have difficulties that affect their school performance. He attributed this, in part, to the difficulty with language that is characteristic of the abused child. This is not to say that all abused and neglected children will perform at a subpar level in school. Dr. Densen-Gerber indicates that some are even overachievers, "losing" themselves in academics as a way of blocking out maltreatment in the home.

However, it is very unlikely that significant numbers of abused and neglected children are faring well academically. As the National Association of Social Workers concluded: "While further research is needed to determine the exact relationship between abuse and special education, it is clear that child abuse and neglect represents a significant impediment to educational excellence."

7
Other Significant Factors

Family Violence

The term *family violence* is generally used to encompass all violence that goes on within the home, including abuse of children by a parent or parental figure (e.g., mother's boyfriend), spousal abuse, sibling abuse, and violence between a parent and the parent's girlfriend/boyfriend. The term usually conjures up physical abuse, but sexual abuse, emotional abuse, and even neglect can have violent elements.

In their research, Dr. Dorothy Lewis and her colleagues concluded that the most significant contributing factor to violent delinquency seems to be having a violent father. Lewis explains the connection as follows:

> First, a violent father furnishes a model for behavior. Second, when directed toward the child his violence often causes the very CNS vulnerability to impulsiveness about which we have spoken. Finally, witnessing and being the victim of irrational violence engenders a kind of rage and frustration that, when directed inward, expresses itself as suicidal behavior. When directed outward and displaced from the father, it manifests itself as homicidal aggression. (Lewis et al., 1979)

In a very recent study, several researchers looked at three different groups of children: twenty-four child witnesses to spouse abuse, thirty victims of child abuse, and twenty-four control children. Each group was compared for a number of variables, including depression, separation anxiety, somatic complaints, and aggressive behavior.

The results showed (1) that "witness" children were more often diagnosed as depressed and as having separation anxiety disorders than the child abuse victims or control subjects were; (2) that both witnesses and victims were diagnosed as having conduct disorders more often than the controls were, although victims are more likely to develop such disorders than witnesses, especially if they are male; (3) that witnesses showed more somatic concerns than either victims or controls did. The researchers concluded that abused children are more apt to identify with the aggressor parent and directly express their own aggressive feelings. In contrast, witness children commonly internalize the perceived aggression, resulting in feelings of passivity, helplessness, and guilt associated with a failure to protect the victim (Brown et al., 1985).

These findings are similar to those of earlier studies, which suggested that male children reared in violent homes tend to emulate their fathers and learn to use violence to solve their problems, whereas girls from such homes are more apt to be withdrawn, passive, and submissive. Straus, Gelles, and Steinmetz (1980) in their well-known study of family violence (*Behind Closed Doors*) concluded: "Each generation learns to be violent by being a participant in a violent family."

Many theories have been put forth over the years about the causes of violence. As noted earlier, the theories can be grouped under one of three categories: individual (e.g., biological/genetic factors), family (e.g., parental alcoholism), and socioenvironmental (e.g., race, poverty). Those that consider child abuse and family violence primary causal factors are now among the more convincing theories. Moreover, at a direct service level, it is uncommon to come across a CHINS or delinquent who has not experienced family violence, either as a direct recipient of abuse or as a witness.

In addition to the long-term developmental harm that family violence causes, there are also some immediate concerns. As stated by one commentator:

> Domestic violence is a problem which is legitimately of direct concern to school staff. Children's learning and concentration are directly affected by their increased stress if they are observing or overhearing violence between the grownups at home. Their fearful thoughts about what may happen next may be very distracting. There is also actual danger to the children themselves; children are frequently injured when they try to protect an assaulted parent or when they inadvertently get caught in the middle. (West, 1979)

Family violence commonly involves other trauma, such as police and judicial intervention (e.g., restraining orders), mothers gathering up their children and seeking protection at a battered spouse shelter, and, all too often, a sudden reunion with the violent partner within a matter of days. The children become involved in a cycle of leaving the home, then returning; of a raging father figure disappearing, then reappearing; of police coming, police going; of the court saying one thing, then seemingly doing another. What a confusing and anger-producing world it must seem to the young people involved, who are expected to appear at school each day, on time, well-behaved, and ready to learn.

Substance Abuse and COAs

Since the early 1970s, much public attention has been given to the widespread use of alcohol and drugs by school-aged children, especially those at the secondary level. And although it is an uncommon delinquent who is not a substance abuser, it is also true that many otherwise nondelinquent youth also use alcohol and drugs. Gaining peer acceptance is recognized as a common motivation for most substance-abusing youth.

It would be a mistake, however, to conclude that the use of drugs or alcohol is meeting all the same needs among young people. Many are able to limit their use of these substances and to avoid police detection for substance-related offenses. Especially when only sporadic or moderate use is involved, such behavior can be interpreted as part of a normal developmental process, although not necessarily healthy and certainly not recommended.

In contrast, chronic acting-out children with long-standing problems often use drugs and alcohol as a means of self-medication—that is, to eliminate tremendous stress and emotional pain. Unlike many of their healthier peers, CACs usually have great difficulty limiting their use of substances to time and place, often resulting in negative repercussions, such as suspensions, expulsions, and appearances in juvenile court. And substance abuse by chronic acting-out students adds yet another deficit to their life condition, leaving them with even fewer resources to pursue educational success.

Substance abuse can therefore be seen as having both cause and effect properties. Certainly, substance abuse can lead to or cause disruptive behavior in school. Viewed from another angle, especially when the abuser is a chronic problem child, substance abuse can be seen as an effect of or response to powerful feelings of anger, hurt, and depression that are simply beyond the individual's ability to contend with absent appropriate intervention. Most disturbing is continued substance abuse that puts the abuser beyond the reach of those who would help.

Another facet of the substance abuse problem is the phenomenon of children of alcoholics (COAs), who are currently the subject of many alcohol training seminars. For years, research and direct service efforts focused on the alcoholic. More recently, attention has been given to the effect the alcoholic has on his/her spouse and offspring.

Models have been developed for identifying typical roles or patterns of behavior that family members adopt in response to the alcoholic parent (Wegscheider, 1979). Of particular interest for current purposes is the "scapegoat" role adopted by some COAs. Some authorities theorize that these children act out (1) to siphon off family attention and anger otherwise intended for the alcoholic parent, thereby preserving the alcoholic's status and everyone else's role, and (2) to force the family to rally together and stay together.

This is not to suggest that all CACs are filling a family scapegoat role or even that they are COAs. However, alcoholism is often present among parents of CACs, and the scapegoat model can be a valuable analytical tool. Regrettably, the COA aspect of these young people's lives is often overlooked by intervenors. Robert Ackerman (1983), an alcohol abuse authority, comments:

> Children of alcoholics themselves have contributed to their being unnoticed. Because of the societal uncertainty surrounding alcoholism, most children of alcoholics have not openly shared their experiences or received help. For many children of alcoholics, more effort has gone into covering up the alcoholism than into seeking help. In fact, only five percent of children of alcoholics are in treatment specifically for those problems that arise from being a child of an alcoholic. Many children of alcoholics are being noticed outside the family, but not for the direct effects of alcoholism. Unfortunately, estimates indicate that as high as twenty percent of the caseloads of juvenile courts and child guidance clinics are children who come from alcoholic homes. In these situations, the children are being seen for problems other than for being the child of an alcoholic. Often the family alcoholism is not taken into consideration by others or is hidden by the child.

At the very least, we know that COAs are under great pressure from living in an alcoholic household. Moreover, family response patterns, such as the scapegoat role, apparently continue long after an alcoholic parent has stopped drinking unless an intervention is made with the child by someone who is knowledgeable about alcoholism. Even with such an intervention, modification of ingrained response patterns is difficult, particularly in cases where the COA has reached adolescence. Furthermore, these children are typically plagued with many other problems, although cessation of parental drinking can often do much to lessen the intensity of these problems.

Another intriguing facet of substance abuse, especially alcoholism, is its relationship to child abuse. Some authorities maintain that parental alcoholism is, per se, psychological or emotional abuse of the child. The explanation here is that a parent consumed with drinking simply is not emotionally available for the child. Worse, some alcoholics become violent when they drink or become sufficiently uninhibited to be sexually and/or physically abusive. It is interesting, notwithstanding the conviction of nearly all mental health and CPS workers that alcohol is involved in most cases of family violence and/or child abuse, that research has yet to reach consensus on whether alcohol plays a significant role in the perpetration of child abuse. However, there is research that suggests that incest victims are more likely than the general population to engage in substance abuse (Garbarino and Gilliam, 1980).

How prevalent are COAs and alcoholism? How pervasive is the problem? Ackerman (1983) estimates that 10 percent of the U.S. population is being raised (or was raised) in an alcoholic home. He further cites common agreement that there are 25–28 million COAs in our society. The Children of Alcoholics Foundation in New York says that there are 28 million COAs (7 million under age 18) and that most have numerous and diverse psychological, physical, and emotional problems. The National Institute on Alcohol Abuse and Alcoholism (NIAAA) in Washington, D.C., indicates that approximately 75 percent of all adjudicated delinquents are believed to have at least one alcoholic parent, and a 1982 Gallup poll revealed that one of every three American families is affected by a family member's drinking. The magnitude of the problem is truly staggering.

Unfortunately, many COAs also become alcoholic and therefore are also reflected in NIAAA's estimate of 10 million alcoholics in the United States. Some authorities estimate that 50 percent of all COAs become alcoholic and that 30 percent marry alcoholics, reflecting the generally accepted belief that alcoholism is both hereditary and far more common in some cultural groups (e.g., Scandinavians) than in others (e.g., Asians). The State of Maine, in a status report to the National Governors' Association (Petit and Overcash, 1983), estimates as many as 80 percent of all adolescent suicides may be COAs. Yet, as Ackerman (1983) has pointed out, not all COAs are affected in the same way. Some even do extremely well—perhaps, as Ackerman and others have suggested, as a means of trying to bring some happiness and positive recognition to a troubled family.

In short, we know that alcoholism is a serious disease that afflicts many parents in our society. We also know that many children in alcoholic homes are adversely affected by their parents' disease and that delinquent children likely have a disproportionate number of COAs within their ranks. And we know—or should know—that for our multiple-problem chronic acting-out students, being COAs further impedes their opportunity to learn and renders them without the parental assistance they need. Less is known about parental drug addiction, although the effects on the child are seemingly much the same as with alcoholism. They may even be worse, in that much drug use is illicit and often involves police contacts and even incarceration.

Ackerman (1983) posits that the educator can do little about the parent's alcoholism or addiction, that intervention involving treatment of parental alcoholism is "outside the school's sphere of authority and probable competency." As for student COAs, he believes that it is essential for educators to identify them, as they often suffer from communication difficulties (including the belief that discussion of home is taboo), shame, and embarrassment—all of which interfere with learning, which is the educator's concern. The reader is referred to Ackerman (1983), *Children of Alcoholics: A Guidebook for Educators, Therapists, and Parents,* for guidance on educator interventions with COAs.

As for students who regularly abuse drugs or alcohol, ultimate concerns include overdosing, masking of underlying problems, school expulsion, and prosecution within the court system. For these children, the question must be "Why are they risking so much?" As those who work with CACs know, peeling back the substance abuse often reveals parental substance abuse as well as other problems.

Teen Pregnancy

Teen pregnancy encompasses sexual acting-out by children who are the subject of this Handbook—and much more. The United States has the highest teen pregnancy rate in the western world and is the only developed country whose rate is still rising. One out of every ten teenagers in the United States between 13 and 17 become pregnant. This translates to one million teenage girls and a similar number of teenage male partners. Some 600,000 teenagers give birth annually. And although teenagers represent only 18 percent of sexually active women capable of becoming pregnant, they account for 46 percent of all out-of-wedlock births and 31 percent of all abortions.

Some disturbing correlates are welfare dependency and school dropout rates. Young women who give birth as teenagers are two to three times more likely to live on welfare. Half either quit school because of the pregnancy or get pregnant after dropping out.

One particularly promising response to the problem of teen pregnancy has been the emergence of school-based health clinics, pioneered in the early 1970s by the Maternal and Infant Care Project in Minneapolis. Currently, there are more than thirty clinics in the United States with another seventy-five in the planning stages. The clinics typically provide students with a broad range of health services, such as physicals for athletic competition, weight control programs, day care centers for student mothers (thereby offering these parents an alternative to dropping out), immunizations, and family planning options. One such clinic in Chicago is housed within Jean Baptista Point DuSable High School. The clinic's services range from sports checkups to eye exams to treatment for bumps and bruises to birth control. About 80 percent of the families in the vicinity live below the poverty level.

Syndicated columnist Ellen Goodman observes that in 1983, 463 babies were born to women in the DuSable area between the ages of 10 and 19. Three hundred of these young mothers were of high school age. She further notes that families such as these, begun when the parents are teenagers, cost taxpayers $16.6 billion.

Goodman interviewed the clinic's nurse practitioner, who wishes that the public and press would care as much about teenage health as teenage sex. She points out that in the clinic's initial two-month period last year, 10 to 15 percent of the students the clinic screened could not see well enough to read. Six students were designated as diabetic, and many had hypertension.

The DuSable clinic completed its first year in June 1986. Current projections are that for every six teenage pregnancies in 1985, there will be only one in 1986. DuSable's principal describes the clinic as a "remedial program for kids at risk."

Another response to teenage pregnancy is the National Urban League's "Male Responsibility Program," which encourages black males to act responsibly so as to avoid fathering children they are unable to provide for. John Jacob (1985), president of the NUL, indicates that "in 1982 black teens had 145,929 births, 87% of them out of wedlock. By their 18th birthday, 22% of black females have become mothers, as compared to 8% of white females. For every 1,000 black teenage girls, there are 163 pregnancies."

Notwithstanding the NUL's focus on black males, teen pregnancy clearly affects all teenage groups, regardless of race, ethnicity, or economic status. In this sense, the problem is much like youth substance abuse. Also, it is a myth to assume that only "problem" youth engage in sexual intercourse and experience early pregnancies. Yet our direct service experience suggests to us that many CACs, be they black or otherwise, engage in more indiscriminate sexual activity than their more educationally successful peers. Moreover, their experiences are apt to be characterized by victimization and exploitation, either as perpetrators or as victims.

Divorce

Divorce statistics are shocking. Each year, more than one million marriages end in divorce in the United States. Seventy-five percent involve children, and 60 percent of the children are under age 12. Divorce directly affects 9 million children. In 1985, there were 1,187,000 divorces, a 3.9 percent increase over 1984. This translates to one couple in every twenty being divorced.

Linda Bird Francke, author of an excellent book on the effects of divorce on children, says: "Now divorce is so common that its very normality may have anesthetized us to our children's pain." She also indicates that "study after study has linked parental in-fighting with behavioral problems in children, which sometimes escalates into delinquency" (Francke, 1983).

A closer look at the research reveals the following:

1. Children reared in one-parent families show increased problems in educational attainment, behavior, and social adjustment (Finer, 1974; Ferri, 1976).

2. Marital discord and breakdown are associated with an increased risk of delinquency and of conduct disorders more generally (Douglas et al. 1968; Gregory, 1965; Rutter, 1971; West and Farrington, 1973).

3. The high school dropout rate for children of divorce is over twice that of students from intact families (cited in Francke, 1983).

4. Behavioral changes in teenagers who feel betrayed by their parents' "indecent" conduct (e.g., father with new girlfriend) sometimes takes the form of delinquency, running away, and acute depression (Francke, 1983).

5. Students whose parents have divorced admitted to more sexual activity with more partners than students from either intact families or families in which one parent had died. Also, teenage girls whose parents have divorced become sexually active at a younger age and more frequently than girls from intact families (cited in Francke).

6. Children of divorce differed most in comparison with children from intact homes in the area of interpersonal skills and relationships (Richards et al., 1985).

Rather than conclusively establishing that increases in divorce cause more delinquency, which is still an open question, research does suggest that some children of divorce become more vulnerable to stress and negative response behaviors. For example, a 1983 report prepared by a Harvard Medical School psychiatrist concluded:

> Poor academic performance, susceptibility to peer influence and delinquent behavior, as well as suicide and homicide, have been found to be more pronounced among children from homes with one or both parents missing or frequently absent. (Nicholi, 1983)

Two psychiatrists at the University of Washington (cited in Francke, 1983, p.24) have developed a "social readjustment scale" in which life events are ranked in terms of required adjustment level—that is, the greater the adjustment, the higher the stress. Next to death of a parent, divorce was the highest stressor tested for, followed by marital separation and a jail sentence for a parent. Other research has shown that whereas parental death is not associated with an increased risk of delinquency, divorce and separation are.

Perhaps the best-known divorce researcher is Judith Wallerstein, director of the Center for the Family in Transition in Corte Madera, California. In 1984, she presented the preliminary findings of a ten-year follow-up study of 60 families and 131 children. She divided the children into four groups:

1. Children forced by divorce to take inordinate responsibility for their own upbringing (e.g., Francke references 5.2 million children under 13 who are on their own after school).

2. Children who become the main source of emotional support for a divorced parent or an entire family.

3. Children who remain the targets of continued dispute and litigation between their parents.

4. A rising number of children who experience a second parental divorce and who cannot cope with the two disruptions.

Wallerstein uses the descriptive term "overburdened children" to describe the research subjects and other children of divorce. She makes the point that they are not always easy to identify, as many appear to be unusually mature or independent. "However," she states "anxiety may be manifested in psychosomatic symptoms, sleep disturbance, underachievement in school, hyperalertness or severe depression."

If the reader is getting the feeling that children do not survive divorce nearly so well as many of us had previously thought, that's precisely the point that Francke, Wallerstein, and others are making. And if we allow ourselves to really think about it, we should not be surprised.

Several related matters are deserving of comment. First, many children have parents who never marry. Other children have experienced a number of mom's boyfriends or dad's girlfriends living in the home for periods of time. In the child's eye, particularly a young child, such parental figures are often as much a parent as if there had been a marriage ceremony. Thus, their coming and going can be just as detrimental as it is when marriage is involved.

Second, our experience is that chronic acting-out children who fail in school are almost always from homes where there has been divorce and/or a series of "mothers" or "fathers." As these children approach adolescence, they typically harbor great resentment for the newest live-in partners, as well as for the biological parent. It is a little overwhelming to consider the confusion, disruption, and anger that exists in their homes over just this one very important factor.

Third, a biological parent often becomes involved with a partner who himself/herself has several children, resulting in a sudden expansion in the number of siblings and a corresponding reduction in the attention a child is accorded. Another phenomenon is young adolescents, with their budding sexuality, suddenly living in the same household with a nonblood relative of the opposite sex. Finally, divorce or a final parting of the ways often results in a child never again seeing the departed parental figure. In such cases, divorce or the equivalent merges with abandonment. This is very common in the cases we have known.

In summary, divorce and its related phenomena illustrate particularly well that child abuse does not occur in isolation—that it is often attended by or even caused by other very important family factors.

Teen Suicide/Self-Mutilation

Within the 15–19 age group, suicide is now the second leading cause of death, accounting for 2,000 deaths a year. For those under 15, the suicide rate has remained fairly stable. Overall, it is believed that approximately 5,000 teenagers commit suicide each year.

Other statistics include the following:

1. Between 1,500 and 2,000 middle school children attempt suicide each year.
2. Male suicides in the 10–14 age group outnumber females four to one.
3. Females attempt suicide more often than males but do not complete the act as often.
4. Nine out of ten suicide attempts take place in the home.
5. Three times as many suicide attempts were made by school-aged children in 1980 as in 1955.

Suicide statistics such as those provided by the National Center for Disease Control are usually considered conservative, and in some cases it is difficult to determine whether a death is the result of suicide. A significant number of teenage auto accident deaths, for example, may actually be suicides. Similarly, some drug overdose deaths may be planned rather than accidental.

Suicide is a sufficiently disturbing problem that the U.S. Government has recently established the Youth Suicide National Center. The director of the National Institute of Mental Health, Dr. Shervert Frazier, calls youth suicide a "major emergency." There is now an American Association of Suicidology, and at least two states (California and New York) have implemented statewide prevention programs in their public schools. In addition, some individual schools, such as the James Mastricola Middle School in Merrimack, New Hampshire, have developed their own suicide prevention units. Lest this problem begin to appear overwhelming, we should keep in mind that only about one in 13,000 teenagers will actually commit suicide each year.

Who are these children who attempt or actually commit suicide, and to what extent do their ranks include chronic acting-out students? Unfortunately, there is not much available research to answer these questions. Some suicidologists believe that risk factors that are sometimes present include school failure, broken homes, substance abuse, domestic violence or child abuse, violent behavior, hyperactivity, or neurological impairment. However, some of these factors might be found among youth who have done well in public school, only to encounter increasing problems in the immediate postsecondary years. In support of this view, Dr. Pamela Cantor, president of the American Association of Suicidology, believes that college students are most at risk for suicide because they come from home environments that typically exert a lot of pressure on their children to succeed. Moreover, Alfred Del Bello, former lieutenant governor of New York and chairman of New York's Council on Youth Suicide Prevention, is persuaded "that suicide knows no geographic, economic, or social barriers. It is not limited to 'problem kids.'" Thus, until more precise data are collected (currently being done by NIMH and the National Center for Disease Control), we are left with impressions and assumptions. In any event, it is not likely that CACs, who tend to come from the lower classes, are overly represented. If anything, as Dr. Cantor believes, they may be less involved in suicide than their more affluent, better educated peers.

Not surprisingly, researchers have identified links between child abuse and suicide. Garbarino and Gilliam (1980) found that incest victims are more likely than the general population to commit suicide. Maisch (1972) and Molnar and Cameron (1975) also found a relationship between incest victims and suicide attempts. These findings are consistent with a broader belief that child abuse is a source of major stress, which causes such psychiatric repercussions as depression, anxiety, and substance abuse.

Related to suicide is self-mutilation, which is common to chronic acting-out children. Several studies have been conducted on linkages between child abuse and violence directed toward self. One study (cited in Smith et al., 1980) compared three groups of children: those who had been physically abused, those who had been neglected, and a control group of so-called normal children. All were in the 5–13 age range. It was learned that 41 percent of the physically abused children engaged in self-mutilative/self-destructive behavior, versus 17 percent of the neglected children and 7 percent of the "normals."

Robert Ross (1980) of the University of Ottawa studied 120 girls sentenced to reform school in the early 1970s for CHINS offenses to learn of possible linkages between physical abuse and subsequent self-mutilations. Of the 120, 96 had carved themselves at least once while incarcerated (e.g., with knives, glass, pins) sufficiently to cause permanent scarring. Among the multicarver group, 48 percent had been victims of parental violence prior to age 12. In contrast, only 19 percent of the single carvers and 2 percent of the 24 noncarvers had experienced physical abuse in the home.

Self-mutilation and suicide can be seen as both nonrelated and linking phenomena. Some mutilators have no intention of committing suicide and never do. For example, tattooing is a form of self-mutilation. Although tattooing frequently constitutes deviant behavior, especially for girls in suburban areas, only a small percentage of people with tattoos attempt suicide. On the other hand, successful suicides often engage in prior suicide "gestures," such as cutting and burning themselves. Consequently, self-mutilation can, in some cases, be symptomatic of children at risk for suicide. Because few people are sufficiently skilled to tell the difference between someone who self-mutilates only and someone who self-mutilates as a prelude to suicide, interventions must be made on the basis of possible suicide.

The State of New York has been especially aggressive in developing suicide prevention materials for public school personnel. The booklet *Suicide Among School Age Youth* provides a management framework for school personnel in responding to the problem of suicide, including a Risk Assessment Checklist. Copies may be obtained from the N.Y. Department of Education, Office of General Education, Albany, NY 12234.

Foster Children/Foster Homes

School personnel need to be aware that a significant number of CACs are placed in foster homes, usually as the result of court action in response to child abuse, CHINS, and delinquency petitions. Sometimes the placements are temporary, and the children remain away from the biological home for a period of several months or less until a crisis has passed. Other times, the placements are permanent. The use of relatives as foster parents, although still done, is far less common today because of the transient nature of the American population and because relatives often do not want to be involved.

Certainly, there are cases when removal from the home brings the child major relief; that is, when leaving the biological parent(s) has almost no negatives associated with it. Far more often, the removal is very difficult for the children involved, especially in cases when a parent advises the court that the child *cannot* live at home. The issue here is not so much the wisdom of removing children from their homes as it is the sensitivity of educators to the fact that many children, including some who are tremendously unlikeable, are going through the experience of not being able to live at home for one reason or another.

Someone must ensure that educators are aware of such a significant change and that these children are given an opportunity to express how they are feeling. Too often, we assume that CACs are little iron people, who either must be delighted to get away from such a bad home environment or are such lousy kids that they can handle and even deserve being bounced around. Adolescents, in particular, often reinforce the "iron" view by claiming to have no feelings about not living in their own homes.

Cynthia Crosson Tower (1984), in her materials on child abuse sponsored by the National Education Association, also makes the point that foster children may need special concern from teachers:

> The biggest issue that the foster child is probably working out is that of separation and loss. No matter how difficult the home situation, this child has experienced the loss of an important element of life. The expression of this loss may differ from individual to individual. One child may be withdrawn or sullen, another difficult, exhibiting behavior problems. Feelings of inconstancy and instability may create a child who seems not to care. The best way to deal with these situations is to contact the social worker and insist on being told something of the child's background. The youngster may have special needs or interests that you can address. Mostly, however, foster children are wondering if you will reject or abandon them as others seem to have done. They may test you or tell wild, unbelievable stories to shock you. Knowledge of their background may help here too. Their need to know that they are all right, no matter what the family situation, is para-

mount for these youngsters. Again, the classroom teacher can be not only an ally, but also an important source of information on the child's progress by maintaining close contact with the social worker and the foster parents.

How many children are in foster care? No one seems to know for sure. Some estimate that 150,000 to 200,000 adolescents are in foster homes and that this is half of the total number. New York City alone has some 16,000 children in foster care. Judith Schaffer of the Center for Adoptive Families in New York notes that older foster children in particular, "come from environments ranging from unsettled to brutal in their own home and in other placements." She also makes the point that placements in foster homes are usually made quickly in whatever is available.

Other problems include financial disincentives for foster parents to adopt, because federal and state assistance payments are tied to foster status only. In the worst cases, foster parents have literally put out a foster child when s/he reached the age of majority. The plight of adolescents who have been in long-term foster care is particularly difficult. They are hard to adopt because they are no longer little and cute. Worse, they often act out, and nobody wants that.

Not all children placed outside the home wind up in private foster homes. Many are institutionalized in hospitals, treatment centers, group homes, reform schools, and the like. No doubt some of these institutions, like some foster parents, do a good job of making a child feel wanted. Others provide nothing more than a cold, lifeless, and even brutalizing environment, where the child gets a strong message that s/he is worthless. More often than not, such children have ceased to attend public schools, although the better residential programs allow for public school attendance once a resident has some measure of control over himself/herself.

Recognizing that so many children drift from one foster home to another, referred to as "foster care drift," Congress passed the Adoption Assistance Act of 1980. The intent of the Act is to require ongoing judicial or administrative review of each case and to achieve permanent placement in the biological or adoptive home within eighteen months. It is too soon to tell how effective this law will be, although the intent is admirable.

Another development is the creation of the National Association of Former Foster Children in New York. In its initial newsletter of June 1985, the editorial cites a 14-year-old Ohio boy who committed suicide after having been in thirty-two foster homes in nine years. It also cites a study by the National Prison Project in Washington, D.C., which found that 90 percent of all men in prison today grew up in some type of foster care or institution. It is hoped that the National Association will draw even more attention to foster care issues. It advocates the presence of a crisis care team whenever a foster placement is made. The team should consist of a trained social worker, a trained foster parent, and a family therapist. It also hopes to give long-term foster children a sense that they are not alone, that someone understands—and cares.

Relocations

As the case histories in this Handbook suggest, chronic acting-out children often have experienced much moving about—within towns and states throughout the country, and even to other countries. There is nothing intrinsically wrong with moving, so long as there are good reasons, such as an opportunity for a parent to obtain a substantially higher paying job. There may even be some beneficial aspects for some children's development.

A second category of movers includes poor people who work hard but necessarily must move on. Migratory workers are one example. Although this moving may not be best for the children, there is a certain life necessity and pattern to it which likely makes sense to them. Unfortunately, our experience is that parents of CACs often move for lesser reasons. Sometimes a parent's thoughtless move is paralleled by a court or state administrative agency decision to place a child outside the home community, without any consideration of how this move affects the child.

Researchers have examined the issue of moving and its effect on delinquent and non-delinquent youth. West (1982) found that delinquents were more apt to have experienced family moves. He also found that recidivist delinquents were particularly frequent movers.

Why should moving matter, particularly when some people contend that some children, such as offspring of military personnel, are quite able to handle shifting home fronts? A quick answer is that some military children do not handle this as well as we think. Dr. Densen-Gerber believes that most children require familiarity of "place and face." Place becomes especially important when there are changing faces because of divorce or abandonment. Sadly, too many chronic acting-out children experience too many places and too many faces, leading to rootlessness, a lack of caring and commitment, and general feelings of despair.

Moving about also has special impacts at school. For one thing, moving makes it doubly difficult for these children to learn. They are always starting over, and there is seldom any continuity between one school experience and the next. Often, prior records are never obtained, creating a situation in which educators are starting anew as if these children had no history.

The whole phenomenon of multiple relocations is best illustrated by actual cases, such as that of a 14-year-old we know. Her school history is as follows:

Kindergarten in Hampton, New Hampshire.

First, second, and third grades in Fremont, New Hampshire, when living with Aunt Lillian.

Repeated third grade in Portsmouth, New Hampshire.

Grade four in Fremont and Portsmouth, New Hampshire, and Amesbury, Massachusetts.

Grade five in Ohio.

Grade five, second semester, in Fremont and Exeter, New Hampshire.

Grades six and seven in Exeter, New Hampshire.

Grade eight in Dover, Hampton, and now Portsmouth, New Hampshire.

Compounding all of this is the presence of learning disabilities among so many chronic acting-out children. Over and over, special education personnel emphasize that educationally handicapped children require predictability and familiarity. One might ask about the right of these children *not* to be moved so they have a chance to succeed educationally. It doesn't take very many years and many moves before failing children are hopelessly behind. All manner of games are played by schools, such as grade promotion for "social" reasons, but the sad reality is that an unstable elementary school experience too often sets the stage for increased acting out and greater failure in the middle schools.

Moving about also retards the efforts of child protection agencies to make helpful interventions. In some cases, such as Susan's (Case 2), the moving is a calculated strategy by the family to escape scrutiny by child protection. As yet, no effective interstate child protective system has been developed, and even if there were such a system, some of these families would never surface again.

Given the constitutional underpinning of an American citizen's right to move about at will, we are left with the unfortunate spector of many CACs, including significant numbers who are abused, continuing to be moved so often that their chances for academic success are ruined. Until the time when a parent's right to move about can be fairly balanced with the right of at-risk children to a meaningful educational opportunity, we recommend that educators stress to these parents that moves are highly detrimental to children who are struggling in school. We further recommend that every effort be made to obtain school records to eliminate needless retesting and new attempts at interventions that were previously discontinued for good reason. At a more fundamental level, children deserve caregivers, including educators, who have a good sense of where they have been as well as where they are going.

8
Case 2:
Susan, Age 14

Summary Assessment Profile

A. CHILD FACTORS
    1. **Academic Performance**
        Public school history: Susan has lived in many different parts of the country, and her current public school has no cumulative academic records. The public school that Susan attended prior to this school did not know Susan's residence within its own district.

        Her mother reports that Susan did not have any early difficulties in school. Susan says that she found school easy and that when she made the effort, she could achieve As and Bs without difficulty. However, her public school records for the most recent two-year period reveal poor grades with predominantly Ds. The record also reveals inconsistent effort. Last year, she enrolled in a different public school, where her grades ranged from F in science to Bs in English and home economics. She withdrew from this school partway through the year and enrolled herself in a new school. Her mother did not accompany Susan, claiming that she could not take time off from work. At this school, Susan initially achieved at a high level in English but failed her other courses, again primarily because of nonattendance. By spring 1985, she was failing English because of truancy.

        a.   *Language competency:* Good, as evidenced by the aforenoted grades in English. Recent individual achievement testing measured approximately one year below grade level. Her grade placement was grade eight, with testing scores in reading comprehension and spelling at the sixth-grade level. Math measured at the eighth-grade level. Group achievement testing indicated ninth- to eleventh-grade levels in reading, language arts, social studies and science and seventh- to eighth-grade levels in math. Total achievement was a few months above grade placement.

        b.   *Areas of success:* Language (in particular), home economics.
    2. **Acting-Out Behaviors**
        a.   *Age of onset:* 12.
        b.   *Types and places:*

(1) *School:* Foremost behavior was truancy and what can best be described as a highly seductive or overly affectionate way of relating to people. It appears that the combination of the truancy, constant moving and changing schools, and her superior intelligence mitigated against her being "typed" by any one school as a major in-school behavioral problem.

(2) *Home:* Increasingly oppositional to mother, running away. She admits to theft while residing with foster parents. Also, her mother says that Susan has acted violently against her and a younger sister.

(3) *Community:* Some sexual acting out and running away.

3. **Medical/Psychiatric Status**
    a. *Size/appearance:* About 5'5", average weight, pretty.
    b. *History of injuries, illnesses, handicaps:* See c. Neurological impairment.
    c. *Neurological impairment:* Susan was born prematurely and had seizures as a young child. Also, her mother reports that Susan was always hyperactive, although doctors did not concur with a diagnosis of hyperkinesis. Her mother is unable to clarify these conditions, as for years she has been very mistrusting of doctors.
    d. *Psychiatric diagnosis:*
       Axis I—adjustment reaction of adolescence with predominantly emotional elements, secondary to chronic physical and emotional abuse.
       Axis II—diagnosis deferred.
       Axis III—none.

4. **IQ**
    a. *Full scale:* 115
    b. *Verbal:* 107
    c. *Performance:* 135

5. **Child Abuse History**
    a. *Source:* Intrafamily.
    b. *Type:* Physical, sexual[a], emotional/psychological, neglect.

    Susan describes both physical and emotional abuse from her mother. She recalls her mother screaming at her, calling her "the devil's child," telling her she hated Susan's guts, and that she (her mother) should have aborted the pregnancy. The physical abuse involved slappings and striking (always the backs of legs and Susan's face) with vacuum cords, dog leashes, and wooden boards. Susan was also kicked and locked in closets and rooms by her mother, who has acknowledged using "harsh discipline." Susan suffered bloody noses, black eyes, bruised ribs, and has some permanent scars. A year ago, her mother chased Susan from the house with a knife. Social workers also describe chronic neglect by the mother.

---

[a]Susan denies any sexual abuse, although several things suggest otherwise: (1) she has a very seductive interpersonal style; (2) her mother has hinted that two of her ex-husbands were incestual; and (3) Susan has made references to her 18-year-old sister recently residing with her (and presumably Susan's) father until the sister found out he "raped her younger sisters."

One social worker who made a home visit stated that Susan is the "bright star" in the family and that the mother resents this, as do the sisters, who also engage in constant criticism of Susan.

    c.   *Severity:* Severe.

    d.   *Frequency:* Regular.

    e.   *Duration:* Susan says that her mother has physically and psychologically abused her for as long as she can remember.

6. **Substance Abuse:** Susan has abused alcohol, although not on a regular basis. She has no known drug use.

7. **Suicide Attempts:** About a year ago Susan could not take any more of her mother and swallowed a large number of aspirins. She was hospitalized for a week.

8. **Educational Handicap:** Insofar as is known, Susan was never coded prior to referral for treatment. At the time she terminated treatment, she was being assessed as a special needs student on the basis of serious emotional disturbance.

9. **Cultural Factors:** Susan's mother was baptized as a Mormon. However, she does not approve of the Mormon religion, now believing it to be a cult. Little is known about Susan's biological father.

10. **Peer Relationships:** Susan was a survivor on the streets and was able to use friends and adults to help her survive; otherwise, she did not hang out in groups.

11. **Strengths:** She is a survivor. She is also articulate and bright and has a very pleasant personality when she is feeling positive.

12. **Other**

    a.   Treatment staff were taken aback by her overly affectionate gestures, her constant requests for hugs and kisses, and her "I love you's" to staff, whom she had known for only a few months.

    b.   Susan experienced two significant losses by death: her uncle died of bone cancer in 1981 and her best friend was killed in a train accident in 1982.

    c.   When a southern state intervened when Susan's mother was hospitalized, Susan (age 12 at the time) was working in a convenience store and was the primary source of money for the children who were left unattended. When she became overwhelmed, she called the police.

    d.   Last year, Susan filed a neglect report against her mother.

B.   FAMILY FACTORS

  1. **Changing Parental Figures**

    a.   *Divorce/remarriage/equivalent:* Susan's mother married a private in the U.S. Army in 1963. This marriage terminated at the time of Susan's birth in 1970, and it is unclear whether the first husband is her biological father. Her mother remarried in 1970, divorced, and then married a third time in 1973. This marriage ended in divorce six years later. In addition, Susan's mother has had many relationships with other men, including a Hell's Angel "bikey" with whom she and her children lived for a while.

    b.   *Adoption:* None.

    c.   *Foster parents:* Susan has lived in eight foster homes in at least four different states. In one state, a family was prepared to adopt her several years ago (something Susan wanted), but the court returned custody to the mother upon her release from a state hospital. The foster father was a policeman who responded to Susan's call for assistance when the children were left unattended while their mother was hospitalized.

    d.   *Deaths/disappearances/abandonment:* Susan's biological father and two stepfathers terminated all contact once they left the home.

2. **Siblings:** Susan is the third of four girls, the others being 19, 18, and 9. Uncertainty exists over paternity. Susan's mother reports that all her children were born prematurely, although the mother claims that only Susan has caused her real problems. The 9-year-old is mother's "pet"; the 18-year-old is living away from home; and the 19-year-old is severely learning disabled, pregnant, resides with her mother, and "mimics and repeats" whatever her mother says.

3. **Economic Status:** The mother is a high school graduate, attended college, but most of her employment has been as a waitress in bars. None of the former husbands contribute any support, insofar as is known.

4. **Spousal/Sibling Violence:** Insofar as is known, Susan's mother was not physically abused herself by the men in her life, nor were her children. Instead investigating social service personnel indicate that Susan has historically been the center of much emotional abuse from her siblings as well as from her mother, who has also been very physically abusive to Susan. The mother states that Susan has threatened to kill her younger sister and fears that Susan may act on the threat. On one occasion, Susan attempted to break her younger sister's arm, and her mother slapped her to make her stop.

5. **Parental/Sibling Substance Abuse:** The mother has a long history of drinking heavily and smoking marijuana regularly. Her drug use, according to Susan, began when they lived with the "bikey." Susan's two older sisters are both heavy drinkers and drug users, including speed and cocaine. Her 9-year-old sister drinks beer at home. Susan's maternal grandfather and uncle are also alcoholics.

6. **Parental/Sibling Perpetration of Child Abuse:** As noted, the mother, in concert with Susan's three sisters, has directed a great deal of psychological abuse at Susan. In short, Susan is a "target child." In addition, the mother has physically abused Susan for years and acknowledges to social service workers that she has always been "too strong a disciplinarian."

7. **Relocations:** Susan's family has a long history of relocations. She was born in state A and resided there until age 7 or 8. The family then moved to state B for one month. The next move was to state C for a short time. From state C they moved back to state A for a summer. After state A, the family moved to state D, where they lived for about two and a half years. They left state D for state E to avoid further investigation when one of Susan's older sisters was placed in reform school. They then resided in state E for three years.

    After the sister's release from a reform school, the family moved to a southern state about the time of Susan's thirteenth birthday. They moved to the Northeast just before her fourteenth birthday to live with her mother's sister. Mother and sister had a falling out, resulting in the mother moving to the apartment where she currently lives. Susan reports she has lived in twelve foster homes over the past five years. Eight of these are documented. The first placements were precipitated by the mother's hospitalizations; subsequent ones were related to Susan's oppositional behavior at home and her own request for intervention.

8. **Psychiatric/Medical Status of Parent(s):** The mother has had several nervous breakdowns, involving at least two hospitalizations since 1979. On a third occasion, she refused to be hospitalized. Susan says her mother stayed at home "acting real crazy."

    The mother also has a kidney problem; however, she has not sought medical assistance, citing no medical insurance and mistrust of doctors.

9. **Integration/Isolation**
    a. *Family:* The mother acknowledges no present contact with any of her siblings or her father, who never married her mother. After her parents split, Susan's mother lived with her father from age 7 to 18 because of an illness her mother had.
    b. *Community:* Her mother has no known community contacts other than those associated with her job as a waitress. She has no means of transportation and walks to work. In addition, she no longer has any religious involvement and has a history of refusing (and even running from) social services. She has had no involvement with the public schools.

10. **Advocacy Capability:** Her mother has very little ability or inclination to advocate for Susan's needs. Compounding matters is her resistance to any social services assistance.

11. **Other:** None.

C. PRIOR SYSTEM INTERVENTIONS
    1. **Public Schools:** The absence of a cumulative scholastic file makes it impossible to determine whether, as Susan and her mother say, no school interventions were attempted. It is plausible that Susan was not eligible or in need of special education services because of her high IQ, although counseling was needed.
    2. **Child Protection:** Child protection agencies in at least five different states have been involved with this family. Because of the many moves, no state CPS has ever been able to have sustained involvement with the family.
    3. **Judicial:** Susan was placed in foster homes by the court system in 1980 and again in 1983; these placements were initiated by CPS because of the mother's breakdowns and inability to care for the children. In these instances, the courts granted temporary custody to the state.

        More recently, Susan was brought to court on a CHINS petition for running away, truancy, and being unmanageable. Susan was first placed in a group home, then in a treatment program. This court became the third state court to temporarily switch custody from the mother to the state child protection agency. In recognition of the mother's history of abuse and degradation of Susan, the court barred the mother from contact with Susan until such time as treatment staff decided Susan was ready.

        The mother filed the CHINS petition approximately one month after Susan filed a neglect petition against her mother. One month prior to this, Susan attempted suicide through an overdose of aspirin.

4. **Mental Health:** Family counseling was provided for a while when the family lived in a western state. This was not a successful experience. The current court of jurisdiction subsequently ordered family counseling as part of the group home placement for Susan. However, her mother did not show for the sessions. Otherwise, it is not known what treatments were provided the mother during her periods of hospitalization.

Interview with Dr. Densen-Gerber

David Sandberg (DS): How does this case compare with Case 1 based on your review of the reports?

Dr. D-G: The most significant difference between this case and George's is that the primary system for Susan should have been child protection, with the public school being a significant adjunct resource. With George, child protection was certainly needed, but, in my view, the public school should and could have been the primary system. Susan needed a new home and geographic stability most of all, which CPS could and should have provided. Her superior intelligence enabled her to do some learning despite all the family abuse and chaos. However, she was also blocked from learning in the sense that she is not progressing from grade to grade as she should and easily could have if all this turmoil was not present in the home.

DS: Notwithstanding the high IQ, I'm still puzzled over the As and Bs, however sporadic they were.

Dr. D-G: It is very difficult to understand how Susan could do well in school given all the chaos in her family life. There may have been a disassociative phenomenon at work.

DS: It is interesting to note that Susan was able to test out at a few months above grade placement.

Dr. D-G: Yes, but if all was well in the home, she probably would have tested three to four years above grade level. The important issue of a child's potential must always be part of any evaluation and assessment planning, in my view.

DS: A child filing an abuse or neglect report against her own parent is unusual in my experience.

Dr. D-G: Yes. Susan filing a neglect petition against her mother is extraordinary. Very few children do this. It takes a lot of guts—and hostility! But she did this only after trying to kill herself, which was another "flag" for help.

After being chased with a knife, Susan had every right to file an assault and battery charge against her mother. It's noteworthy that if anyone else except a parent had threatened her with a knife, an assault and battery charge would normally result. But in our society, we still allow parents to behave this way against their children without criminal repercussions.

DS: This case is a "systems failure" case as I see it. Do you agree?

Dr. D-G: Yes. The child protection system allowed this family to move about without putting together a "trail," resulting in Susan's continually appearing anew without a history. This is not in her best interest. Child protection in at least one state knew of the abusive home condition but unfortunately either could not or chose not to find out where Susan's family had moved.

DS: Is this a case the public schools could have handled given adequate backup by child protection?

Dr. D-G: There is no question that Susan could have been educated in the public schools, but she needed major, ongoing support by the child protection system and the courts. This is a parental termination case. Susan needed a foster/adoptive home at an early age. Susan's family is so chaotic, including the running from state to state, that the child protection system, in conjunction with the courts, needed to be the primary intervention agent. Even the best school-based intervention could not work, because this family runs whenever people move in to help the children.

DS: Susan clearly appears to be a target child. Any explanations?

Dr. D-G: It is very important to know her paternity; Susan may have been differently fathered by a man whom her mother grew to detest. Also, she is very bright and attractive, qualities that have not been observed in her other family members. She is what I call a petunia in an onion patch.

DS: I note, too, that she was a hyperactive child.

Dr. D-G: The very bright are often hyperactive as children but are not necessarily ADD children. They just have more curiosity and energy.

DS: What about the childhood seizures?

Dr. D-G: For one thing, seizures are terrifying to the child and to the parent, who often does not know what to do. The seizures can set the child apart as different, even as a burden. An EEG should be done to see if she continues to be epileptic and if medication is in order.

DS: As in Case 1, there is a discrepancy between the verbal and performance scores.

Dr. D-G: Yes. It is unclear whether the verbal score is low because of organicity or deprivation. In any event, frequently, frustration results from being able to do tasks well but not being able to communicate at a similar level of complexity. It should also be noted that deprivation, abuse, and neglect adversely affect the verbal scores more than performance. Susan's testing clearly shows an ability to use language but suggests a lack of encouragement, particularly in the home, to do so. Such a wide discrepancy pattern is noted as an antecedent to acting out, conduct disorders, and later sociopathy.

DS: Aren't there pretty clear indicia of sexual abuse here, even though Susan denies that?

Dr. D-G: One explanation is that Susan may be disassociative. She may have totally denied or blocked memories of any sexual abuse, such that she really believes it never occurred. We need additional clarifying information to be sure. For example, what does the mother mean when she "hints" that her ex-husbands were incestual. When and with whom? Also, we need to know more about her sister learning that their father had "raped" the younger girls, which presumably includes Susan.

DS: What about Susan's overly close interpersonal style? Others have described it as "overly affectionate" but not seductive.

Dr. D-G: The clinging child is always a possibly abused child. It's one of the indicia of abuse when the child behaves this way to all adults without discriminating who the adults are.

DS: I'm struck by Susan working at age 12 in what must have been a futile attempt to keep the family together when her mother was hospitalized.

Dr. D-G: Yes, she apparently tried desperately to keep everything together, despite rejection, abuse and neglect by the mother. She is much like Cinderella—again, the petunia in the onion patch. Let me make the additional point that Susan also suffers from not knowing who her father is. She does not know for sure whether her siblings are full or half-siblings; we think they are likely half-siblings. Plus, there is all the moving about. Rootlessness and a lot of energy devoted to "Where did I come from?"

DS: How disturbed is her mother?

Dr. D-G: Very disturbed, in my opinion. She rejects her heritage and her own child. Since we know about the hospitalizations, we must assume that she is not a bad person but rather that she is experiencing significant psychiatric difficulties. Clearly, this mother is unable to parent properly. Also, let us not forget that this mother experienced considerable trauma as a child, including long-term separation from her own mother. There may be a genetic predisposition to severe mental disease.

DS: Such that it is very difficult to understand how one court could have returned Susan to her mother, especially when there was a foster family ready to care for Susan long-term.

Dr. D-G: More systems abuse. How much abuse and neglect must a child be subjected to before permanent removal is ordered?

DS: Where does Susan's giftedness come from given other family members who are not her equal IQ-wise?

Dr. D-G: Giftedness is usually genetic, but it can occur in isolation. However, it is more probable that Susan was fathered by a high-IQ man, although her mother attended college and may be quite bright but malfunctioning because of her psychiatric problems.

DS: To me, it borders on the criminal that CPS kept intervening, trying to assist Susan and her siblings, and the mother kept denying the assistance by moving to another state. Do you have any thoughts about how this could be prevented?

Dr. D-G: I'm not sure, but this is a most serious problem that must be addressed nationally.

DS: In one state I know of, it is a Class B felony for a noncustodial parent to remove a child from the state with the intent to deprive the other parent custody. Susan's mother was in an analogous situation in three different states where CPS had custody. I would like to see this law apply to such situations. Also, the federal Missing Children Act could be amended to include such cases. Do you agree that such legislation is needed?

Dr. D-G: Yes, I do. The juvenile interstate compact system must also be properly adapted and applied. However, nationally, we Americans are opposed to tracking. Nonetheless, I believe that it must be done. Susan's case illustrates why.

DS: It occurs to me that just the relocations alone would be enough to prevent Susan from succeeding academically.

Dr. D-G: Absolutely. These were not well-thought-out, necessary moves. They were always for the purpose of escaping from child protective services. The mother, a distrustful, paranoid, and suspicious person, wanted no one to intervene. It is herself and three of her children against the world. She, in my opinion, is a very disturbed, confused person who has been allowed to circumvent the system, all contrary to Susan's best interest. Permitting this situation to happen is contrary to Susan's ability to have an opportunity to be educated and a reasonable chance to be a well-functioning adult.

DS: Let me ask you about the preliminary diagnosis. Do you concur in light of the additional information we now have about Susan?

Dr. D-G: No, I believe she suffers from some type of disassociative disorder; adjustment reaction of adolescence isn't strong enough. To me, Susan exhibits a number of characteristics of disassociation, including her ability to do very well in school in the face of an extraordinary home situation. I can not fathom how else she would have coped with all that she had to endure unless she had the capacity for disassociation and massive denial, mechanisms that are adaptive to maltreatment but in the long term maladaptive to healthy living. We need to understand that many abused children do not perceive any way to escape. They are thus left to extraordinary means to respond to all the maltreatment if they are not to go insane. Becoming disassociative, psychiatrists are learning more and more, is one such extraordinary means. Also, I consider diagnosis a part of a fluid process, subject to change as the child alters his/her course of behavior as a result of such things as therapeutic intervention or worsening life events.

DS: When Susan swallowed a bottle of aspirins, this was more than just a suicidal gesture, wasn't it?

Dr. D-G: Yes. She was and is deeply distressed. It can also be seen as one additional type of "flagging" behavior.

DS: How do you explain Susan's absence of major substance abuse, particularly when all her siblings and mother are abusers?

Dr. D-G: I don't know why, but it does further illustrate her being the petunia, or "Cindersusan."

DS: Therapeutically speaking, what does Susan need foremost?

Dr. D-G: First, an updated diagnosis. Then she needs a psychiatric foster home and psychotherapy. She needs to be parented by well-educated people who also have insight into who Susan is. Again, I believe she may be disassociative, a budding multiple personality.

DS: Finally, what accounts for Susan's remaining a reasonably honorable person in the face of a life experience that often dictates delinquency, substance abuse, and so forth?

Dr. D-G: I point to a genetic predisposition to what I have termed "withstanding toughness." She is a *survivor*. Some humans survive adversity; others don't. And if I am right that she is disassociative, this would further explain her surviving an extraordinary life ordeal, living in an emotional concentration camp. An Auschwitz evokes this type of response, and disassociation gets you "over the wall," so to speak.

Part III
Barriers to
Intervention

The following chapters are concerned with analysis of what we consider the foremost barriers to more effective interventions on behalf of CACs, many of whom may be abused or neglected. The barriers fall under four main headings: legal, psychiatric, educational or "interinstitutional," and resource.

We address these issues recognizing that the nation's educators should not be asked to take on new burdens without thoughtful consideration of potential or actual barriers. We also want to better understand just how imposing these barriers are.

Consequently, we asked Henry Beyer, assisted by Margaret Daley, to address a number of legal issues directly bearing on CACs and on greater public school participation in their lives (Chapter 9). Dr. Judianne Densen-Gerber was then invited to participate in a question-and-answer dialogue with the principal author to explore potential danger areas in pursuing psychiatric/emotional issues, including abuse and neglect, with students (Chapter 10). A paramount consideration for us was possible widespread educator resistance to being asked to do yet one more thing on behalf of the nation's increasingly troubled students. We gave this task to Cynthia Mowles, a superintendent of schools (Chapter 11). Finally, although we could not do much given the limited scope of our project, at least some mention needed to be made of resources and resource limitations (Chapter 12).

Chapters 9 through 12 are not concerned only with addressing potential barriers to intervenors. Chapters 9 and 10, in particular, provide positive guidance to educators on how to proceed legally and safely in the effort to be more helpful to CACs. In addition, Chapter 10 offers important information about CACs, child maltreatment, and classroom adjustments that may have to be made with abused or neglected children.

9
Legal Barriers

Henry Beyer

A 1962 article by Dr. C. Henry Kempe in the *Journal of the American Medical Association*, describing the "battered child syndrome," first generated national awareness of the problems of abused children.[1] Within a short time, all fifty states[2] had enacted legislation to provide an institutionalized mechanism to protect children against domestic violence and other forms of abuse.[3] This swift response, demonstrating a strong national commitment to protecting children against violence, is especially noteworthy when viewed against the historic lack of legal rights for children.[4]

The child abuse statutes enacted by the states are by no means identical. They vary, for instance, in delineating the span of years throughout which children are protected, the maximum age ranging from 16 to 21.[5] The statutes are similar in many respects, however. Nearly every state encompasses within its definition of the term *child abuse* the infliction of serious bodily injury by a parent or by others in loco parentis—that is, standing in the place of a parent. Most states also include sexual intercourse with, and molestation of, a child within the scope of the definition. Some states include not only the actual infliction of physical injury but also the creation of a *risk* of serious injury, as well as the infliction of psychological injury. Others consider the infliction of *any* injury to be abuse, regardless of whether it is "serious."[6]

Mandatory Reporting

To promote the goal of preventing future harm to children who have already been abused, every state requires specified professionals to report suspected cases of abuse.[7] Those explicitly mandated to report abuse are individuals who normally come in contact with children, who possess information regarding the child and his/her physical condition, and whose professional role places them in a situation in which they may detect early signs of, and may suspect the existence of, child abuse.[8]

In every state, doctors and hospitals are required to report suspected abuse cases.[9] In all states, teachers are also specifically mandated to report.[10] The rationale is that a teacher may be the first person outside the child's home to discover a child's injuries, especially since abusing parents often do not seek medical attention for their injured children for fear of prosecution.[11]

It has been suggested that mandated reporters may sometimes wish to forgo an abuse report out of concern for possible retaliation directed toward the child. Research has disclosed no case law on this issue, and the statutes appear to make no provision for such an exception to the reporting requirement. The abuse reporting system is based on the principle that the state agency statutorily responsible for receiving abuse reports shall investigate their validity[12] and shall take whatever action is necessary to protect the child from further abuse, including any abuse that might be termed retaliation.[13]

Nothing in the reporting laws require more than one report from a mandated reporter. The main purpose of the laws is to prevent future abuse.[14] If a mandated reporter suspects that an abusive situation has been terminated, it is unclear whether a report must still be filed under the rationale that the child still has an abused status requiring treatment. Most statutes are framed in a way that requires reports of suspected *instances* of child abuse[15] rather than in terms of known continuing situations. A reporter who declines to make a report because of a personal evaluation that the abuse was terminated may be placing the child's health at risk and may be denying to the family counseling services provided by the state. One of the premises on which the child protective services system rests is that such services play a key role in breaking the intergenerational abuse cycle.[16]

Confidentiality

Mandated reporters (that is, individuals who are legally required to report suspected abuse) must do so despite any special relationship that would under other circumstances be recognized as a confidential one and thus not subject to such a statutory obligation.[17] Because society has made the detection and prevention of child abuse a preeminent public policy, many state legislatures have specifically abrogated the privileges associated with special relationships that ordinarily protect communications against disclosure.[18] Legislatures are able to do this because the reason for creating such privileges in the first place was to further particular public policies.[19] It is therefore entirely proper for them to negate such privileges in furtherance of an even higher public policy, such as the prevention of child abuse.

Although extensive research has failed to discover any case yet decided regarding the effect of a child abuse allegation on the teacher–student relationship, other even more traditional immunities (such as those between husband and wife, priest and parishioner, or doctor and patient) have, on occasion, been voided by legislatures or courts for the sake of protecting children.[20] It seems clear, therefore, that if it were pitted against a statutory duty to report, the teacher–student relationship would not be recognized as a valid excuse for failing to report.

Liability for Failure to Report

As of 1981, thirty-two states had imposed criminal liability for failure of a mandated reporter to report an instance of suspected child abuse.[21] Although only five states made specific provisions for civil liability,[22] under the "presumption of negligence" doctrine, violation of a criminal statute will also frequently lead to civil liability.[23] Several other states have created a duty to report, but without specifying any penalty for its breach.[24]

Although the failure to report a reasonable suspicion of child abuse is punishable in most states as a misdemeanor,[25] criminal penalties are almost never enforced.[26] As of 1984, it appears that not one professional had ever been convicted of willfully failing to comply with child abuse reporting laws.[27] A survey of recent cases turned up only one attempted criminal prosecution of a teacher for failure to report a case of suspected child abuse.[28] In that case, a Clairmont, California, teacher was brought up on misdemeanor charges for failure to inform police about a 12-year-old boy's fondling of an 8-year-old girl. Surprisingly, the case generated a great deal of public support for the teacher, on the grounds that the reporting statute was meant to apply only to abuse inflicted by adults.[29] Also, the teacher had consulted the school's psychologist, who had advised her to keep the information confidential. She was not convicted.

Perhaps the major reason that criminal charges are rarely brought for failure to report is that all states except Michigan require proof of *willful* misconduct in order to convict.[30] This subjective standard requires a showing that the defendant actually knew of or suspected the abuse.[31] Clearly, this is a much more difficult burden of proof than the objective negligence standard adopted by Michigan, which imposes liability upon a showing of "constructive" knowledge. Thus, in Michigan, if a rational person who is statutorily required to report knew *or should have known of or suspected* the abuse,the actual state of mind of that person is irrelevant.

Research of recent case law has disclosed no instance of a civil action brought by or for a student against a teacher for failure to report suspected abuse. This is not, however, because such a suit does not state a claim upon which relief can be granted. In the California case of *Landeros v. Flood,*[32] a child brought an action against a physician and a hospital for their 1971 failure to properly diagnose the battered child syndrome and for failure to report these findings to the authorities.[33] This was the first U.S. lawsuit seeking recovery for injuries under an abuse reporting statute.

In *Landeros,* the lower state court found no basis for imposing a legal liability upon the medical people involved, because "the battered child syndrome . . . has not become—at least as yet—an integral and demonstrable part of the skill and learning of an everyday medical practitioner."[34] The justices of the California Supreme Court, however, in their 1976 review of the decision, said that they "simply do not know whether the views [on the battered child syndrome] espoused in the literature had been generally adopted in the medical profession by the year 1971, and whether the ordinarily prudent physician was conducting his practice in accordance therewith. The question remains one of fact, to be decided on the basis of expert testimony."[35]

As a result of massive national publicity during the decade and a half that have elapsed since the reporting failures in the case, the skills and knowledge required to detect child abuse are presumably now much more common in the medical profession. Whether they are sufficiently widespread in the teaching profession, however, to be used as a standard of behavior for the "ordinary prudent teacher" would probably still be considered by most judges to be a question of fact to be decided by the jury.

A review of representative child abuse reporting statutes[36] reveals no specifically delineated indicia of abuse and neglect. Nor does case law provide much guidance as to what signs a mandated reporter must observe in order to satisfy the requirement of "suspicion."[37] This is not surprising, considering that suspicion has been legally defined as the "apprehension of something without proof or upon slight evidence which does not amount to proof."[38]

Teachers are required to report their suspicions because they are able to observe, on a regular basis, children who might not otherwise come to the attention of any representative of the public.[39] In the absence of actually observing an incident of abuse or having a child confide that abuse is occurring, teachers must base their suspicions on circumstantial evidence. Medically documented psychological responses that are frequently exhibited by abused children may properly give rise to such suspicions. For instance, common behavioral indicators of children who are sexually abused have been reported to include withdrawal, fantasy, or infantile behavior; bizarre, sophisticated, or unusual sexual behavior or knowledge; delinquency or running away; and poor peer relationships.[40] Any such behavior may be indicative of sexual abuse. Obviously, not every child with poor peer relations is sexually abused, but such behavior should "alert one to the possibility that abuse or neglect is taking place and should be investigated. Clearly, if several indicators are present, or if they occur repeatedly, the probability of maltreatment is greater."[41]

Except in cases where evidence of abuse is clear and conspicuous, it would appear quite difficult to enforce the reporting statutes by penalizing educators who fail to file reports. Greater success in increasing the number of reports can probably be achieved by educating teachers as to the importance of their role in alleviating child abuse and by providing them with positive incentives to file reports. One such incentive might be the implementation of procedures for increasing the level of feedback to the reporter from the child protection agency. Educators have noted that they are rarely informed of the status or disposition of abuse reports they have filed.[42] At least one state task force[43] has recognized this as a disincentive to mandated reporters and has recommended administrative action to "improve [the] system of feedback to reporters."[44]

Currently, many states allow disclosure of information concerning abuse investigations to certain professionals. In New York, for instance, the "person in charge of an institution, school, facility or agency making the report shall receive, *upon request,* a summary of the findings of and action taken by the child protective service in response to the report."[45] This provision has been criticized, however, for not clearly requiring that mandated reporters be given such feedback automatically.[46] Furthermore, the reporting statute appears to forbid the person in charge from passing on this information to others, including the teacher who initiated the report.[47] In California, however, at the completion of an investigation of abuse, the investigating agency is statutorily required to inform the mandated reporter "of the results of the investigation and of any other action the agency is taking with regard to the child or family."[48] It thus appears that statutory changes would be required in some states but not in others in order to provide individual teachers with feedback that might provide additional incentive to report suspected abuse.

Liability for Filing an Erroneous Report

One reason often cited for mandated reporters' failure to report is their fear of possible civil action, such as for slander or defamation, brought against them for an erroneous report.[49] In an effort to relieve such fears and to promote reporting, most state statutes explicitly provide immunity to mandated reporters who, in "good faith," inform authorities of suspected abuse.[50] One typical provision reads:

> The identity of a reporting person shall be confidential subject to disclosure only with the consent of that person or by judicial process. A person acting in good faith who makes a

report or assists in any other requirement of this act shall be immune from civil or criminal liability which might otherwise be incurred thereby. A person making a report or assisting in any other requirement of this act shall be presumed to have acted in good faith. This immunity from civil or criminal liability extends only to acts done pursuant to this act and does not extend to a negligent act which causes personal injury or death or to the malpractice of a physician which results in personal injury or death.[51]

Reporters in most states are thus not subject to any criminal or civil liability unless they knowingly turn in a false report.[52]

It is remotely possible that a teacher could be penalized in other ways for filing a good faith report of suspected abuse. In *Maus v. National Living Centers*,[53] a nurse's aide was discharged from her job at a Texas nursing home in retaliation for reporting suspected abuse and neglect of patients at the home. The Texas Court of Appeals ruled that the firing was permissible under the state's "employment at will" doctrine, even though the state's institutional abuse reporting statute granted her immunity from civil and criminal liability and actually would have subjected her to criminal prosecution if she had not reported![54] It should be noted, however, that in this case it was the mandated reporter's employer who was being reported as the suspected abuser; a teacher would be in a rather different situation in reporting a parent as a possible abuser.

Student Records

Public school systems are required by state and federal law to maintain records pertaining to the health and academic status of enrolled students. Among the items that student records should contain are dates of school attendance, numbers of days absent, the student's health record, results of vision and hearing screenings, results of and reports from any special evaluations (e.g., speech, hearing, psychology test results; socialworker, guidance counselor, special teacher reports), all standardized achievement test results, and copies of all due process notices provided the family and all consent forms concerning special education that are signed by the family. The question arises whether any of these records might be useful in detecting instances of child abuse and, if so, whether teachers and other potential abuse reporters have a right of access to them.

Information in student records is protected by the federal Family Educational Rights and Privacy Act (FERPA), commonly referred to as the Buckley amendment.[55] This amendment, enacted in 1974, is designed to protect the privacy of both parents and students.[56] Under its provisions, parents (and students over age 18) have the rights to inspect and review all written records, to deny access to persons who do not have a "legitimate educational interest" in reviewing the records, to obtain a hearing on their complaints concerning the records, and to have corrections and amendments made in the records where appropriate. These rights apply not only to records directly related to education but to *any* records regarding the student that the school system may be keeping. If, for example, a school system receives a student's medical report from a physician and maintains the report in the record file, it must be made accessible to parents, even though it may be stamped "confidential."[57]

Certain records are excepted from this accessibility rule. One exception encompasses documents that are "in the sole possession of the maker thereof and . . . not accessible or revealed to any other individual except a substitute."[58] This exception would apply to notes a teacher may make and keep personally, showing them to no one except possibly another teacher who substitutes for the author of the notes.

Under the Buckley amendment, no permission is needed for the release of records to teachers within the educational system in which the child is enrolled who are determined to have a "legitimate educational interest";[59] to state and local authorities to whom such information is specifically required to be reported or disclosed pursuant to state statute adopted prior to November 19, 1974;[60] or to organizations conducting studies for the purpose of "improving instruction."[61] Most significantly, the statute includes an explicit exemption allowing the release of information *without parental consent* if such information is "necessary to protect the health or safety of the student."[62] Schools must maintain a record, accessible to parents, of all persons requesting access to a student's records. The record need not indicate, however, which teacher or other "excepted" individuals have reviewed the records.[63]

Thus, although research has disclosed no case law regarding the right of teachers to inspect student records for the purpose of detecting child abuse, the Buckley amendment does not appear to present any obstacle to such inspections.

The Education for All Handicapped Children Act

The Education for All Handicapped Children Act[64] provides federal funds to state and local education agencies to assist them in providing special education to children with mental or physical disabilities. The act guarantees handicapped children the right to a free, appropriate, public education in all states that accept such assistance; all states currently participate in the program.[65]

The act is intended to serve children with mental retardation, hearing impairments, visual impairments, speech impairments, specific learning disabilities (such as dyslexia), serious emotional disturbances,[66] orthopedic or physical impairments, or other health impairments.[67] School systems are required to evaluate any child exhibiting characteristics of these designated handicaps in order to determine whether he/she is eligible for special education services, to decide upon an appropriate educational placement, and to design an individualized education program for the child.

Might a special education evaluation be used by a school system as part of its attempt to strengthen or refute a teacher's faint inkling that abuse might be a possible explanation for a child's substandard performance or unusual behavior? Although some observers have condemned the use of the special education process for purposes not related to educating students with handicaps,[68] it is also recognized that the practice occurs with considerable regularity.[69]

It appears, however, that no perversion of the process would be required in order to institute an evaluation in many instances when there is a concern that does not rise to the level of a "suspicion" of abuse. This is because abused children frequently exhibit the characteristics of "serious emotional disturbances,"[70] one of the handicapping conditions covered under the Act. "Seriously emotionally disturbed" children are defined as those who exhibit, over a long period of time and to a marked degree, one or more of the following characteristics that adversely affect their educational performance: (1) an inability to learn that cannot be explained by intellectual, sensory, or health factors; (2) an inability to build or maintain satisfactorily interpersonal relationships with peers and teachers; (3) inappropriate types of behavior or feelings under normal circumstances; (4) a general, pervasive mood of unhappiness or depression; or (5) a tendency to develop physical symptoms or fears associated with personal school problems.[71] Teachers may thus properly refer for evaluation a student exhibiting any of these signs in the hope of determining not only the child's educational needs but also whether he/she is being subjected to abuse. Such a referral, however, may never be substituted for the filing of a report with a child protective agency when abuse is actually suspected.

Evaluation testing usually consists of a battery of tests—measuring intelligence, aptitude, or ability—by a school psychologist or psychometrist. A child may also be tested for speech and hearing impairments, tested by a school nurse to determine if the child has any health problems, and tested by a school social worker to determine the nature of the child's family and developmental background. The child may also be referred to a physician for detailed analysis of any medical problems. It is certainly possible that evidence of abuse might be discovered in one or more of these tests or examinations, especially if the examiners are trained in recognizing signs of abuse.[72]

Under the special education regulations, however, families must be notified of a proposed evaluation. This notice must include a full explanation of the procedural safeguards available to parents and children under the law, a description of why the evaluation is being proposed, a description of the legal and educational options available, and a description of other factors relevant to the school's proposal.[73] A possible impediment to using the evaluation process to investigate child abuse lies in the regulation that requires that written parental consent be obtained before the conduct of such an evaluation.[74] In at least one case, however, it has been held that a state administrative hearing officer may override a parent's refusal to provide such consent.[75] The Illinois state education agency ruled: "When a parent refuses to consent to an initial evaluation, that refusal is a reviewable action. The administrative review may determine that a sufficient basis exists to warrant the overriding of the refusal and may override it with an order that an evaluation occur. . . . [T]he parent . . . may seek judicial review in such cases."[76] Although a parent's refusal would not seem to present an insurmountable barrier to the conduct of a special education evaluation when some mild intimation of possible child abuse exists, the delays involved in obtaining a hearing officer's order for the evaluation may make such an approach impracticable in many cases.

Limitations on an Educator's Investigatory Activities

Generally, state child abuse reporting statutes do not require that mandated reporters do anything more than inform the proper authorities of their suspicions.[77] As discussed earlier, the state reporting statutes confer immunity from civil liability on individuals making reports. This immunity is preconditioned, however, on the filing of a report. Therefore, teachers who are interested in conducting a personal investigation are not protected by the statute from civil actions (such as for slander or invasion of privacy) until they have actually filed such a report with the proper authorities.

Teachers should thus be extremely wary of conducting their own investigations. The abuse reporting statutes confer investigational responsibilities not on local school systems or their employees but on child protective and law enforcement agencies. The legislatures' intent that these latter agencies conduct the required investigations is conveyed both implicitly, by the particular reporting and investigations systems established by the statutes, and explicitly, in the statutes themselves.[78] Child protective and police agencies are likely to be familiar with the law in the area and generally better prepared to approach and discuss the situations with the actors involved. The doctrine of *ultra vires*, which requires that agencies limit their activities to those that are legislatively authorized,[79] may thus bar some of the actions a teacher may wish to perform in the course of a personal investigation. If a teacher's action (e.g., an investigatory visit to the home) is *ultra vires*, then the teacher may not be acting officially as an agent of the school system but may be, in the law's quaint phrase, "on a frolic of his [or her] own."[80] In such case, the teacher may be personally liable for any injury (e.g., defamation, invasion of privacy) that he/she might cause. Following the same reasoning, it would be most unwise for a teacher to attempt to regulate a student's behavior and/or whereabouts at times that are unrelated to school activities.[81]

The U.S. Supreme Court upheld the validity of investigatory home visits by state administrative agencies in its 1970 ruling in *Wyman v. James*.[82] The Court held that agency staff visits to the homes of recipients of AFDC (Aid to Families with Dependent Children) was a reasonable administrative tool and did not violate the Fourth or Fourteenth Amendments of the U.S. Constitution. It should be noted, however, that the *Wyman* visits were not conducted for the purpose of collecting evidence of a crime and that their constitutionality could be upheld on the basis of the state's distribution of government benefits to the families visited. Most important, in *Wyman*, state law specifically authorized and required an agency case worker to visit the home; an investigatory home visit by a teacher or school social worker would be conducted under no such authority.

Although the U.S. Supreme Court ruled in 1985 that a school official's search of a student's purse was not unconstitutional because he had a reasonable suspicion that it contained cigarettes, the Court continues to recognize a school child's Fourth Amendment right to a "legitimate expectation of privacy."[83] Furthermore, many jurisdictions impose significant restrictions on the types and extent of investigations teachers may conduct, even within the confines of the school. For example, although an alert physical education teacher might note telltale bruises on a child changing clothes in the locker room, that teacher is legally prohibited in some jurisdictions from asking the child to strip for the purposes of seeing whether such marks exist.[84] Furthermore, some states allow only police officers to have children given medical examinations, such as X-rays, without parental consent, and then only after receiving authorization from a magistrate.[85]

Besides the possible use of a special education evaluation (discussed earlier), what may a teacher properly do when he/she first realizes that abuse may be a possible explanation for the behavior, academic performance, or condition of a particular student? Although we have found no case law on the subject, it is almost certainly permissible for the teacher to ask the child, discreetly and considerately, if abuse or neglect is occurring. Such an inquiry should be made privately (to avoid, insofar as possible, the potential for defamation) and with due care for the student's sensibilities (to avoid any perception or actuality of harassment or infliction of emotional distress). If the teacher has any reservations about his/her ability to ask such a question with sufficient tact or to deal properly with the student's possible reactions to the question, the teacher should consider having the school psychologist ask the question. Although the involvement of another person may increase the possibility of a charge of defamation (which is possible, however remotely, even when the student alone is asked a question that implies that his/her parent may be a child abuser), such great weight is currently being given to public policies aimed at detecting and preventing abuse that it would appear unlikely in the extreme that two mandated reporters would be held liable for discreetly sharing information as a prelude to the possible filing of an abuse report. The educators' good faith in attempting to fulfill their reporting duty responsibly should serve as an effective defense.[86]

The foregoing assumes, however, (1) that there existed some grounds prompting the teacher to make the inquiry; (2) that the question was posed in a discreet, considerate manner; and (3) that the teacher acted in good faith in all other respects. If, after the inquiry, the teacher suspects abuse and files a report, then the reporting act's immunity clause will provide additional, statutory protection.

Although the possibility appears extremely slight of a successful action against a teacher making a good faith inquiry of the student about whom he/she is concerned, it would behoove the teacher not to extend such inquiries to other individuals. Educators should bear in mind that, under existing laws, they have the legal duty only to *report* suspicions of abuse; others have the legal responsibility and authority to investigate such reports.[87] Teachers and, it is hoped, students will be best served if all parties fulfill their assigned roles.

Congressional Prohibition of Examinations in Certain Programs

The U.S. Congress has decreed:

> No student shall be required, as part of any applicable program, to submit to psychiatric examination, testing or treatment, or psychological examination, testing or treatment, in which the primary purpose is to reveal information concerning: . . .
>
> (2) mental and psychological problems potentially embarrassing to the student or his family . . .
>
> (5) critical appraisals of other individuals with whom respondents have close family relationships.[88]

At first glance, this prohibition would appear to present a serious obstacle to use of special education evaluations as proposed herein. Upon closer inspection, however, the statute appears to apply only to "research or experimentation" programs or projects intended to explain or develop new or improved teaching methods or techniques. Although the precise statutory applicability is far from clear—and no case law yet exists that interprets the scope or application of the section—it appears most unlikely, given the high national priority assigned to the reduction of child abuse, that it would ever be used to prevent examinations designed to uncover such abuse.[89]

Principal Author's Note

The current statutory provisions that allow disclosures of information concerning the status of abuse investigations to certain professionals are by no means uniform. Some states still do not authorize a CPS feedback; others, though allowing such feedback, are very limiting as to whom can be informed.

Elsewhere in this Handbook Jaclyn Adams comments that lack of CPS feedback is one of the most serious problems she has encountered as a public school special education coordinator. Jeannette Gagnon, also a member of our project, had indicated that the CPS reluctance to disclose information to other professionals often has more to do with concern over a family's complaints about disclosures than with any laws forbidding disclosure.

One of the most thorough assessments of the problem was done by José Alfaro, director of the (New York) Mayor's Task Force on Child Abuse and Neglect. Alfaro recently surveyed 131 school personnel, among others, to determine the foremost impediments to the mandated reporting of suspected child abuse and neglect. He concluded:

> Steps to improve the relationship between mandated reporters and the child protective agency, as well as steps to improve the quality of the program, are likely to be the most effective means of improving reporting. The most potent means of improving the relationship will be activities to strengthen feedback and communication—the most frequently made recommendation among those surveyed. (Alfaro, 1984)

The precise role confidentiality plays in breakdowns in communication among CPS workers, educators, and others is unclear. However, Jaclyn Adams cites a current imbalance in which CPS workers are almost uniformly authorized to have any information bearing on child maltreatment, whereas other professionals working with a child often are not. This is true even in the case of special education teachers, who are supposedly attending to the child's handicapping conditions. Given the documented links between child abuse and developmental disabilities, this outcome is hard to defend.

In effect, we have a system in which those charged with investigating maltreatment have access to virtually all information except attorney–client communications, whereas those charged with treating and educating certain children have limited access. The road to correction, therefore, lies with legislative recognition and implementation of several principles:

1. Child maltreatment, like chronic acting out, is beyond the ability of any one agency or system to handle.
2. The maltreated child's remedial opportunities are enhanced by the open sharing of abuse/neglect-related information among all his/her professional intervenors.
3. The maltreated child's right to fully informed caregivers transcends the parents' rights of privacy.
4. The maltreated child's educational records should indicate which educators are entitled to maltreatment-related information.
5. Clear violations of a broadened confidentiality approach should result in monetary

sanctions, as criminal penalties are apparently too severe to encourage prosecution of violators.

At least two states (Maine and Maryland) have recently addressed problems related to CPS confidentiality/feedback and have made legislative recommendations. Also, the problem is beginning to be discussed at national child abuse conferences. In addition, some states already allow for broad access to child abuse/neglect records. For example, under New Hampshire's child protection statute, all case records are considered confidential, subject to rules of access promulgated by the state child protection agency. The statute (RSA 169-C:25) requires that any such rules shall include provision for (1) multidisciplinary evaluation teams; and (2) "other service agencies involved in the exchange of information with the [state CPS agency]."

Until such time as all state legislatures have corrected the current imbalance in information access, we suggest that educators obtain the clearest possible explanation from their superiors regarding what the law allows for in their states. It may be, in some instances, that educators are entitled to more information about a child than they had thought.

Ideally, the issue should be put to a school's attorney in the form of a request to identify all federal and state laws bearing on access to maltreatment information. If this is not feasible, the question should be directed to the state board of education, which can consult its own attorney or the state's attorney general.

Notes

1. "Reporting Child Abuse: When Moral Obligations Fail," 15 Pac. L. J. 189, 189 (1983).

2. For a discussion and listing of these statutes see J. Costa and G. Nelson, *Child Abuse and Neglect: Legislation, Reporting and Prevention* (1978); Paulsen, "Child Abuse Reporting Laws: The Shape of the Legislation," 67 Colum. L. Rev. 1, 1 (1967).

3. Ch. 217 §1, 1965 Iowa Acts 352 [current version at Iowa Code §232.67 (1979)].

4. "Iowa Professionals and the Child Abuse Reporting Statute: A Case of Success," 65 Iowa L. Rev. 1273, 1281 (1980).

5. *ACLU Handbook: The Rights of Young People*, 109 (1985).

6. *Id.* at 110.

7. Paulsen, "The Law of Abused Children," in *The Battered Child* 153, 158 (2d ed., 1974).

8. "The Family Educational Rights and Privacy Act of 1974 vs. Child Abuse Reporting Laws: The Teacher's Dilemma," Juv. Just. 15 (August 1975); V. Fontana, *Somewhere a Child Is Crying* (1973).

9. *ACLU Handbook, supra* note 5, at 114.

10. "Note: Civil Liability for Teachers' Negligent Failure to Report Suspected Child Abuse," 28 Wayne L. Rev. 183, 187 (1981). Vermont and New York do include teachers within the group of professionals required by statute to report. See N.Y. Soc. Serv. Law §413 (McKinney 1976 & Supp. 1985); Vt. Stat. Ann., title 13, §683(a) (Supp. 1985).

11. People v. Bullard, 75 Cal. App. 3d 764, 768–69, 142 Cal. Rptr. 473, 476 (1977); "Reporting Child Abuse," *supra* note 1, at 189; Brown, Fox, and Hubbard, "Medical and Legal Aspects of the Battered Child Syndrome," 50 Chi.-Kent. L. Rev. 45, 67 (1973).

12. In fiscal year 1984, for example, the Massachusetts Department of Social Services report-

edly received 40,000 reports of abuse and neglect, of which 16,000 were "substantiated." According to Massachusetts Assistant Attorney General William Pardee: "Substantiation does not mean that anyone has been determined in a judicial sense to be a child abuser . . . [but] that the department has found some credible evidence that an incident of abuse or neglect has [occurred]." "Suit Claims Family Rights Suffer in Abuse Probes," *Boston Globe* (11/1/85), 21. A study by the Child Welfare League of America reported that nationwide reports of child abuse and neglect rose 16 percent from 1983 to 1984. "Reports of Child Abuse in Mass. Increased 20 percent Last Year, National Study says," by J. Dietz, *Boston Globe* (2/26/86), 84. See, also, "When Sex Abuse is Falsely Charged," Children & Teens Today (February 1986), 6.

13. See, e.g., Md. Family Code §5-906, "Temporary Removal from Home without Court Approval."

14. R.W. ten Bensel et al., "Reporting Child Abuse," 35(4) Juv. & Fam. Ct. J. 41 (Winter 1984–85), at 5.

15. See, e.g., Cal. Penal Code §11172 (West 1982).

16. ten Bensel, *supra* note 14, at 5.

17. See, e.g., Maryland reporting statute, which provides: "Notwithstanding any law on privileged communications, each . . . educator . . . who contacts, examines, . . . a child and who has reason to believe that the child has been subject to abuse shall [make a report]." Md. Code of Family Law §5-903(a).

18. Minn. Stat. §626.556, subd. 8 (1982).

19. In the Matter of a Handicapped Child, 460 N.Y.S. 2d 256 (Supp. 1983).

20. Colorado v. Corbett, 456 P. 2d 687 (1983) (husband and wife immunity disregarded); Commonwealth v. Kane, 388 Mass. 128, 445 N.E. 2d 598 (1983) court refused to recognize confidentiality between priest and parishioner); Commonwealth v. Collett 397 Mass. 424, 439 N.E. 2d 1223 (1982) (confidentiality between social worker and client); Minnesota v. Andring, 342 N.W. 2d 128 (1984) (communication between physician and patient).

21. "Note: Civil Liability, *supra* note 10, at 188.

22. *Id.*

23. "Reporting Child Abuse," *supra* note 1, at 194. See, also, Prosser & Keeton, *Torts,* §36 (5th ed., 1984).

24. "Note: Civil Liability," *supra* note 10, at 188.

25. *ACLU Handbook, supra* note 5, at 114.

26. *Id.*

27. ten Bensel, *supra* note 14.

28. L.A. Daily J. (Aug. 13, 1984), at 1, col. 1.

29. *Id.*

30. "Note: Civil Liability," *supra* note 10, at 188.

31. ALA Code §26-14-3 (1977); Cal. Penal Code §11165-66 (West Supp. 1981); Del. Code Ann. title 16, §903 (Supp. 1980); N.M. Stat. Ann. §32-1-15 (Supp. 1980).

32. 50 Cal. App. 3d 189, 123 Cal. Rptr. 713 (1975), *reversed,* 131 Cal. Rptr. 69 (1976).

33. See, generally, "Comment: Physicians Liability for Noncompliance with Child Abuse Reporting Statute," 52 N.D.L. Rev. 736 (1976).

34. 123 Cal. Rptr. 713, 719 (1975).

35. 17 Cal. 3d 399, 410, 131 Cal. Rptr. 69, 74 (1976).

36. See, e.g., Cal. Penal Code §1172 (West 1982); Mich. Comp. Laws §722.625 (1975); N.M. Stat. Ann. §32-1-15 (Supp. 1980); N.Y. Social Service Law §422 (McKinney 1983).

37. See *Landeros, supra* note 35.

38. Black's Law Dictionary 1298 (5th ed., 1979).

39. Text *supra* note 8.

40. L. Fischer and G. Sorenson, *School Law for Counselors, Psychologists, and Social Workers,* 186 (Longman, 1985).

41. *Id.* at 184.

42. See "Principal Author's Note" at the end of the textual portion of this chapter.

43. State of Maryland, Governor's Task Force on Child Abuse and Neglect, Preliminary Report (Jan. 1984).

44. *Id.* at 14, Long-range recommendation (A).

45. N.Y. Social Service Law §422(4) (McKinney 1983) (emphasis added).

46. Jose D. Alfaro, "Impediments to Mandated Reporting of Suspected Child Abuse and Neglect in New York City," Unpublished report, on file at Center for Law and Health Sciences, Boston University School of Law (May 1984), at 18.

47. *Id.*

48. Cal. Penal Code §11170 (West 1984).

49. "Torts: Civil Action Against Physician for Failure to Report Cases of Suspected Child Abuse," 30 Okla. L. Rev. 482, 485 (1977).

50. See, e.g., Md. Fam. Law Code Ann. §5-909 (1984). But see Minn. Stat. Ann. §626.556 (West 1985), which includes proviso that reporters exercise "due care" to qualify for immunity:

> *Subd. 4. Immunity from liability.*
>
> (a) Any person, including those voluntarily making reports and those required to make reports under subdivision 3, participating in good faith *and exercising due care* in the making of a report or assisting in an assessment pursuant to this section has immunity from any liability, civil or criminal, that otherwise might result by reason of his action.
>
> (b) A supervisor or social worker employed by a local welfare agency, who in good faith exercises due care when complying with subdivisions 10 and 11 or any related rule or provision of law, shall have immunity from any civil liability that otherwise might result by reason of his action.
>
> Any public or private school, facility as defined in subdivision 2, or the employee of any public or private school or facility who permits access by a local welfare agency or local law enforcement agency and assists in good faith in an investigation or assessment pursuant to subdivision 10 has immunity from any liability, civil or criminal, that otherwise might result by reason of that action.
>
> This subdivision does not provide immunity to any person for failure to make a required report or for committing neglect, physical abuse, or sexual abuse of a child. (emphasis added)

51. Mich. Comp. Laws §722.625 (1975).

52. "Reporting Child Abuse," *supra* note 1, at 213. The Massachusetts Appeals Court has recently reviewed the immunity provisions of that state's child abuse reporting statute as applied to a psychology intern and has upheld them in exceptionally strong language: "The writer of a report is immune from liability regardless of the correctness of his belief as to the child's injuries or their cause. *Even the absence of good faith* in making a report *is immaterial to liability* so long as the report is one which is mandatory under the statute." Hope v. Landau, 21 Mass. App. Ct. 240, 486 N.E. 2d 89 (Mass. App. Ct., 1985) (dicta; emphasis added). See, also, Evans v. Commonwealth 14 Mass. Law. Weekly 357 (Suffolk Cnty., Mass. Super. Ct., reported 11/25/85).

53. 633 S.W. 2d 674 (Tex. Ct. App. 1982).

54. *Id.* at 675.

55. P.L. 93-380, 20 U.S.C. §1232g (1978).

56. 45 C.F.R. §99-1-99.

57. Bersoff, "Confidentiality and the Family Rights to Privacy Act," *School Social Work and the Law,* Papers from the National Invitational Workshop on School Social Work and the Law, May 29–31, 1980, Ann Arbor, Mich., published by National Association of Social Workers, Silver Spring, Md.

58. *Id.* at 145; 20 U.S.C. §1232g(a)(4)(b)(i) (1978).

59. 20 U.S.C. §1232g(a)(6)(b)(1)(A) (1978).

60. 20 U.S.C. §1232g(a)(6)(b)(1)(E) (1978).

61. 20 U.S.C. §1232g(a)(6)(b)(1)(F) (1978).

62. 20 U.S.C. §1232g(a)(6)(b)(1)(I), (1978); 45 C.F.R. §99.36(a).

63. 20 U.S.C. §1232g(a)(6)(b)(4)(A) (1978).

64. P.L. 94-142, 20 U.S.C. §§1401-1461 (1978).

65. See, generally, Board of Education v. Rowley, 102 S. Ct. 3034 (1982).

66. 34 C.F.R. §300.5(b)(8) (1985).

67. 20 U.S.C. §1401(1), (15) (1978).

68. See, e.g., J.A. Calagan, "Psychological Testing: Turn Out the Lights, the Party's Over," 52 Exceptional Children 288 (1985).

69. *Id.* at 289.

70. 34 C.F.R. §300.505(b)(8) (1985).

71. 34 C.F.R. §300.5(b)(8) (1985).

72. Training is important, not only to enable evaluators to recognize probable abuse but also to keep them from concluding incorrectly that it exists. Experts in the field have noted, for example, that "investigating the parents to determine culpability in child abuse cases has been characterized as 'clinically unhelpful, ethically absurd and intellectually unsound.'. . . The clinician may find himself playing a detective game for which he is professionally unprepared." E.H. Newberger and J. Daniel, "Knowledge and Epidemiology of Child Abuse: Critical Review of Concepts," 5 Pediatric Annals 140 (1976), as quoted by B. Bursten, "Detecting Child Abuse by Studying the Parents," 13 Bull. Amer. Acad. Psychiatry and Law 273 (1985), at 280. D.J. Besharov, director of the American Enterprise Institute's Social Intervention Project—remarking on the tenfold increase in child abuse reports during the past twenty-two years—also recently cautioned against "overzealous" reporting. He pointed out that it puts innocent families through the anguish of an investigation and also overwhelms the limited resources of child protective agencies. "65% of Reports of Child Abuse Said to Be False," *Boston Globe* (12/18/85), 17.

73. 34 C.F.R. §300.505(a) (1985).

74. 34 C.F.R. §504(b)(1)(i).

75. Case No. SE-34-84, 1984-85 EHLR Dec. 501:111 (Supp. 129) (Ill. State Board of Education, Dept. of Specialized Education, decided Sept. 10, 1984, reported Sept. 28, 1984).

76. *Id.* at 113.

77. People v. Strntanger, 34 Cal. 3d. 505, 573, 668, P. 2d 738, 744, 194, Cal. Rptr. 431, 437 (1983).

78. "The legislature intends that in each county the law enforcement agencies and the county welfare or social services department shall develop and implement cooperative arrangements in order to coordinate existing duties in connection with the child abuse cases." Cal. Penal Code §11166.1 (West Supp. 1986). See, also, Md. Family Code §5-905, Investigation.

79. Center for Law and Education, *The Constitutional Rights of Students: Analysis and Litigation Materials for the Student Lawyer* 9 (1976).

80. Joel v. Morrison, 6 C. & P. 501, 172 Eng. Rep. 1338 (1834).

81. *The Constitutional Rights of Students, supra* note 79, at 10.

82. 400 U.S. 309 (1970).

83. New Jersey v. T.L.O., 105 S. Ct. 733, 742 (1985).

84. "No child shall be subjected to a search at school which requires the child to remove his or her clothing to expose his buttocks or genitalia or her breasts, buttocks or genitalia unless the department [of social services] has obtained an order from a court of competent jurisdiction permit-

ting such a search." Mich. Comp. Laws Ann. §722.628, Sec. 8(8), P.A. 1984, No. §1, effective March 29, 1985.

85. See, e.g., Cal. Penal Code §11171.5 (West Supp. 1986).

86. Slander is defined as the "speaking of false and malicious words concerning another, whereby injury results to his reputation" (Black's Law Dictionary 1245, 5th ed., 1979). A question asked in the good faith fulfillment of a legal duty can hardly be termed malicious. Any action based on negligence (e.g., negligent infliction of emotional harm) could be defeated by a showing that the educator acted reasonably and prudently. An element in a prima facie case of harassment is that the action serve no legitimate purpose of the actor (Black's Law Dictionary 645, 5th ed., 1979). Clearly, as a mandated reporter, the prevention of child abuse is a most legitimate purpose.

87. See, e.g., Opinion of the Michigan Attorney General, No. 5443 (2/20/79): "Inasmuch as the Child Protection Law specified that Department of Social Services may obtain the assistance of law enforcement officials and the Probate Court in conducting its investigation of abuse and neglect, the Department may not delegate the responsibility of conducting the investigation but may seek the assistance of other agencies in the conduct of its investigation." Mich. Stat. Ann. §25.248(8), Annotation 18, Cum.Supp. 1981-82.

88. 20 U.S.C. §1232(h)(a) [*sic*] [apparently should be designated §1232(h)(b)] (1985).

89. An indication of the "overwhelming interest" courts currently assign to "protecting and promoting the best interests and safety of minors" is provided by a recent New York state appellate court decision that even the sacrosanct exclusionary rule should be disregarded in a child protective proceeding in order to remove a 13-year-old girl from her abusing mother. In re Diane P., 54 U.S.L.W. 2273 (N.Y. Sup. Ct., App. Div., Oct. 28, 1985, reported Nov. 26, 1985).

10
Psychiatric Barriers: A Dialogue

Judianne Densen-Gerber
David Sandberg

DS: I would like to first ask you some general questions about chronic acting-out children and child maltreatment and then proceed to more specific questions about educator involvement in child abuse cases or cases in which abuse is suspected. A threshold question concerns whether, from a psychiatric view, educators should be expected to assume responsibility for chronic acting-out students.

Dr. D-G: First, it is important to consider this project within the context that chronic acting-out children are blocked from learning unless the necessary interventions are made, much as is the case with sightless or hearing-impaired students. If children cannot learn because they are impaired, regardless of the cause, it is the responsibility of educators to see to it that their students become unblocked. This is not to imply that a teacher must himself/ herself achieve this, but I strongly advocate that s/he has the responsibility to ensure that someone with the necessary skill (e.g., school social worker, psychologist, psychiatrist) evaluates the child's situation to determine what is preventing the child from learning. Given normal intelligence in a child, there has to be a reason the student is not learning. It's institutional neglect for schools not to find out why a child is unable to learn. It's also a non-delegable duty.

DS: How far does the educational system's responsibility extend? When are educators justified in giving up on a child?

Dr. D-G: I say never. Every child deserves an education, and every child needs to be part of the learning experience. Rather than suspending or expelling, we need new techniques and resources, even with those children whom others cannot tolerate. Sometimes a child can clearly be beyond the school's ability to handle. In fact, educators, like any other group of true professionals, should resist when they are asked to do something for which they haven't had sufficient training. But the responsibility to ensure an appropriate placement in which a particular blocked child can learn remains, as does the responsibility to visit the placed child so s/he does not feel abandoned by the school system. As can be seen in the case histories in this Handbook, these children have often experienced abandonment. Systems should not inflict additional damage.

DS: You seem to be suggesting a type of ultimate responsibility that some adult must assume if a parent can't or won't.

Dr. D-G: A child in any system, including schools, needs one person who is primarily responsible for him/her. Persons in authority are there, in part, to negotiate the system on behalf of the child. Such negotiation is part of the educator's inherent role definition. This is especially true when we are dealing with K–6 students. A K–6 student may have to spend a good part of the day in special resource rooms, but it is the homeroom teacher who is ultimately responsible, not the special education teacher. In addition to seeing that the child's needs are being met, the homeroom teacher also has a responsibility to ensure that next year's homeroom teacher receives a full feedback on the child's status. Obviously, all of this is much less necessary in homes where there are not major problems. But to expect multi-problem, abusive, or neglectful parents to properly advocate a child's need is a fundamental denial of an obvious reality.

Allow me to interject here my essential three tasks of parenting, which must be present in at least minimal amounts if children are to develop normally:

1. To provide the child a minimum of love and security
2. To negotiate systems on behalf of the child
3. To be an appropriate, responsible role model

DS: I would like to pick up on your statement about information flow and continuity of a case and educational services. My own feeling is that we need someone who is ultimately responsible for students throughout their stay in elementary and middle schools, not just during an academic year.

Dr. D-G: I agree. Individual schools know best who is well positioned to ensure year-to-year continuity and flow within a particular school. Another dimension to this is devising better ways to get information from one district or state system to another when families move, which is often the case with chronic acting-out children from chaotic, dysfunctional family sets. Information flow and ensuring continuity in a case are crucial, yet as we see in the case histories, the new receiving school frequently seems to have few or no accompanying records. It's as if these children materialize out of nowhere, only to disappear again.

My recommendation is that all parents must present an educational transfer sheet, prepared by the sending school, as part of enrolling a student in a new school. Such a sheet would provide such basics as name and address of previous schools, behavioral and other problems, interventions attempted, and so forth. The medical counterpart is the off-service, on-service note that one treating physician prepares for the next.

DS: It seems to me that disruptive, sometimes offensive, and even illegal behaviors are what make these children particularly at risk. Such behaviors drive away nearly all of those who would help and even seem to justify systems people abandoning them. It's akin to being a leper, very unlike other at-risk children who do not turn off adult caregivers.

Dr. D-G: The analogy is to the AIDS victim-children. These students engender fear, guilt, and anger within the helpers, who finally want to flee from their role as caregivers. They are telling us we are powerless; they make those of us in helping professions feel impotent.

Our feelings need to be ventilated so that they don't get acted out on the students. The answer is not to tell educators simply to be nicer. Their frustration is real. At the same time, teachers can't teach children they dislike or with whom they are angry. All of us in the helping professions, including educators, must ask ourselves if we dislike a particular client or student. When dislike is present, or when educators do not have tolerance for those who act out, they should remove themselves from these children. It's not that these adults are always insensitive or wrong. Some people just can't work with this type of child and shouldn't be allowed to abuse or neglect them. However, we should not negate our real feelings but should compensate with others when we ourselves are inappropriate. We must always be actively aware of countertransferential issues, and we should not be ashamed to delegate or transfer to another helper.

DS: Granted, patience is a prerequisite for working with these students, but there are limits to anyone's patience—which brings to mind issues of punishment and discipline. Are you suggesting that these students cannot or should not be disciplined?

Dr. D-G: First, let me distinguish between punishment and discipline. They are not the same to me. Punishment—or a punitive approach such as suspending, expelling, using corporal punishment—is, in my view, a positive dynamic in a very small number of cases, but certainly not with children who are being abused or subjected to great turmoil in the home. To do so in most instances is to reinforce the problem. In contrast, keeping students after school for extra instruction and discussion about their behavior, and even placement in a special class within the school—is more effective. This has to be done over and over, as children with well-established patterns of misbehavior simply aren't capable of "cleaning up their act" overnight. Ultimately, there are four options with chronic acting-out students: (1) retaining them in a regular classroom with supports; (2) referral to a resource room or alternative school; (3) placement in a residential program; and (4) incarceration (hospital or reform school).

DS: Does trauma in the home, such as physical or sexual abuse, ever justify acting-out behavior in school?

Dr. D-G: No, but such trauma does make the behavior understandable in a psychiatric context. The trauma helps explain why the acting out is occurring and what is needed in the way of therapeutic intervention. But regardless of the severity of the victimization, it does not give any child the right to act out and interfere with the rights of others.

DS: We've spent some time on acting-out behaviors. Two other key components of this project are the school experience and child abuse. First, how important is school to a child's development?

Dr. D-G: It is indispensable. It is half the "work" of childhood. This is particularly true for children under 16. Occasionally, a release from years of school failure may be desirable in some cases, but the failure is always regrettable. The other half of childhood "work" is play, without which children are deprived of fantasy. Schools must develop opportunities for doing things simply for their enjoyment. Creating is an essential element for healthy human development. Abused and neglected children often have been denied playtime at home.

We also need to recognize that schools are one of the most important socializing institutions in a student's life, more so in many cases than the family and the church, which, historically, have been dominant. More than learning the basics is involved. There are four "Rs" to be taught in a good educational environment: reading, writing, 'rithmetic, and human-relatedness.

DS: Now I would like to ask you several questions about child abuse, beginning with some general observations you may have on each type of abuse.

Dr. D-G: In terms of damage to the child, I am most concerned about incest and severe, life-threatening physical abuse. If either or both are present, it is imperative that child protective intervention and treatment occur at the soonest possible opportunity. This is not to deny that less severe physical abuse, sexual abuse involving a nonfamily member as the perpetrator, emotional abuse, and neglect are potentially very damaging experiences and should be addressed quickly as well. For some children, they can be as harmful as incest or severe physical abuse, depending on these children's ability to cope and adapt. So-called benign neglect, for example, doesn't shock anyone, but it can be very harmful.

However, in terms of weighing initial severity, I do look first to homicidal physical abuse and incest. An immediate concern is that the child may be killed or may commit suicide. Beyond this, children who have been subjected to these extreme types of abuse have serious intimacy disorders, including an inability to trust others. Moreover, as we described in our earlier NCCAN project on the child abuse–delinquency connection, physical abuse victims commonly have great difficulty sorting out what is loving and nurturing versus what is violent. Similarly, we saw how incest victims confuse love and nurturance, on the one hand, with violence and sexual exploitation. This helps explain why some victims, as they grow into adolescence, often enter into very destructive relationships.

Another dimension in determining the severity of incest involves such issues as who the perpetrator is, his/her relationship to the child, the age of the child at the time of the incest experience, and whether penetration of any kind is involved. If the answer to any of these is in the affirmative, these are usually the most destructive cases. Also important to evaluate is the duration of the incest and the support or rejection of other family members. All incest is not equally traumatic.

Let me elaborate a little more on physical abuse. As for a slap on the behind, there's not much to recommend it, but most children will survive it, and the U.S. Supreme Court endorses it. This is, nonetheless, mild abuse, because there is no justification for inflicting pain on another. With "moderate abuse," the child fears punishments that may become especially violent. These children can be remediated. Children who have been subjected to severe, life-threatening abuse are very difficult to help. Abusive parents in these cases lose total control, having homicidal impulses. This is not to say the victims can never be helped or that all act out. Many become withdrawn and even suicidal. However, it is obvious, the more severe the abuse, the more damage results and the more difficult it is for the child to trust and trust is the essential ingredient to progress.

As for emotional abuse, I, like so many others, have difficulty providing a good definition. Certainly, we all can recognize blatant forms, such as constantly telling a child s/he is "stupid" or "ugly." A parent who tells a young female child that she is ugly directly attacks the child's ego—her sense of self—and clearly is destructive to her healthy development. Emotional abuse can also be in the form of unreasonably high parental expectations, followed by chastisement when the child doesn't meet those expectations. Also, emotional abuse often accompanies the other abuses, as well as neglect, so it cannot be so easily compartmentalized as, say, incest. You've indicated that Dr. Garbarino is working on developing a framework for better understanding emotional abuse, so I will defer to him at this point. However, we must not underestimate its destructiveness.

Concerning neglect, there are several types of neglectful parents. Some have psychotic or borderline states such that they are unable to provide their children with essential life necessities including a minimal amount of love. This should be obvious to educators and to other mandated reporters who must make a CPS report, so that such families can receive the support they desperately need. Others may be better off yet so preoccupied with their careers that they give their children insufficient attention, although usually in such homes the natural necessities are provided. Nonetheless, regardless of type of parent, the children involved perceive the message, day-in and day-out, that they are not worthy of their parents' attention. And if your parents pay you no attention, it is very difficult to believe that others will, and if they do, surely their motives are suspect.

In addition to these abuses, we must also talk about peer abuse. Chronic acting-out children, especially in K–6, are frequently the subject of tormenting by classmates as seen in Case 1 (George). The targets are often hyperactive kids, those with ragged clothes, those who smell because they are enuretic or for some other reason, and those with a physical handicap. Whichever system is involved has a paramount responsibility to deal with this as a serious institutional issue. We must teach respect and concern for all life forms, even "unpleasant" human ones.

Finally, all educator colleagues must be forthcoming, as all other systems personnel must be, where institutional abuse and neglect is present. If we want to make gains on the child abuse–acting out front, we all must recognize that one's own system often aggravates the situation, with very harmful results. Maltreatment is not perpetrated only by parents. Although some physical and sexual abuse is perpetrated by educators, it is apt to be relatively infrequent compared to educator perpetration of emotional abuse, neglect, and abandonment. To illustrate: (1) it is emotional abuse for an educator to call a student "stupid" or "dumb," especially when the student is having academic difficulties; (2) it is emotional abuse for an educator to put a student out of school and feel good about it; and (3) it is neglect if a school system fails to make a meaningful intervention when children such as those in our case histories present themselves.

Like it or not, the fact is that educators have a great impact on young students. Through their conduct and the way they deal with people, educators present to their students a model of how to be and how to treat others in this world.

DS: I suppose that educators, like other professionals, are about as defensive as parents when they are asked to examine whether they are abusive or neglectful.

Dr. D-G: Of course, but they, like the rest of us, must do so if we are serious about helping children. All of us—maltreated child, maltreating parents, and system intervenors—also need to avoid blame-assessing. We need to enlarge our response repertoire.

Let me add that, if nothing else, we need to see abuse—regardless of type or source—as a powerful stressor on children that robs them of their ability to concentrate properly.

DS: Attention deficit disorder is commonly seen in chronic acting-out children. Dr. Hochstedler discusses ADD at some length in Chapter 2. Is there anything else educators should know at a basic level?

Dr. D-G: Four things immediately come to my mind:

1. Minimal brain damage is present.

2. If the problem is organic it can and must be treated.

3. The child usually outgrows the problem if properly treated.

4. School peers often make fun of an ADD child.

DS: You mentioned enuresis a while back as leading to peer abuse. In my experience, a small but significant number of CACs are enuretic. Can you provide some guidance here?

Dr. D-G:

1. It is usually a clear sign of a child under great stress, with emotional immaturity as a component.

2. Part of an enuretic assessment is to learn how the family is responding to the problem.

3. It can be treated with medication, by limiting nighttime fluids, and by taking the child to the bathroom on a fixed schedule at least once a night. There are numerous ways to deal with enuresis. Most children can get the enuresis under control with proper help.

4. School peers can be brutal if they know about the problem a peer is having, especially in a residential setting.

5. It is always humiliating to a child.

6. It is not necessarily limited to children—some adults continue to be enuretic and/or encopretic.

7. Often, such elimination behaviors are clear indicators of extreme hostility plus a lack of control.

8. Enuretic children, though frequently appearing helpless and mild, can be dangerous.

DS: Given these and other important developmental factors outlined in our Summary Assessment Profile (Chapter 13), how would you rate the child abuse factor?

Dr. D-G: Not all child abuse is the same. There is mild, moderate, and severe abuse. With severe abuse, where physical safety and the sense of bodily integrity are at stake, everything else pales in comparison. Also, "mild" child abuse (e.g., a parent telling a child she is stupid or ugly) may not be so damaging as some other conditions, but each child responds differently. To some, even mild abuse can be devastating. This is why it's so hard to set up a formula. The most hopeful prognostic sign is the presence of an adult whom the child can love. Basic safety always comes first. Also, most interventions don't have to be individually tailored to exact cause, in the sense that what we want to do in most cases is raise the child's coping mechanisms, make the child less depressed, and give the child hope.

David Sandberg and Dr. Densen-Gerber then began an analysis of psychiatric barriers to educators becoming more involved with CACs who are abuse victims or for whom abuse is suspected.

DS: The first question to ask is whether—from your vantage point as a lawyer, psychiatrist, and therapist for many abuse victims—educators should do more than file abuse reports.

Dr. D-G: I cannot give you a simple yes or no answer. Let me explain. The reporting laws require educators to report abuse whenever it is known or suspected. So there is no debate about this type of involvement. Next, I have no problem with educators presenting abuse information to children as part of a health or human-relatedness course. In fact, I think it is necessary that schools do this as part of society's overall effort to reduce levels of violence and exploitation. Such courses are a key to good prevention work.

But if you are asking me whether the average classroom teacher should seek out chronic acting-out children—or any other children, for that matter—to ask them if they are being abused or neglected, I am not in favor of this for several reasons. For one thing, it can interfere with the teacher–student relationship and the student's opportunity to learn if s/he knows that the teacher knows about the abuse. Remember, frequently, shame and embarrassment are associated with the abuse. Another reason for the child victim's teacher not becoming involved in this manner is that it creates a situation in which the abusive parent may begin to target the teacher for hostility, further complicating the already tenuous relationship between teacher and student. It is better for the guidance counselor, school psychologist, or social worker to be the parental target. These people are better trained to deal with parental anger, and if things go wrong, there may not be a direct spillover into the classroom. Yet another reason is that personal involvement by a teacher in a student's abuse experience can intensify transferential feelings about the parent to the teacher. A good academic environment has an element of emotional distance, even in the presence of true caring.

Teachers should report suspicions, and someone else, such as a school social worker, can follow up. Teachers should then be given feedback so that they can make an adjustment in dealing with an abused child. For example, if a student is a sexual abuse victim, teachers need to know that such a child often has trouble distinguishing between good and bad touching. Issues of trust are involved. On the other hand, emotionally and neglected children often respond well to touching. Physically abused children should not be punished or reprimanded but rather should be guided, "stroked," and rewarded. Teacher responses need to remediate, not subconsciously repeat the threatening behavior or transgressions in the home. A child who lives in a home with too many rules needs a nonrigid teacher who can free up the child.

DS: What about a situation in which a student seeks out a classroom teacher to talk about personal things, including abuse at home?

Dr. D-G: That is a very different situation. The first governing principle is that whoever the child selects to confide in must not abandon the child. At that moment, the teacher must recognize that s/he has been selected because the student has trust in him/her. Avoiding the student, or simply telling the student "I am not trained to talk about these things," or pushing the student off onto someone else is a betrayal of that fragile trust. And we need to remember how sensitive many of these children are to abandonment and betrayal, as the case histories illustrate.

What I advocate is teachers telling a student (1) that they feel honored that the student thinks enough of them to want to share important, personal information; (2) that they will be glad to talk with the student; and (3) that they will do anything they can to help. They should also tell the student that some problems are beyond their training but that they will go with the student to those persons who do have the training. A strong message of "I will stand by you" needs to be given to the student.

DS: What should educators to when a student then confides that s/he is being abused or neglected?

Dr. D-G: At least three things: (1) reassure the student that this is, indeed, very important information; (2) confirm that the student did the right thing to share this with someone; and (3) tell the student that this is the kind of problem that the teacher will need assistance with. Once at the counselor's, the teacher should ask the student if s/he would like the teacher to stay or wait outside the counselor's office. I want to emphasize that the teacher's responsibility does not end at the point that the "right" person has been brought into the picture. There is a continuing responsibility to ensure that the counselor or principal files an abuse report and to ensure that the child receives ongoing counseling. I realize that this is asking a great deal, given everything else a teacher has to do, but like it or not, if the child has chosen a particular teacher to help, the child will continue to look to that person no matter who else is brought in on the case. A teacher so chosen should handle the honor, though often horrific, with tender, loving care.

DS: How likely is it that these children will view the abuse report as a betrayal?

Dr. D-G: It depends on the individual child and on what is communicated to the child. No promises should ever be given to the child that a teacher or counselor will not reveal anything the student tells them. Furthermore, it should be explained to the child that there are some things that must be reported. Even with K–6 children, a concerted effort should be made to explain why this is so and what the basic steps are in a home investigation by CPS. In more severe abuse cases, the police may also have to be involved. This is never an easy task, but it can be less traumatizing to the child if educators refrain from attacking the parents, rather than the situation, and they must give assurance that the school will stand with the child throughout the ordeal.

DS: You say that educators should never promise a student not to tell. But we know that some children do approach a trusted adult with an initial request for such a promise and that sometimes that promise is given. What does an educator do who makes the promise, then is told by the student that s/he is being abused?

Dr. D-G: There is no choice. The abuse must be reported as required by law.

DS: Even though this is a betrayal?

Dr. D-G: There is a choice between two betrayals here: betrayal of the child, based on the promise not kept, versus betrayal of the child abuse reporting system, thereby becoming a partner in the conspiracy of silence. So reporting, in my view, is the lesser of two betrayals. Can the betrayal based on the broken promise be repaired? Probably not, although once educators perceive the dilemma, they should make every effort to explain to the student that they have done something wrong by promising not to tell, that they must, by law, inform, but that they are still prepared to stand by the student. However, damage has been done, which is why educators should never put themselves in this position in the first place.

DS: What's a good response when a student initially says, "I have something important to tell you if you'll promise not to tell anyone"?

Dr. D-G: A good response would be: "I will keep private everything I can, but some things I can't. I cannot make a promise I cannot keep. Also, I now want to know what you want to tell me, because I know it is very important and I feel good you have chosen me to tell. You trusted me to tell me something important. Trust me one step further—that I will only tell if it's absolutely necessary. You must trust that I will do the best I know how to help you."

DS: I want to return to your earlier statement that classroom teachers should not initiate discussion with chronic acting-out students about possible abuse in the home. You're not suggesting that teachers should not initiate other kinds of personal discussion, are you?

Dr. D-G: No. It is entirely appropriate for a teacher to sit down after class with such students, tell them that their behavior is a sign that something is bothering them and that if they don't want to talk with the teacher, the school has special people who know how to help. That's very different from a specific probe about abuse. One is an invitation to talk; the other is in the nature of a specific confrontation about a highly charged matter that the student most likely is completely unprepared to handle. This is not to say that trained professionals, such as a school nurse or counselor, should not question the student, but it should be done within a certain framework. Ordinarily, I see classroom teachers as being in that framework but, as discussed earlier, in the role of liaison to other professional staff and as an ultimate advocate to see that the child's needs are met. I say "ordinarily" because I realize that in some schools, counseling staff are either lacking altogether or are not effective; consequently some teachers assume a dual role. When it is necessary, I applaud them.

Let me emphasize that teachers should not have to become whizzes at psychiatry, social work, and mental health interventions. These are not teacher roles and responsibilities. Their job is to teach *and* to see to it that any of their students who cannot learn receive the help they need. And, of course, they, along with school administrators, have an ultimate responsibility for students whose parents cannot or will not advocate for their own children.

DS: If educators do talk along personal lines with a student, such as about child abuse at home, can they inadvertently trigger traumatic reactions?

Dr. D-G: Yes, especially if teachers untrained in therapeutic principles and procedures initiate questions about child abuse. We have to understand that it takes a certain amount of emotional preparation, especially for very young K–6 children, to respond to and talk about something as nightmarish as intrafamily abuse. Children, and even adults, can decompensate or fragment when they are unprepared for an untimely confrontation, although the chances of this happening are much less if a trained counselor does the questioning. Therefore, my basic advice to classroom teachers is to err on the side of caution and use school counseling personnel—but, again, do not abandon the child.

DS: What comes to mind are some adolescent and adult abuse victims, who, in retrospect, say that they wish some adult had asked them about abuse at a much earlier stage. Are you concerned that your approach may result in some children's abuse situations not being uncovered.

Dr. D-G: No. What I am saying is that every educator should "think" child abuse as a *possible* contributing factor in every case of a chronic acting-out student and that these students must be guided into counseling with people who are better equipped to evaluate abuse and make other assessments. I am not talking about avoiding the issue. Rather, I am articulating roles, procedures, and assignment of responsibilities. In addition, we have previously recognized and discussed situations in which the classroom teacher has been selected by a student to receive very important personal information and how these situations can best be handled.

DS: I was struck by your earlier observations about personal involvement by teachers clouding or adversely affecting the teacher–student relationship. This might be interpreted by some people to mean that teachers are warranted in being interested only in the academic aspects of a student's life.

Dr. D-G: That is not what I intended to imply. I believe that teachers have a responsibility to ensure that all of their students learn. If learning is not occurring because of emotional or other kinds of blockage, teachers are responsible for having such students properly assessed and remediated. This doesn't mean that they have to do the testing, the home visit, the special education instruction, and so forth—but simply that they should ensure that someone appropriately trained does it.

To be able to meet this basic educator responsibility, teachers obviously need feedback from those conducting the intervention about what the child's affliction is. This includes information about any abuse or neglect at home. Without this information, teachers haven't the data to formulate an opinion about whether a student's needs are being adequately met. Furthermore, if the child is abused or neglected, the primary teacher, as I said before, may well have to make an adjustment in response to the child's newly discovered condition. As I indicated earlier, a child who has been physically abused by the father will be especially sensitive to a male teacher who appears to be punishing the child. A child who is an incest victim will likely be very sensitive and confused over what others would perceive as a reassuring pat on the back. Their sense of good and bad touching is blurred, and issues of trust are immediately involved when touching occurs. All of this is to say that teachers' knowledge about abuse at home—given to them by school counseling personnel—can help prevent their unintentionally repeating types of behavior that, to the child, are similar to the abuse at home. If a child overidentifies the teacher with the abusive parent because of style, age, and/or sex, the child's acting out in class may become worse. We call this *transference*.

Teachers with problem students have to become personally involved if they expect to help the students learn, but the personal involvement should usually be other than an intimate, counseling type of relationship. Also, as I mentioned earlier, it is often better that students not know that teachers have very negative information about their parents. No matter how neglectful or brutal the parents, they are the only parents the child has, and usually the child is quick to defend them against the world. Too frequently, the child internalizes that s/he is deserving of such parental treatment and that s/he is the one at fault.

DS: You are calling for feedback of abuse or neglect information to classroom teachers, yet, as discussed in Chapter 9, educators have long complained that they often receive no feedback from CPS once an abuse report is filed. Usually, CPS cites confidentiality laws.

Dr. D-G: To the extent that such laws prevent a free flow of information in the child's best interest, we need amendments. We need a mantle of confidentiality over the entire multidisciplinary, multiagency system that deals with children at risk, not over individual disciplines and agencies within this larger system. Common sense alone tells us that the special education teacher, for example, has limited ability to help a coded student who is abused or neglected if s/he does not know the status of the abuse investigation and the nature of the interventions being made, as well as the type of abuse and by whom.

That's looking at things from a "best interests of the child" perspective, which should be the main criterion for assessing confidentiality laws. Also, we need to weigh professional morale as a critical factor. An open system of feedback among systems people attempting to help a child learn is essential. Without it, the sense of futility and cynicism that you refer to begins to build, and information sources plus the case findings so vitally needed tend to dry up.

DS: I am persuaded that isolation and secrecy are diseases associated not only with abusive families but also with the systems that have been created to help children. "Interagency coordination" is the remedial buzzword, but it is a very serious problem. My own view is that confidentiality laws, as much as turfdom and competition for limited resources, are at fault.

Dr. D-G: Narrow confidentiality laws are akin to the radiologist who refers a patient to a specialist without telling him what the X ray reveals. We have to mature as a society to the point where we are consistently willing to make interventions involving "unacceptable" child handicaps, such as abuse victimization, in the same way we intervene with "acceptable" handicaps, such as hearing and sight deficits or even learning disabilities. Sometimes we get very hung up blame-assessing the parents or someone else rather than protecting the child, yet every day that goes by without the child's receiving help is one more day that the child does not learn. Most of these children are already developmentally delayed by the time they reach grade K, and they need intervention as soon as possible. This is why I strongly endorse grades K–6 interventions.

DS: Please elaborate further on an intervention strategy that is heavily focused on K–6?

Dr. D-G: This is where the focus should be for a number of reasons. I concur in your feeling that caregivers become increasingly turned off to these children as they get older. Aside from this, adolescents are defensive by nature and become increasingly adept at covering up the home situation. Also, they are frequently using drugs or alcohol, which complicates the intervention process. Most child abuse commences long before the junior and senior high years; therefore, a child abuse–related intervention strategy should be implemented at the earliest possible stage. A related consideration is that child abuse is a progressive disease, meaning that it magnifies as it progresses. That is, the longer the incest, violence, and school failure continue, the greater the cumulative effects on the child. Yet another reason is that it is easier and more acceptable for child protection workers to go into the home where there are preadolescent children. Even though adolescents are often abused, it is more difficult to perceive them as victims.

Also, waiting to intervene until junior and senior high school makes the task very difficult because of the prior abuse and escalation in the child's behaviors. Furthermore, one faces the normal adolescent distancing issues—such as individuation, separation, and autonomy—coupled with normal oppositional teen rebellion, plus the special distancing problems we discussed earlier including intimacy disorders and lack of trust.

I want to emphasize, however, that these older children should not be abandoned as lost causes, because most are capable of recovery with the proper kinds of assistance. It's just more difficult at this age.

DS: I would like to ask you a few questions about assessment factors other than child abuse. One concerns IQ measurements—whether they are essential.

Dr. D-G: I believe they are. They provide at least three very important pieces of information: (1) whether a child is retarded or borderline retarded (below 80); (2) whether a child is gifted (120 and above); and (3) whether there is a significant discrepancy between verbal and performance scores. Of the thousands of adolescents and adults I have worked with who are behaviorally disordered, no more than 5 percent were in the borderline range, approximately 20 percent were in the superior range, and the rest were average. It is helpful—probably essential—to know where a child fits, as treatment techniques vary, particularly in reference to high verbal and extractual skills.

DS: What is the significance of discrepancies between the verbal and performance scores?

Dr. D-G: Usually, acting-out people, young or old, score considerably higher on performance than on verbal, which is indicative of underdeveloped language skills and symptomatic of buildup of underlying frustration based on the discrepancy. One of the special education remedial tasks is to raise the verbal score so that it approximates the performance score. Therapy, particularly insight therapy, is based on verbalization of conflicts.

DS: What about the "dreaded diagnosis of conduct disorder," as Dr. Lewis puts it? Will most chronic acting-out students become conduct-disordered?

Dr. D-G: It depends on new inputs and changes. Without any significant interventions in the home and at school, most will. It's a very serious disorder, often accompanied by a severe intimacy disorder. Isolation, substance abuse, and violence are often associated factors. A CD child—and they can be as young as 7 and 8—has a disease that, without intervention, usually progresses to adult sociopathy. The acting-out behavior becomes an increasingly ingrained way of life, taking its toll not only on the victim but on society as a whole as crime rates rise.

DS: Specific intervention methodologies are being developed for incest, COAs, children of divorce, substance abuse, and so forth. How much expertise do school-based personnel need in order to intervene in a competent manner?

Dr. D-G: Most interventions do not have to be individually tailored to precise causes. What we need are more generalists rather than more specialists. We need people who can motivate systems to do their jobs. Increasing a child's coping mechanism, helping a child to be less depressed, and giving a child hope are essential tasks.

Highly specialized inputs are obviously needed in some cases, such as where incest or severe physical abuse is present, but for the most part these children need adults who will advocate for them.

We need to remember that many, if not most, chronic acting-out children have multiple problems. As the case histories illustrate, often a child has experienced such things as child abuse, an alcoholic parent, and at least one divorce or loss of a parental figure, and is adopted. To think in terms of a specialist for each of these is not feasible from a psychiatric or resource point of view. I would like to emphasize, however, that, if at all possible, someone at the child's school should visit the home to see the environment the child leaves and returns to each day.

DS: One last question concerns schools, especially junior and senior high schools in some inner city areas where there is a substantial amount of violence. I can hear educators saying that they have their hands filled just trying to remain safe in school, let alone visiting homes.

Dr. D-G: They are right, and I'm familiar with schools that have armed guards at the door, but fortunately this is not commonplace. Of course, the types of interventions we are advocating are not going to happen until the more basic issue of people being safe in school is addressed. Learning cannot occur where everyone in the institution feels threatened. Schools must be happy places where maximum learning can occur.

11
Educational Barriers

Cynthia Mowles

Cynthia Mowles was asked to answer seven questions based on her knowledge of the educational field and a survey of the major educational trade journals. Our feeling at the outset was that as busy educators currently are trying to meet an ever-expanding list of student needs, child maltreatment is so disturbing an issue that most educators want to do whatever they can to help. To the extent that CACs are seen more in terms of their behavior than their maltreatment, we anticipated mixed feelings by educators about reassessing interventions.

More than just being busy, some educators—perhaps many—have a feeling of being under seige. This feeling seems to be primarily due to an increasing number of children's problems to which educators are expected to respond.

With this in mind, Dr. Mowles, assisted by Jo-Ann Paveglio, commenced her inquiry. This chapter consists of her findings in response to the seven questions plus her recommendations and suggestions. The chapter concludes with some notes bearing on educators as intervenors and schools as intervention sites.

Questions and Answers

1. Is there consensus among educators nationally that there are significantly more "problem" students now than in the past? What student problems are most often cited as of greatest concern?

There is no national consensus that there are more "problem" students now than in the past. Educators do feel, however, that the problems they are currently facing have changed over the last decade. One of the "newest" issues that educators are facing is that of missing children. Schools are now utilizing time and resources to ensure, every day, that they can account for every absent child.

At the elementary school level, especially in rural areas, school violence and vandalism are not critical issues; however, overall school discipline is an issue. Gallup polls continue to list discipline as a citizen issue as well. The acting-out child is a constant source of concern to educators, with an increased awareness of the strong relationship between students' acting-out and the presence of learning problems, such as learning disabilities in these students.

The use of drugs and alcohol remains a concern to educators, and the consumption of alcohol by elementary age children is a significant concern. This is a concern because of its direct relationship to the student's behavior in school as well as its relationship to the child's long-term health status.

The influence of television on children has been a concern since the 1960s. This concern has evolved from the relationship between TV viewing and violence to more current concerns relating to the portrayal of stereotypes and human relationships on TV.

The final concern, but by no means a lesser concern, is the presence of a large number of abused and neglected children in our schools. The consensus of educators is that there are probably no more abused children than in the past but that the awareness is much greater and that, in particular, sexual abuse is now more openly discussed.

2. What is the current mood of educators about assuming a broad versus narrow responsibility for educating children? Is there consensus that some students are so adversely affected by family-related problems that the broad approach must be taken if these students are to succeed?

Educators are currently caught in a dilemma. On the one hand, they express concern about the whole child, including the child's family situation and nutritional status. On the other hand, teachers are being pressured to increase student academic achievement and to prepare a high percentage of students for college. This academic focus tends to divert the teacher's energies from the personal/developmental issues. The most successful teachers are those who recognize and address the interrelationships between the two aspects. Another way of expressing this concern is that the recent national reports on excellence in education stress the need to combat mediocrity and seek excellence. This has led many teachers to demand more time to concentrate on teaching with "fewer distractions." Most teachers do not feel that they receive support from their local school boards for academic accomplishments.

Teachers are very aware that they have the children with them more than anyone other than the family. This places teachers in a very strong position to intervene in a child's life. Students tend to go to someone who is familiar, and teachers are in a position to provide day-to-day support. Teachers are also accessible to adults, since schools are part of everyday life in the community, and many families are able to relate more easily to schools. For some students, the school counselor and/or the school nurse remain the constant figures in their lives as teachers change.

There are some educators, especially educational administrators, who feel that schools should focus on those tasks for which they were established—the basic skill areas. This focus on the school's prime role should, according to these educators, lead to success, leaving the other needs to be addressed by other agencies.

Although teachers continue to attempt to balance academics and student personal needs, there are situations in which a teacher feels that a child's family condition is so severe that the teacher should continue to provide a supportive classroom environment but should refer to an outside agency, such as the local mental health center, for more in-depth assistance.

3. Does child abuse/neglect ring a particularly responsive chord with educators? If yes, does the concern extend to compliance with reporting laws or beyond?

Child abuse and child neglect are issues that elementary teachers find particularly disturbing. Because elementary school teachers spend long blocks of time with their students, they are particularly responsive to changes in a child's behavior and/or appearance. Compliance with child abuse reporting laws is the *minimum* response from teachers. There appears to be little reluctance to report; however, many teachers still need training in the identification of abuse and neglect. Beyond compliance, those elementary teachers who have had training in child abuse and neglect do attempt to meet the special needs of these children, either within the classroom or through outside referrals.

Examples of schoolwide efforts that extend beyond compliance are primary prevention programs such as parenting courses, health education programs, and multidisciplinary teams.

Virtually all state departments of education—as well as professional organizations such as the National Education Association (NEA), the National Association for the Education of Young Children (NAEYC), the American School Counselor Association (ASCA), the Parent–Teachers Association (PTA)—have resolutions and materials that indicate a commitment to serve abused and neglected children that extends far beyond simple compliance with reporting laws.

4. What are the foremost problems educators encounter or anticipate encountering in making helpful responses to abuse/neglect?

The foremost problem facing educators is the need for training in the identification and treatment of abused and neglected children. A recent poll indicated that 74 percent of all teachers had received no specific training in child abuse and neglect. Some additional problems are:

> Teachers fear getting involved, especially in relation to losing the rapport previously established with parents; this is a more intense relationship than for other professionals, since teachers must continue to work with parents.

> Teachers fear litigation because of its cost and time away from class.

> Teachers feel that they are already overburdened.

> Teachers wish to protect the image of the school.

> Teachers lack procedural knowledge.

5. What role can special education play in the schools' answer to chronic acting-out students exhibiting school failure and possible underlying child abuse or neglect?

All schools have pupil placement teams (terminology may differ) whose task is to review, assess, and program all special needs students. If a child is to be coded and hence eligible for special education services, the child must have an educational handicap. Studies have shown that many abused and neglected students have handicapping conditions. One study shows that 25 percent of abused and 64 percent of neglected students demonstrated delays in motor development, 39 percent of abused and 72 percent of neglected students show delays in language development affecting their academic performance, and 53 percent of abused and 82 percent of neglected children evidence below-average or failing grades in school.

Since there does appear to be a strong relationship between school failure and abuse and neglect, the pupil placement teams should consider abuse/neglect as a factor whenever a student is referred to them. This would give the school another opportunity to screen for potentially abusive or neglectful situations. In addition, special education staff members are trained to help parents set realistic goals and expectations for handicapped children; this skill would also be very valuable in working with abusive or neglectful parents. If these children are coded as educationally handicapped, the services of the school counselor and psychologist would be available. Unfortunately, in most districts, the only mechanism that triggers the availability of these services is the child's qualifying as an educationally handicapped student.

The special education role is strongest at the elementary school level, where children have contact with fewer teachers and the school maintains closer contact with the families.

6. Are educators "turf-minded" to the point of resenting other systems personnel (e.g., CPS workers, social workers) basing themselves within the schools?

Educators express strong feelings that the regular classroom teacher is the primary resource for the elementary age abused or neglected child. The main reason is that the teacher offers continuity and consistency to the child. Educators express concern that coordination becomes an issue as more individuals are involved and that great effort should be given to provide follow-up. The position of school social worker is given the strongest support by teachers. The teachers look upon the person in this role as one who can improve communication with parents.

An additional, although mundane, concern is that most schools do not have any additional space for offices or classrooms to be used by personnel from outside the school system.

In summary, any resistance to the presence within the schools of personnel from outside agencies stems from concerns about offering an integrated approach, rather than from turf protection.

7. In assessing the foregoing issues, does the analysis differ when considering elementary versus secondary levels or when considering teachers versus administrators versus support personnel (e.g., school nurse, guidance counselor)?

When reviewing staff roles, two issues must be considered: the staff person's training and that person's primary focus.

On the training issue, elementary teachers usually have a more extensive background in child growth and development than secondary teachers do. Administrators often lack training in family issues, whereas support personnel such as counselors and many nurses have training in working with children within the context of the family.

The primary focus of elementary teachers is the child, whereas secondary teachers often stress content and/or program. For these reasons, elementary teachers usually have a greater impact on the total student than secondary teachers do. This fact compounds the situation for an abused secondary school student, in that conditions may be more severe yet the secondary school environment may be much less supportive. In comparing the role of administrators to the role of support personnel, it is clear that the administrators are much more removed from the student.

Despite the differences in training and focus, the severity of child abuse and neglect statistics should dictate that all educational personnel have more training in normal child growth and development as well as specific training in the area of child abuse and neglect. It is also apparent that all educational personnel should become more student-centered. Although acknowledging the pressures to attain academic achievement, a student-centered approach ultimately enhances academic success via stronger student–teacher relationships.

Recommendations for Schools

Every pupil placement team should include screening for abuse and neglect within the special education procedures.

Schools should offer primary prevention programs in the area of parent and health education.

All students in teacher education programs should be given preservice training in identifying and servicing abused and neglected children.

Educators in general should go beyond the immediate manifestations of academic difficulty (the symptoms) and focus more on underlying causes.

Information Needed by Teachers

Signs/indicators of abuse and neglect.

Community resources available to children and parents.

Available primary prevention programs.

Family life education information.

Available self-help groups and hotlines.

Means of protecting themselves from litigation.

Principal Author's Note

In assessing the current climate of schools, two widely acclaimed books on the crisis in American education were especially helpful. The first, *A Place Called School* (Goodlad, 1984), is at times a far-reaching analysis of public schools. Of particular interest for our purposes are the data from a study in which teachers, parents, and students were asked to rate the seriousness of a list of problems in their elementary, junior high, and senior high schools. All three groups answering the questionnaire identified student misbehavior as the foremost school problem in each type of school. However, "teacher's failure to discipline" was ranked relatively low as a problem, leading Goodlad to conclude:

It appears that all three groups tend to view the misbehavior of the young as pervasive, existing as a condition apart from efforts, including teachers', to control it. This hypothesis is strengthened by the data on students' concern for their own safety. The demand by segments of the public and many school board members that teachers exert stronger discipline appears, then, not to go to the roots of what must be viewed as a community-wide responsibility. The school alone cannot handle problems once shared and controlled by home, church, and school working hand-in-hand. If these earlier collaborations cannot be rebuilt, then perhaps we need new configurations of agencies and institutions sensitive to changing circumstances.

The second book, *The Great School Debate* (Gross and Gross, 1985), consists of essays by such well-known educators as Mortimer Adler, Ernest Boyer, Albert Shanker, and Goodlad. Unlike most of the special reports on education (e.g., *A Nation at Risk*), this book includes some thoughtful analysis of children's problems that prevent learning. We were especially heartened by a chapter entitled "The NEA's Plan for School Reform." Seven thousand delegates to the 1984 NEA annual convention endorsed the plan, which features ten essential steps. The second step is "Ensuring Each Student's Rights to Learn and to Succeed." To achieve this, the NEA believes that the following concerns must be addressed:

Pressures causing students to drop out or to be pushed out.

Situations fostering truancy.

Interruptions by disruptive students and the factors that make students disruptive.

Shortages of learning materials for students with special needs.

Communication problems for students who cannot speak English.

Problems for students who lack adequate health care.

The NEA plan continues:

We urge schools to back up their student behavior codes with comprehensive programs to help problem students become academically productive. In some cases, this may require the placement of particularly disruptive students in short-term alternative settings designed to move them back into mainstream classrooms.

We also believe school districts should provide programs for the early detection of student problems. Information about these problems should be shared with teachers, who will use it to plan appropriate instruction. As teachers, we have learned that students who misbehave often see themselves as academic failures. Individualized programs, remedial education, health services or counseling, as well as disciplinary action, may all be appropriate means to help these students.

The plan's ninth essential step for improving education in America is "Coordinating School and Community Services." In this connection, the NEA points to four issues that must be addressed:

Abused children.

Hungry children.

Latch-key children.

Alcohol-affected and drug-affected children.

The plan's supporting analysis is as follows:

As teachers, we know that abused children have difficulty learning. Hungry children cannot concentrate on their lessons. Children whose families are going through a crisis cannot devote their full attention to instruction. Consequently, over the years schools have accepted increasing responsibilities for the health and welfare of children.

The rationale behind this increased responsibility was simple: If the schools didn't help, who would?

Schools will continue to have noninstructional responsibilities for the health and welfare of their students. But the problems students bring to their classes are becoming more diverse and complex each day. Their solution demands the experience, training, resources, and time that school staff members simply do not have.

These problems cannot be addressed without the active help of appropriate service agencies. What schools can do is help coordinate the services these agencies offer. Schools, after all, are the natural focal point for reaching children and young adults. We recommend that local governments coordinate badly needed health and welfare services for our students through the school. This coordination should be carefully planned to make sure no instructional time is lost.

Balancing this position of the NEA is its call for consistent enforcement of school rules by students, parents, teachers, and administrators.

In further assessing the scope of public school interventions, there are important attitudinal differences, depending on whether CACs or maltreated children are the focus. There is greater unanimity of thought concerning CACs, but society has just begun the effort to define the scope of educator involvement in abuse/neglect cases.

The history of public school involvement with CACs is not a proud one. When these children are viewed primarily in terms of their behavior, which inevitably occurs when they reach the adolescent years, the outcomes are almost always suspensions, expulsions, and dropping out. About all that has ever curbed this pattern is P.L. 94-142 (the Education for All Handicapped Children Act), but even its limited protections apply to coded students only. And legally, school officials have always been granted broad authority to rid the schools of students who will not behave.

When the focus shifts to maltreatment, however, with CACs being viewed primarily as victims of abuse or neglect, schools often construe the scope of their involvement much more broadly. Moreover, awareness of child maltreatment has an ameliorating effect on educators, who otherwise are inclined to punish or expel students for repeated misbehavior.

Now that schools are beginning to confront the problem of child abuse and neglect, a question arises of how much they should be involved. During the 1970s, educators were told to report suspected maltreatment. Presumably, their responsibility ended there. However, midway through the 1980s, there are growing signs that educators can and should do more. Increasingly, teachers themselves want to know more about students' abused or neglected status solely so that they can make appropriate adjustments in the classroom.

We offer here the thoughtful analysis of two experts on the scope of public school involvement in child maltreatment cases. First, Dr. James Garbarino, president of the Erikson Institute for Advanced Study in Child Development in Chicago, poses and answers four questions (Garbarino, 1979):

Q: What is the responsibility of schools to identify and report suspected abuse?

A: Notwithstanding significant problems in reporting, there is a legal mandate for school personnel to report suspected maltreatment.

Q: Are schools culpable as perpetrators of or accessories to maltreatment?

A: Yes, insofar as schools use corporal punishment and refuse to provide services to children who deviate from the norm.

Q: Are schools in a position to significantly affect either the necessary or even the sufficient conditions for maltreatment in the home?

A: Given that there is an increasing concern about the ability of the schools to master their core tasks—teaching basic academic skills—there are grounds for deciding that they cannot realistically be asked to do more.

Q: Can schools realistically be expected to contribute directly to the prevention or treatment of child maltreatment.

A: If we are speaking about school-initiated efforts on any broad scale, the answer is probably no. Schools seem hard-pressed to do what they see as their fundamental goal, teaching basic academic skills. . . . Except for specific individuals who develop a special commitment and/or expertise, or special grant programs that permit the addition of staff, schools seem unlikely to take the initiative.

Garbarino goes on to say that he finds it more reasonable to think in terms of schools being a key component of prevention and treatment initiated within the larger community in which the school is sited. Within such a framework, he envisions schools as contributors in these areas: parent education, identifying developmentally dangerous conditions in the home, and use of the school facility as a center for providing services to families.

A second thoughtful analysis of the potential of schools to be (or not be) effective child abuse intervenors is provided by Dr. Richard Krugman (1985), director of the C. Henry Kempe National Center for Child Abuse and Neglect in Denver. He identifies four roles for schools and grades each of them:

1. Recognition and reporting—doing reasonably well.
2. Therapeutic—not doing well, although resources are available if school personnel elect to use a broad definition of "emotionally disturbed" under the Education for All Handicapped Children Act.
3. Prevention—some schools are doing this reasonably well; others don't want any part of it.
4. Eliminating their own contribution to the problem—ignored by all school districts and, not surprisingly, the most difficult to obtain educator involvement.

Although Krugman seems to be more inclined than Garbarino to look to schools to initiate broad interventions, it is interesting to note that, independent of one another, they have identified the same intervention focuses: recognition/reporting, treatment, prevention, and institutional abuse/neglect. This Handbook is concerned with all four, as follows:

Recognition/reporting—educators becoming more aware of the child maltreatment aspect of many CACs lives.

Treatment—educators, in conjunction with other systems personnel, ensuring that maltreated CACs receive the educational and therapeutic services they need to succeed academically.

Prevention—educators promoting the earliest possible interventions to reduce further incidence of maltreatment and acting-out behavior.

Institutional abuse/neglect—educators addressing their own contribution to both the maltreatment and the acting-out problem.

Thus, we believe that the scope of educator involvement in child abuse and neglect is necessarily broad. Regarding Garbarino's more narrow forecast for schools, we concur that schools face other pressures and responsibilities, which may limit their involvement with maltreatment issues. However, we are not persuaded that this will turn out to be the case. Furthermore, even if Garbarino should be proved correct, he still sees the public schools as playing a key role in a comprehensive, community-based prevention/intervention strategy.

Concerning the scope of educator involvement with behavioral problem students, it is time to call an end to years of warfare between CACs—especially those in their teens—and educators. The war has produced no victor; CACs eventually drop out or are thrown out, and weary educators wonder why they ever chose the educational profession.

12
Resource Barriers

Society has a crucial interest in the proper socialization of its children.
—Judge Lindsay Arthur,
Senior Judge of Hennepin County, Minnesota

One inevitable obstacle that arises when improved interventions in children's lives are contemplated is limited resources—or, at times, no resources at all. Regrettably, as school budgetary belts are tightened, it is often so-called support services (e.g., school social worker, resource room worker, teacher aide) that are the first to go. There is an implication that these are nonessential services. But as Judge Arthur's statement suggests, we are not talking about frills when we talk about improved services to chronic acting-out children. On the contrary, such services are essential to prevent a further increase in the disturbing number of dysfunctional people in our society. As noted in Chapter 11, the NEA concurs in this view.

Nonetheless, the issue of limited resources within the child development sector, including public schools, is exceedingly complex and difficult. We can do no more than offer some summary thoughts on several different ways to view the problem.

One way to approach the resource problem is to consider the number of manhours expended each school day by principals, assistant principals, and front office personnel on a disproportionate number of acting-out students. One such person recently told us: "The nine or ten behavioral problem students in our school are always the major topic of conversation—and we have over 500 students." There doesn't seem to be much doubt that a relatively small number of such students siphon off a very substantial portion of administrator time and energies. Of course, this is all time that otherwise could be invested on behalf of other students.

There is also a problem of substantial burn-out experienced by counselors and special education teachers, often related to chronic acting-out children. In addition, court appearances are now a regular part of many educators' days, with cases usually involving these students as CHINS, delinquents, abused or neglected children. Often, the educators' involvement is linked to truancy and special education issues.

All of this denotes a great investment of resources in terms of staff time, expenditure of emotional energy, and financial outlays that are already being made. One question is whether the investment has been carefully thought out or is simply reactive in nature. In most instances, it appears to be the latter, suggesting the need for educators to take a step back and reconsider how they wish to allocate the resources they are currently committing to chronic acting-out students. This Handbook offers a number of suggestions about what might be done.

Another question is whether an investment in a teacher aide at $4 to $5 per hour or a school social worker at $20,000 per year is a cost-effective strategy. A good argument can be made that it is.

As for the pursuit of entirely new resources in tight economic times, the answer does not always lie with additional staff or equipment. We talk elsewhere in this Handbook about the significant strides the juvenile court system has taken with the use of volunteers from the Court Approved Special Advocate (CASA) program. Educators, particularly at the elementary level, would be well advised to consider implementation of the CASA model or some similar model within the schools. Also, we chanced to review a book on sexual abuse treatment in connection with our project. The authors, citing a model treatment program in Santa Clara (California) County, comment: "The most essential exportable ingredients are the will to begin and a 'can do' attitude to put against the inevitable obstacles." The message seems to be that if you wait for the financial resources to start a sexual abuse treatment in your community, you'll probably never have one. In fact, the Santa Clara County program became a meaningful reality largely on the basis of attitude.

It is also important to remember that significant resources do exist. Under P.L. 94-142, for example, all "educationally related" services for coded students must be provided as a matter of law. Furthermore, most states make a variety of services available through agencies related to juvenile justice, child protection/welfare, and mental health. In fact, if more of these agencies entered into agreements, available funds and services could be extended to a broader client base.

However, attitude and ingenuity alone are sometimes not sufficient to do effective intervention work. Moreover, our society needs to realize that children today are subjected to many more problems than before and that the schools, along with the juvenile court, mental health and CPS systems, are now being asked to do what the home, churches, and community used to do. Once this is understood, we believe there will be a willingness to increase funding for supportive services. Also to be considered is what it costs society in the long run for not carrying out effective interventions.

Ultimately, we see an essential need for the United States to rethink its crisis-oriented, limited funding approach to children in need of services. This position was eloquently stated by Richard Munro, chief executive of Time-Life, Inc., in a 1984 presentation to the Children's Defense Fund:

> *We have a choice:* The millions of boys and girls in need today can either be a source of new economic growth—or a roadblock to that growth. We've put off investments in human capital for too many years. And unless we make those investments, that bright future won't happen.
>
> I submit that, as a nation, we need to reverse our declining education and support of disadvantaged children. We need to stop thinking of these as expenses. We need to regard these instead as crucial investments in our economic future—as well as a moral good, which they clearly are.

Part IV
Improving
Interventions

13
The Summary
Assessment Profile

This chapter presents, first, the Summary Assessment Profile we developed for our project, followed by a brief elaboration of the items in the Profile.[1]

We strongly recommend the use of this profile or a similar assessment tool with all CACs. Particularly important is an evaluation process that considers the child, his/her family, *and* the social systems that affect the child's life for better or worse. It should be kept in mind that the Profile is a brief summation of what, in most cases, will be considerable information from records maintained by the school and other agencies. Too often, valuable diagnostic and assessment information becomes forgotten, buried within files that grow larger and larger. The Profile is intended to keep key information within sight of intervenors. If school officials decide they cannot record particular items, the Profile can serve as an agenda of issues requiring clarification.

The Profile

A. CHILD FACTORS
    1. **Academic Performance**
        a. *Language competency*
        b. *Areas of success*
        c. *Results of other educational testing*
    2. **Acting-Out Behaviors**
        a. *Age of onset*
        b. *Types and places*
            (1) School
            (2) Home
            (3) Community
    3. **Medical/Psychiatric Status**
        a. *Size/appearance*
        b. *History of injuries, illnesses, handicaps, pregnancy*
        c. *Neurological impairment*
            (1) Attention deficit disorder

(2) Hyperactivity
(3) Other
   d. *Psychiatric diagnosis*
4. **IQ**
   a. *Full scale*
   b. *Verbal*
   c. *Performance*
5. **Child Maltreatment History**
   a. *Source* (intrafamily, stranger, peer, institutional, other)
   b. *Type* (physical, sexual, psychological/emotional, neglect)
   c. *Severity*
   d. *Frequency*
   e. *Duration*
6. **Substance Abuse**
7. **Suicide Attempts**
8. **Educational Handicap**
9. **Cultural Factors**
10. **Peer Relationships**
11. **Strengths**
12. **Other**

B. FAMILY FACTORS
1. **Changing Parental Figures**
   a. *Divorce/remarriage/equivalent*
   b. *Adoption*
   c. *Foster parents*
   d. *Death/disappearance/abandonment*
2. **Siblings**
3. **Economic Status**
4. **Spousal/Sibling Violence**
5. **Parental/Sibling Substance Abuse**
6. **Parental/Sibling Perpetration of Child Maltreatment**
7. **Relocations**
8. **Medical/Psychiatric Status of Parent(s)**
9. **Integration/Isolation**
   a. *Family*
   b. *Community*
10. **Advocacy Capability**
11. **Other**

C. PRIOR SYSTEM INTERVENTIONS
1. **Public Schools**
2. **Child Protection**
3. **Judicial**
4. **Mental Health**
5. **Other**

D. CURRENT STATUS
1. **Academic**
2. **Behavioral**

 3. **Disciplinary**
 4. **Significant Others**
 5. **Other**
E. REMEDIAL PRESCRIPTION
 1. **What does this student need?**
 2. **Which systems need to be involved?**
 3. **Which essential resources are available/unavailable?**
 4. **What is the plan?**
 5. **Which system's person is ultimately responsible for this student?**
F. SUPPLEMENTAL NOTES

Elaboration of Items in the Profile

A. CHILD FACTORS:

 1. **Academic Performance**
 We are persuaded that language competency is critical to educational success; therefore, we have singled it out. Although CACs are usually failing in most or all academic areas, any successes should be examined as possible clues to student strengths that can be built upon.

 2. **Acting-Out Behaviors**
 There is value in knowing whether the child acts out only in school or also in the home and community. If only in school, this may be an indicator of a learning disability as the primary or even sole source of the behavioral problem. Once age of onset is determined, the question should always be asked, "What else was going on in the child's life about this time?"

 We include here some behavioral signs of maltreatment from *Child Abuse and Neglect: A Guidebook for Educators and Community Leaders,* by Edsel (Erickson, Alan McEvoy, and Nicholas Colucci, Jr.):

 Being unduly hostile to authority

 Being excessively disruptive or overly aggressive

 Being violent toward classmates

 Contemptuously refusing to do or complete schoolwork

 Destroying school property and stealing personal belongings

 Being frequently absent from school without apparent illness

 Being unable to attend to lessons for any reasonable length of time

 3. **Medical/Psychiatric Status**
 Dr. Densen-Gerber has noted that average size and normal appearance at least put a child within a certain mainstream. The concept of collecting information on injuries, illnesses, and handicaps is rooted in some of the aforenoted research on delinquents, who often have extensive histories that undermine their opportunity for educational success and even for normal behavior. Pregnancy issues

should always be part of a female intervention. Neurological impairment should be assessed with chronic acting-out children, especially hyperactivity and attention deficit disorder (ADD). Psychiatric diagnosis has a limited but important role in, for example, identifying a psychotic or conduct-disordered (CD) child. The reader may wish to review Dr. Hochstedler's observations in Chapter 2.

4. **IQ**

   The need here is to identify whether a child is retarded, has normal intelligence, or has superior intelligence. Notwithstanding some research that suggests low IQs among chronic acting-out children, our experience is that the great majority of these children are of normal intelligence, with 10 to 20 percent in the superior range and only 0 to 5 percent in the retarded or "dull normal" range. However, it is important to know who the children are who are at the extremes, keeping in mind that a low score may be more indicative of great emotional turmoil than of an actual low IQ. One other thing to look for is a significant discrepancy between the verbal and performance scores. Often, the verbal score is much lower, which can be indicative of major anxiety and inner turmoil.

5. **Child Maltreatment History**

   Although this history is a vitally important assessment area, each school will have to determine where and how it will collect and record this information. Dr. Mowles's recommendation is that every pupil placement team should screen for abuse and neglect. Regardless of how it is assessed, the maltreatment question must be faced up to, because terminating maltreatment is usually a prerequisite for other interventions to be successful. Also, there are certain specifics about maltreatment that are necessary in understanding how to protect and properly treat a maltreated child. We have noted some of the more basic ones.

6. **Substance Abuse**

   If a child is repeatedly and seriously abusing drugs and alcohol, some type of substance abuse intervention is essential. For young addicts or alcoholics—and they can be found even in the elementary schools—addressing the substance abuse is a first order of business.

7. **Suicide Attempts**

   There is no research on the number of chronic acting-out children who commit suicide. Our experience is that they are not the type of children who kill themselves with a gun or via a suicide pact with a girlfriend or boyfriend. Rather, CACs seem more the type that kill themselves gradually through substance abuse, by experiencing a high rate of injuries and illnesses, and by generally not taking care of themselves. Many would seem to be candidates for suicide in adulthood via drug overdose, alcoholism, and accidents. However, it is also our experience that these children often admit to "feeling like" killing themselves, and such statements should be taken at face value. Also, CACs frequently put themselves in highly risky situations (e.g., a 12-year-old girl hitchhiking at night), which can be interpreted as a form of suicide.

8. **Educational Handicap**

   P.L. 94-142 provides a framework and resources to make determinations of such handicaps. All chronic acting-out children should be referred for such an evaluation, based on the documented high incidence of learning disabilities and other developmental disabilities among maltreated and delinquent children.

9. **Cultural Factors**

Our various intervention systems (educational, judicial, mental health, CPS) are often very deficient in understanding the cultural realities of a child's life. Although we Americans refer to ourselves as "the great melting pot," the fact is that cultural differences continue to play a significant role in how we see the world. We are reminded of this by the many Hispanic families that now populate much of the western regions of the country. Also, we must accept that growing up in American society as a black child is still fundamentally different from growing up as a white child. It is important to make such distinctions in the overall attempt to understand a child. However, they should not be used to excuse outrageous behavior.

10. **Peer Relationships**

There are at least two things to note here. Does the child have any friends? If so, who are they? Having no friends is almost always more alarming than having negative friends. Also, it is helpful to determine what role a child has within his/her peer groups—leader or follower. Most of the CACs we know are not loners. Instead, they hang out with children who have the same kind of problems.

11. **Strengths**

At one of our project meetings, Fred Nader commented on all the negative factors in these children's lives that "wash over" them. The truth is that most CACs do have many problems. But it is also true, as Fred pointed out, that we should look for their strengths and find ways to build upon them. Fred also suggested that an "all-negative" mindset can adversely affect the intervenor, especially regarding unduly low expectations for the child. We heard a similar view expressed by Maria Ramirez, assistant commissioner of education in New York, who refuses to accept that many of these children are "handicapped." She believes that some simply are not allowed to learn at their own pace or do not retain what they are taught because it has no meaning to them because of violence, alcoholism, and other problems at home.

12. **Other**

This is a catchall subcategory to note anything that stands out about a child that is not readily slotted under one of the foregoing categories.

B. FAMILY FACTORS

1. **Changing Parental Figures**

As evidenced by our subcategories, there are several processes by which a child can experience loss of a parent. It should not be assumed that such a loss is always harmful to the child—sometimes children experience relief, especially when a non-biological person is involved—but often it is. We restate here Dr. Densen-Gerber's "familiarity of face" principle.

2. **Siblings**

It is usually enough to note the number of siblings, the assessed child's ranking, and the status of the siblings. However, if maltreatment is suspected, the evaluators must also consider whether any siblings are at risk.

3. **Economic Status**

   A shocking number of America's children fall below the poverty line. Such children are helped by ensuring that their families receive whatever economic assistance they are entitled to and want. Where poverty is not present, a child's parents may be able to contribute toward the expense of a needed resource for which there is no other source of funding. Our experience is that most CACs come from low-income homes, although often above the poverty line.

4. **Spousal/Sibling Violence**

   Children who are especially aggressive or violent at school may well be imitating or repeating behavior they witness or experience at home. Whether it is spouse assaulting spouse or an older sibling assaulting another sibling, the effect on the child being assessed is much the same. Parents should be asked whether this is going on in the home. They should also be told that such home behavior greatly reduces a child's opportunity for normal behavior and academic success. Unlike confronting a parent about abusing a child, questions about these types of family violence can be more readily directed to parents.

5. **Parental/Sibling Substance Abuse**

   Parental alcoholism and drug addiction are ruining many American homes. If alcoholism, for example, is the principal family problem, school personnel and adjunct professionals (e.g., mental health counselors) need to know so that the child can be addressed within a COA framework. Perhaps nothing can be done about a parent's drinking, but knowledge of the situation sheds considerable light on the child's condition. Our experience is that parental substance abuse is present in a high number of chronic acting-out cases. Similarly, many of these children have substance-abusing siblings, which make it very difficult to impress upon a child that using drugs or alcohol is not O.K.

6. **Parental/Sibling Perpetration of Child Maltreatment**

   Although we included child abuse under CHILD FACTORS, we also include it under FAMILY FACTORS as a reminder that child abuse is both an individual and a family phenomenon. A central issue concerns the present status of the perpetrator.

7. **Relocations**

   In our opinion, this is one of the most overlooked factors in assessing impacts and needs of CACs. The relocations we have in mind are family moves, especially those that necessitate a change in schools. Multihandicapped students cannot tolerate frequent changes in school environments, and parents should be so advised. Dr. Densen-Gerber puts it in terms of a child's fundamental need for "familiarity of place."

8. **Medical/Psychiatric Status of Parent(s)**

   Although this information may not be available to educators, or a school's attorney may advise against it being recorded, someone in the intervention process should know whether a parent has a history of psychiatric hospitalization. It is also helpful to know whether a child has a disabled parent and the nature of the disability.

9. **Integration/Isolation**

   We have found that many CACs come from families that have few or no community ties. Also, there is often estrangement within the extended family, such that these children seldom seem to have an aunt or uncle who takes an interest in them. Also, researchers have repeatedly found that abusive families are badly isolated families who require assistance in becoming part of a community. Thus, isolation—which is frequently attended by depression, anger, and dysfunction—can be seen as a root phenomenon underlying maltreatment of children and chronic acting out.

10. Advocacy Capability

To succeed, every child needs an advocate. If parents possess this capability, they should be encouraged to exercise it on their child's behalf. It is often necessary to tell parents how much this can help the situation. If parents can't or won't, someone has to. Sometimes a classroom or resource room teacher, lawyer, or therapist self-designates and fills the role. Other times, there is no obvious person, and it becomes necessary to identify someone.

11. Other

This is a catchall subcategory for any other significant family factors.

C. PRIOR SYSTEM INTERVENTIONS

It is important to know what prior system interventions have been attempted. Too often, the intervention process targets the child only or the child and his/her family. Especially if a child has reached adolescence, there have usually been numerous attempts at intervention. In most instances, they have not been enough or have not worked at all. We need to spend the time to identify those interventions and learn something about why they weren't effective. Otherwise, there is a tendency to repeat processes that don't work as well as to forge new interventions that overlook useful information resting at the center of prior interventions.

Perhaps most significant, we need to admit that systems play a very significant role in all children's development. When a child is in trouble, s/he often comes into contact with several systems that are not well prepared to meet the child's needs. The juvenile justice system faced up to this in the 1970s when it adopted a deinstitutionalization policy. The child protection system has responded similarly through the Adoption Assistance Act of 1980, which is intended to curb "foster care drift." The educational system needs to take a closer look at those CACs who are not eligible for special education assistance under P.L. 94-142. Most difficult of all—but necessary—is that schools must face up to any maltreatment they perpetrate against CACs.

D. CURRENT STATUS

1. Academic

What grade level has the student reached and what are the prospects for successfully completing the academic year? These are the main things we want to know.

2. Behavioral

At the time of the assessment, has the acting out lessened, has it become worse, or is it taking the same form?

3. Disciplinary

What responses have been made to the acting-out behavior? Filling in this section of the profile should be more than rudimentary noting of reprisals. Also needed here is an honest answer to whether the reprisals mesh with the child's special needs. Acting-out behavior requires sanctions. The question is what type is appropriate for this child? Elsewhere in this Handbook, we have expressed our thoughts about corporal punishment and suspension/expulsions. And although it is true that many CACs stimulate a desire within us to "punish" them, it is our job to control these impulses.

4. **Significant Others**
    Starting with the family, who are the people who can help us with this child? It is far better that families help themselves whenever possible. After family, the query should be widened to include nonfamily members, such as a foster parent. Knowing something about prior interventions can be useful in identifying someone who may have a bond with the child. The issue here is human resources and a child's bonding to a positive, caring adult.

5. **Other**
    Is there anything else about the child's current status that is important to know?

E. REMEDIAL PRESCRIPTION
    1. **What does this student need?**
        Special education personnel are required to specify in an IEP what a student needs and what remedial response is to be made. Although these tend to be narrowly construed, the fact is that most other professionals engaged in child care work do not make any such systematic formulations. We have to get in the habit of identifying and articulating what a child needs in terms that mean something to the child—and us—and in such a way that we can measure whether an intervention plan is achieving something.

    2. **Which systems need to be involved?**
        It would be an unusual chronic acting-out student who does not need at least two systems. School intervenors should expect representatives from the juvenile justice, child protection, and/or mental health systems to be partners in virtually all cases.

    3. **Which essential resources are available/unavailable?**
        Often we are in the position of saying, "What the child really needs is X, but it just doesn't exist." Being pragmatic, we move ahead with second best. At other times, we have the resources that are needed. Usually, a child requires at least two or three essential resources. We should record these in shorthand fashion at the outset of a case to remind ourselves what we are and are not able to do for a child.

    4. **What is the plan?**
        First, there should be a plan for each child, which the intervention team can use to monitor the case at regular intervals. The plan has to be written, however abbreviated, so that everyone downline is clear about what the agreed upon plan is. Again, special education is quite good at this, as are some courts. Therapists who work with adolescents have increasingly resorted to written "contracts," which is another way of concretizing a plan. Without such a plan, our experience is that case management becomes largely a matter of finding a place for the child to live, and "no news is good news."

    5. **Which system's person is ultimately responsible for this student?**
        Intra- and interagency coordination is hampered by many things, not the least of which is well-intentioned intervention teams too often failing to designate a co-

ordinator or case manager. Instead responsibility for each component of a plan is commonly divided among several professionals. The problem here is that there is a "sum of the parts" reality that gets lost. In the worse cases, no one follows up.

Note

1. Express permission is given for duplication and use of the Summary Assessment Profile.

14
The Management Framework

With respect to chronic acting-out students, it can be seen that bits and pieces of a management system are already in place: child abuse reporting laws and intraschool reporting protocols, special education, suspensions/expulsions, community-based support groups (e.g., task forces for child abuse, school attendance review boards for truants), COA groups, the courts, school guidance counselors, school social workers, and more.

What is lacking is a unified school-based management system that ensures that each acting-out student is responded to through a carefully thought out policy. How a child fares often depends upon whether s/he has the good fortune to get into one of the subsystems that have clear-cut rules and due process safeguards: child protection, special education, and the juvenile court. However, each of these systems has limitations and deficiencies. At times, they are even abusive and neglectful. Perhaps most common is a crisis management approach, which increasingly relies on putting the child out of school.

So where lies the answer to making more effective and earlier responses to children whose behavior tips off great inner turmoil? After considering this question at length, project members have concluded that the answer does not lie with our designing a new system. For one thing, there are significant differences in the makeup of every school. For another, systems imposed from without run the risk of being rejected by those within. Consequently, we chose to identify some governing principles that we believe are applicable to all schools and can form the foundation for a school to develop a new management framework or system for dealing with CACs. These principles are as follows:

1. Chronic acting-out behavior is symptomatic of inner distress and frequently of maltreatment.

2. Chronic acting-out children are entitled to a reasonable opportunity to learn, which their behavior prevents, much as learning disabilities and visual handicaps do.

3. Whoever is primarily responsible for educating the child is also responsible for seeing to it that the child receives whatever interventions are needed to allow learning to occur.

4. Chronic acting-out children require and are entitled to an advocate.

5. No one system is capable of properly handling a chronic acting-out child by itself.

6. An essential starting point is development of an assessment profile that focuses on individual, family, *and* socioenvironmental factors, including the school's role.

7. Chronic acting-out children should be asked by trained school-based personnel whether they are being abused or neglected in the home, at school, or in the community.

8. Chronic acting-out children are entitled to each of their systems' caregivers having access to otherwise confidential information about them.

9. A propensity to reject, abuse, neglect, and punish chronic acting-out children needs to be acknowledged—and never acted upon.

10. Major intervention strategies, heretofore targeting the adolescent in difficulty, need to be expanded downward to grade K.

11. Suspensions and expulsions should be used sparingly, if at all (see Chapter 23).

12. Educators should receive training in alternative methods of disciplining and limit-setting.

We believe that any school or school system that allows itself to be guided by these principles will be able to design a management strategy that will result in significant reductions in the amount of acting out. Some schools face larger obstacles than others, and in Chapter 18 we discuss successful strategies in many different environments.

We leave it to the reader to bring about whatever changes are possible within his/her system. A good starting point is getting principals and superintendents to take a hard look at the disproportionate amount of time and human energy CACs currently drain away from teachers, support staff, and administrators every day of the school year.

15
The Need for an Advocate

One of Dr. Densen-Gerber's standards for child rearing is the essential need for a parent to have at least some ability to "negotiate the system" on behalf of the child. By "system," she means the world at large and several key institutions, including the educational system. Otherwise, the young child is wholly at the mercy of a society whose capacity to reach out to such children is matched only by its capacity to abuse or neglect them.

Some parents of chronic acting-out children are entirely capable of negotiating systems. Unfortunately, they often negotiate for something other than the best interest of the child. Other parents simply have no ability to talk with systems people. Even parents who have a sense of what needs to be done often do not understand the inner workings of the courts, the school, child protection, and the mental health system. And in most cases, the parent is also part of the problem.

The net effect is that the chronic acting-out child needs a systems advocate. If these children were assigned an advocate as early as first or second grade, we believe acting out in schools would substantially decrease. Tasks of the advocate include: (1) preventing abuse/neglect, whether originating in the home, school, or community; (2) preventing systems rejection of the child; (3) interpreting the child's behavior and needs to others; (4) insisting that evaluations and services be provided; (5) ensuring year-to-year and system-to-system continuity; and (6) facilitating parent–system and parent–child cooperation.

In short, the time has come for the educational system to widely implement the advocacy concept, utilizing members of the professional and lay community on a paid or unpaid basis. Part of an advocacy foundation is already in place in the form of the ombudsperson (see Chapter 18), the "surrogate parent" under special education laws, and, of course, those educators who have taken it upon themselves to advocate for a student.

Two other systems—juvenile justice and child protection—are already making extensive use of advocates. Examples include:

The Massachusetts Department of Youth Services (DYS) Youth Advocate Program. The DYS brochure states: "A new breed of one-to-one volunteer—the youth advocate—is matched with a particular client at the beginning of the DYS process. As a youth advocate, you can follow the client through the facility program, then back into the community where you can continue to be a supportive friend when needed. You can monitor the client's progress and alert the caseworker in case of a breakdown in the fulfillment of the program description."

The highly regarded CASA (Court Appointed Special Advocate) program, which is being used by many states to assist courts with abuse and neglect cases. CASA tasks include such things as helping to ensure that various parts of a court-ordered plan are carried out (e.g., prodding the CPS caseworker to make a medical appointment for the child or making it himself/herself).

The guardian ad litem (attorney or nonattorney), who has been used by a juvenile courts for years to advocate the best interest of juveniles.

The business sector has also involved itself with advocacy on behalf of acting-out youth. Highly touted examples are Partner's Inc., in North Carolina, Colorado, and California; and Cities in Schools, in Atlanta. A forerunner of these initiatives is the national Big Brother/Big Sister program.

The CASA model points the way in limiting a volunteer advocate to no more than one or two children and in providing training for volunteers. Also to be noted is that a CASA does not replace key actors; s/he serves as an invaluable *additional* resource. Another source of advocates is the medical and legal community, whose state associations, should seriously consider a policy whereby each member is assigned to advocate for one acting-out child.

Beyond individual advocates, Garbarino (1979) reminds us of the school's duty to serve as advocates for all children:

> Although schools are, in principle, the natural allies of children, child advocacy has been problematic for educators who see children's rights as a threat to their authority and obligations. Nonetheless, one of the most important roles to be played by schools is as advocates for children, for their right to a secure and nurturant environment. This implies that schools become active (and some already are) in prodding the larger community to support the basic right of children to personal security and nurturance. Involvement in community-wide child abuse and neglect councils, in legislative action on behalf of children, and in public education on behalf of child protective services can all be part of the advocate role.

16
School Social Workers

In Chapter 1, we referred to Cynthia Crosson Tower's *Child Abuse and Neglect: A Teacher's Handbook for Detection, Reporting, and Classroom Management*. The book begins with a summary statement on the role of several school-based professions—teacher, nurse, counselor, social worker, and health educator—in responding to child abuse and neglect. Ms. Tower's essential point is that each has a unique role to play and that child maltreatment, as much as any other children's problem, requires a multidisciplinary, multistrategy response. Anyone who has worked in the maltreatment field can attest to how even one case can quickly overwhelm teams of lawyers, therapists, and CPS workers. Consequently, there should never be a conflict within schools about which of the school-based professionals are to be involved with maltreatment problems. They are *all* needed.

Having said this, we want to share with the reader our "discovery" of the school social worker profession. At the outset of the project, some of us were not aware that such a profession existed. Subsequently, the principal author met Isadore Hare, senior staff associate of the National Association of Social Workers (NASW), in Silver Springs, Maryland. Ms. Hare's materials on school social workers were remarkably relevant to CACs and to this Handbook.

One of the NASW's publications lists the following school social worker services to students, parents, and educators:

Helping pupils overcome barriers to school attendance and achievement and promoting responsible behavior.

Counseling pupils and parents individually and in groups on topics such as problem-solving skills, parenting, family crises, abuse of drugs and alcohol, family violence, teenage pregnancy, depression and suicide, and other problems that affect learning.

Intervening early in problem situations to prevent development of more serious difficulties.

Consulting with teachers and pupil services personnel about student life situations and home/neighborhood circumstances.

Maintaining open communication between schools and community agencies to facilitate common objectives—for example, serving as case managers to coordinate a program for a child being admitted to a residential institution—or for many other situations requiring interagency collaboration.

Working with problems in a child's living situation (home, school, and community) that affect the child's adjustment in school.

Gathering data and preparing an assessment of the child's social and developmental history to fulfill one crucial aspect of the mandated multidisciplinary evaluation. Areas covered include family background, developmental milestones, social and emotional functioning, health history, school history, evaluation of the learning environment, cultural and socioeconomic factors, and results of application of adaptive assessment tools.

Preventing inappropriate labeling and placement of children in special education programs by, for example, interpreting cultural and socioeconomic factors that might be depressing pupil's academic performance; comparing adaptive behavior of the child in school with his/her behavior in the home and community; or providing services to disruptive and nonconforming children within the school.

Serving as liaison between school and parents to interpret school procedures and policies to parents and to explain family circumstances to school personnel. This has added significance when cultural differences complicate communication between school staff and families.

Fulfilling case management functions by serving as liaison between the school and community-based agencies to coordinate case services, interpreting school procedures and policies to external service providers, and explaining policies of agencies to school personnel.

Our view is that it is not just the *presence* of school social workers that will solve all problems. Rather, given the number of problem students requiring attention and the present commitments faced by other school-based professionals, it becomes essential to have someone on site who is trained to carry out the foregoing tasks. Otherwise, the schools are largely in the position of making limited inputs involving the student only while school is in session, usually at a time of crisis.

In New Jersey, school social workers are given a key role in child study teams that are used to evaluate handicapped children in a comprehensive manner. They are mandated to communicate with parents and students, and state law requires an evaluation of the influences of family, social, and cultural factors in the pupils' "learning and behavior in the educational setting."

This gets to the cornerstone of the school social worker's contribution: no other school-based professional is prepared, by training or professional orientation, to become involved in the student's home and with such community systems as CPS, mental health, and the juvenile court. These are the vital links that must be made. Moreover, when these linkages are made, we believe that the efforts of other school professionals will be enhanced.

Are school social workers a frill? We think not. If just one student is prevented from residential placement, a yearly savings of at least $25,000 can be realized. Our own experience is that social workers who become involved in the home offer the best chance of preventing removal of a child.

At the national level, there is growing recognition of the essential services provided by the school social worker. For example, at NASW's Third National Conference on School Social Work, in 1984, an impressive list of plenary speakers acknowledged the important contribution of the school social worker:

Senator Robert Stafford (R-Vt.), chairman of the Senate Subcommittee on Education, Arts and the Humanities.

Mary Hatwood Futrell, president of the NEA.

Rep. Lindy Boggs (D-La.), member of the House Select Committee on Children, Youth and Families.

Dr. Norman Francis, member of the National Commission on Excellence in Education.

Ann Kahn, first vice-president of the national PTA.

As reported by the *School Social Worker Information Bulletin*:

President Futrell advocated the formation of "a new, stronger, unbreakable partnership" between teachers and school social workers as "first class citizens in the school hierarchy" and stated that NEA was committed to seeing that social workers become an integral part of the schools' operations, with adequate compensation and resources. "Together with teachers, social workers can take the lead in establishing a network of cooperation, among school employees, parents and community services," she said.

The emergence of the school social worker, the newest of the school-based professionals, coincides with the rise in student problems and the decline of both the home and church as child care/child development institutions. Schools are now de facto partners with the CPS, mental health, and juvenile justice systems in filling the void created by the decline of these institutions. And we note that these other systems have for some time recognized the essential need to utilize social workers and social work principles. Cynthia Mowles, a school superintendent and member of our project, concludes that "the position of school social worker is given the strongest support by teachers."

Readers interested in learning more about the school social worker profession, which is now active in more than thirty states, should obtain a copy of *The Human Factor: A Key to Excellence in Education*, a twenty-eight-page booklet prepared by the 1985 NASW School Social Work Conference Planning Committee. (Contact the National Association of Social Workers, 7981 Eastern Avenue, Silver Springs, MD 20910.) The remainder of this chapter briefly references especially pertinent parts of *Human Factor*.

The NASW's central point is that the national goal of academic excellence is obtainable only if there is a corresponding attention to the emotional and behavioral factors that significantly interfere with a growing number of children's ability to learn. Drawing from its findings of a thirty-state study, it categorizes these factors under five general headings: family-related barriers, student personal barriers, school-related barriers, community barriers, and legislative/funding barriers. Based on input from 500 professional respondents—including teachers, superintendents, and principals—the lead issues under four of these headings, in order of priority significance, are as follows:

Family-Related Barriers
   Child abuse and neglect
   Divorce/separation
   Parental apathy
   Family crisis
   Poverty

Student Personal Barriers
   Low self-image
   Problems with parents or other family members
   Truancy
   Underachievement

School-Related Barriers
   Lack of positive relationships between and among students, staff, parents, and administration
   Inadequate discipline policies and/or procedures
   Lack of alternative schools to meet needs of special at-risk groups
   Lack of collaborative teamwork among school professionals

Community Barriers
   Lack of support services

Human Factor notes the particular need for innovative services on behalf of a lengthy list of at-risk groups—for example, the racially isolated student, the "socially maladjusted" student, the potential dropout, the pregnant adolescent or teenage parent, and the student with a history of academic failure. These students are often not eligible for existing school-based services, such as special education, or have indifferent or inadequate parental figures who either can't or won't advocate for their needs. Furthermore, many students belong to two or more such at-risk groups.

We believe that *Human Factor* properly targets these and other problems as the business of educators because the problems are known to interfere with academic success. The NASW adopts a comprehensive view of student, family, and institutional issues that emphasizes root causes and early intervention, as opposed to a narrow view that targets the student only on the basis of a "safe" issue, such as school dropout. We contend that dropout is rooted in numerous individual, family, institutional, and community factors that usually are clearly operative in the elementary years. The same is true of most other symptoms, such as truancy, underachievement, and acting-out behavior. We, again make reference to research that links many of these phenomena, with child abuse often being a central ingredient.

17
Interagency Cooperation

I notice that you have had coming before your committee police, school people, psychiatrists, psychologists, and on and on and on. Are they talking to
each other? Are they building programs together? Are they looking at other
things that interrelate? That really is an issue. In our community we have
trouble getting the doctors to talk to the social workers and to the teachers.
Everybody has got a piece of the action but nobody wants to do anything
about it, because they are so stubborn, or because they don't want to change,
or they are not sure that what they are doing is right—and on and on it goes.
—Robert ten Bensel, M.D., M.P.H., testimony before
Canadian Senate Subcommittee on Early Childhood
Experiences as Causes of Criminal Behavior, 1978

As stated earlier, many CACs require the assistance of at least four systems—educational,
child protection, mental health, and juvenile justice—in order to succeed. This is consistent
with the view that these children have multiple problems, often of a serious nature. To the
extent that these systems cooperate with one another on behalf of a child, the child is usually
better served.

Unfortunately, these systems often do not work well together. In some instances, they
war with one another. Help may be on the way, however, because of a widespread acceptance among professionals that child maltreatment is a special problem requiring special
responses. One illustration is the proliferation nationally of multidisciplinary, multiagency,
community-based task forces on child abuse and neglect. To the extent that CACs are considered more in terms of being victims of maltreatment, these children will be better served
as a result of a multiple system intervention.

As further comment on interagency cooperation, we cite here just a few of the many
statements we came across about the essential need for coordination among systems
personnel:

A major cause of child battering and death is the lack of coordination, cooperation and
communication between hospitals, schools, police, child protection agencies and the
courts. All communities should establish multidisciplinary teams to review every childhood death due to maltreatment and every accidental death or death due to unknown
causes. The team should include the professionals who are responsible for children, e.g.,
social workers, police, physicians and teachers. A multidisciplinary inquiry into child fa-
talities will hopefully identify the currently undetected at-risk indicators that can be used
by those responsible for reporting, investigating and helping the abused child. (Presentation by Dr. Vincent Fontana and Dr. Richard Krugman at the Sixth National Conference
on Child Abuse and Neglect, Baltimore, 1983)

Encourage coordination among school personnel, families, support agencies and the juvenile justice system in efforts to assist troubled youth. (Recommendation of California
Commission on Crime Control and Violence Prevention, 1982)

State staff in both the education and human services departments find that the coordination between local school districts and child protection agencies is occasionally well-organized, but usually undefined and often tension-producing. . . . State staff feel that some of the defensiveness and hesitation to become involved which is often shown by school personnel is due to lack of information. (A Cooperative Program to Increase Involvement of Public School in Child Abuse and Neglect," NCCAN project, Minnesota Department of Human Services, 1986)

There are many reasons why agency overlap needs to be attended to. First, if several agencies are involved with a single family, they need to coordinate their intervention. Agencies may be working with a family without knowledge of other agencies involved. Different agencies may be working at cross purposes or they may be duplicating services. Further, agencies may benefit from past histories other agencies have had with the family. Moreover, lack of service coordination may encourage certain families to manipulate agency contacts in a way not conducive to the family's well functioning. (M. MacMullan, "Children at Risk Study," Ann Arbor, Michigan, Probate Court, Juvenile Division, 1984)

BE IT RESOLVED, that the American Bar Association, recognizing that there is a correlation between children who suffer from the handicap of learning disability and children who are involved in the juvenile justice and child welfare systems, encourage individual attorneys, judges, and state and local bar associations to work more actively within the juvenile and family court system, as well as their communities, to improve the handling of cases involving children with learning disabilities. (Resolution of the House of Delegates of the American Bar Association, adopted August 1983)

There must be recognition that putting the whole burden of responsibility [for child abuse] on the social worker will no longer work and that a broadly based team effort—using experts from many disciplines—should take the place of that system. (Kempe and Kempe, 1978)

The reporting of suspected abuse or neglect does not transfer responsibility to one agency, the child protective service. It fulfills a legal obligation to report and thus cause a protective (social) investigation to occur but the need for coordination and cooperation remain. (Alfaro, 1984)

The Association and its affiliates should cooperate with community organizations to increase public awareness and understanding of child abuse. (Resolution adopted by the National Education Association)

As an additional exploration into the world of interagency cooperation (or noncooperation), project member Jeannette Gagnon, assisted by Betsy Singer, contacted each state's CPS agency. They asked four questions and had a 56 percent response rate. The results, stated in terms of percentage of those who responded, are as follows:

1. In your state are there any statutes requiring or encouraging cooperation between child protection services and the school systems? If yes, which statute(s)?

   75%—reporting laws
   29%—statutes calling for cooperation between schools and child protection agencies
    8%—no
    4%—no response

2. Are there any child protection workers who work directly in schools?

    93%—no
    4%—yes, but state funding cuts wiped out the position
    3%—no response

    Common trends: Although the majority of states had no child protection workers directly in schools, many reported that there are multidisciplinary teams, consisting of school personnel and child protection workers, whose purpose includes investigations of child abuse and neglect reports and training of school personnel.

3. Is there any inservice training concerning child abuse, in the schools? If so, by whom is it conducted?

    100%—yes

    Common trends: Training is conducted by a variety of personnel, including child protection workers, boards of education, departments of health and welfare, and divisions of children, youth, and families. Training is provided upon request, and structure varies from state to state and within each state. Frequently, training consists of teaching school personnel how to detect possible child abuse (e.g., physical symptoms and emotional components as manifested through overt behaviors). Training can be in the form of workshops, films, lectures, role-plays, and booklets.

4. Do child protection agencies have any informal linkages with the education system? What are they?

    93%—yes
    4%—no
    3%—no response

    Common trends: Respondents indicated that the existing informal linkages consist of what they described in earlier questions. That is, although there are no child protection workers placed directly in the schools, both organizations work jointly in the detection, investigation, and reporting of suspected child abuse—via, for example, multidisciplinary teams and training opportunities—as required by state statutes that call for the cooperation between various organizations that service children in one way or another.

In addition to the questionnaire, our two CPS project members conducted a search of the child welfare literature to determine how much attention is being given to the CPS–public school interface. They report:

> After an extensive search through a variety of periodicals, we have reached the conclusion that there is little written information regarding the relationship between the child protection workers and personnel in the educational systems.
>
> In many states, there are statutes requiring cooperation between school personnel, child protection workers, and other professionals in the reporting and investigation of possible child abuse. In addition, child protection workers and school personnel in many states work together in training teachers to recognize signs of child abuse. Teachers are becoming more attuned to the possible presence of child abuse in the home, through lectures, films, workshops and role-playing. However, as further revealed by the question-

naires, there are apparently no states in which child protection workers, working out of their own agencies, routinely enter the educational system upon the request of school personnel.

In conclusion, many authors suggest that placing a child protection worker in schools would facilitate the awareness, reporting, and investigation of child abuse and neglect. However, the authors conclude that such a structure is highly idealistic due to insufficient funds.

Although our questionnaire and literature searches are not definitive on the subject, they do confirm our personal experience, which is that very little attention has been given to the critical relationship between the CPS and educational systems. We therefore strongly recommend that this very important relationship continue to receive attention. And although we primarily examined the CPS–educational systems relationship, we are mindful that similar deficiencies exist in important relationships involving the mental health and juvenile justice systems.

Accepting that all agencies and institutions will be concerned about their own interests to varying extents, we have identified six ways to achieve greater interagency cooperation that are practical and reasonable to implement:

1. *Create legislation that mandates key agencies to coordinate their efforts.* We have cited statutes, such as Florida's, that command the educational and child protection systems to coordinate a statewide child maltreatment prevention plan. The major advantage of this strategy is that coordination is compelled. A potential weakness is that compelled coordination may not be as effective as that which is voluntarily sought. Nonetheless, we recommend this approach as potentially the most efficient way of promoting inter-agency cooperation.

2. *Base personnel from one system in another.* Examples include mental health and special education personnel in the court system (see, e.g., Project L.E.A.R.N. in Chapter 18), and social workers and child protection workers in schools. We are particularly supportive of this approach, as it greatly enhances the chances for effective communication among key professionals. Also, educator morale is apt to be higher in the face of troublesome students when there is easy access to someone who is known and has the needed expertise. A variation of this plan is for one person within a system (e.g., CPS) to be designated as liaison to another system (e.g., education). This can be done more readily and is common practice in some places.

3. *Establish interagency, community-based organizations.* In Chapter 18, we reference such groups as School Attendance Review Boards (SARBs) for chronic truants and child abuse task forces. Usually, these are volunteer initiatives, and therein lies a potential weakness; that is, can ad hoc organizations, lacking a paid staff, survive after the last of the initial founders has departed? It is hoped that they will, as such efforts come closest to reflecting true community concern about at-risk children.

4. *Agencies make speakers available to other agencies.* We refer to Joanne Testaverde's observation (in Chapter 19) that the relationship between the child protection and educational systems could be enhanced by CPS workers addressing educators in the schools. She makes the point that more than needing to hear one more lecture on

reporting, educators need to know a CPS worker at a personal level. Jaclyn Adams indicates that educators and CPS workers are mostly ignorant about each other's day-to-day realities, a situation that could be improved by a member of one profession spending a day "shadowing" a member of the other profession.

5. *Agencies collaborate in developing resource information.* The best example we came across is *Children, New York's Greatest Resource: The School's Role in Preventing Child Abuse and Neglect,* put out by the New York State Department of Education, Albany.

6. *Modify confidentiality laws.* Each children's problem area—be it substance abuse, child abuse, or delinquency—has developed confidentiality laws that apparently are premised on the notion that a child has only a single problem. Thus, the drug counselor treating a young drug abuser is privy to this personal information about the child, but no one else is. Similarly, many states have child protection statutes that authorize CPS agencies to have access to a child's school and mental health records, but the reverse is not allowed. This issue is discussed in some detail in Chapter 9.

18
What Others
Are Doing

"Are there others out there who care for these kids who are so good at turning people off?" We believe there are many such people, and we have put together a list of some of the more interesting projects, new laws, and other initiatives directly or indirectly related to responding to CACs. Although we are unable to verify the continuing existence of all, we do believe that each represents a building block in the continuing effort to make better responses to chronic acting-out students.

1. *New York State Department of Education training seminars* for school systems address "problems that impact on the family: child abuse and neglect, adolescent pregnancy, domestic violence, sexual abuse, divorce, substance abuse, and student dropout." Provided in conjunction with the Regional Health and Nutrition NET/work's Family Life Training and Resource Center.

2. *Rich's Academy, run by Cities in Schools (CIS) of Atlanta,* a partnership between that organization and Rich's Department Store, Atlanta Public Schools, and Fulton County. The Academy's program is based on the concept (developed in 1974 by Exodus, Inc.) that many dropouts would stay in school if they received both educational and social service support at the instructional site, particularly if it were delivered in a coordinated and caring fashion.

3. *Recommendation of California Commission on Crime Control and Violence Prevention* (1982): ". . . to further develop methods for early identification, on the part of school and juvenile personnel, of children and families *at-risk for violent behavior;* and to identify those factors in early childhood associated with self-esteem and various types of violence."

4. *Educational Vocational Programs of the St. Louis, E. Missouri Juvenile Court.* This court offers three educationally based programs for juveniles: G.E.D. Program, Youth Opportunities Unlimited (Y.O.U. has an educational/job placement rate of 91 percent), and Project L.E.A.R.N. (intensive remedial instruction in reading, writing, and math).

5. *A suicide prevention protocol* for public school personnel developed by the New York State Education Department and the New York State Council on Youth Suicide Prevention.

6. *Protective Behaviors: Anti-Victim Training for Children, Adolescents and Adults,* (West, 1979). This concise, highly readable manual presents a prevention method against

violence and abuse, both physical and psychological, that has attracted much positive attention nationally. Ms. West observes:

> School staff are rightly and legitimately concerned with violence at home. Violence at home is a direct detriment to a child's school learning in that it interferes with ability to concentrate, decrease a child's ability and interest in the risk-taking involved in active learning and undermines sense of self (self-concept). Even putting humanitarian considerations aside (and why should we?), these stated reasons alone sanction and validate school staff concerns and intervention with violence in children's lives.

The West manual includes, among other things, training materials on substance abuse, because of its frequent presence in maltreatment situations, and a sample letter to be used by a principal, teacher, or school social worker in involving parents.

7. *Family Teaching Center,* Helena, Montana. This program focuses on "aggressive or out-of-control" children, ages 4 to 12. Center staff target "significant others" who wittingly or unwittingly agitate these children. Usually this means the home (parents) and school contexts (teachers).

8. *Learning Alternative Program,* Tampa, Florida. This program's rationale is that early school-based interventions with disruptive students will reduce the likelihood of their committing delinquent acts. It is based within a regular junior high school and provides intensive academic and counseling services in the school and in the home. The program is a collaborative effort of the state's Youth Services Program (Department of Health and Rehabilitation Services) and the county school board. Summary statistics for the initial fall term (1985–86 school year) include: (a) 928 unexcused absences, versus 7,382 for the 1984–85 school year; (b) 617 out-of-school suspension days, versus 1,638; (c) 24 delinquency referrals, versus 174; (d) 7 status offense referrals, versus 81; and (e) 8 abuse/neglect referrals, versus 52. Program counselors conducted 1,980 field and home contacts during this period.

9. *School Youth Advocacy (SYA),* Lansing, Michigan. We note SYA's analysis of the problem and program rationale:

> *Cause of the Problem:* Students with unmet emotional and academic needs may show their frustration through disruptive behavior. Dropping out of school is "one of the last stages in a chain of failures for these students. Typically students who drop out have a poor self-concept, are shy about taking risks, lack skills in handling interpersonal relations and conflicts, and express their frustrations through withdrawal or hostility." Such students are likely to become delinquents.
>
> *Program Rationale:* Guided group interaction will help students improve attitudes toward self, others, and school and will help improve academic achievement. Acquisition of skills to effectively manage behavior can eliminate the need for disciplinary sanctions. A structured peer support group can prove a viable alternative to traditional disciplinary action, and may prevent disruptive behavior. Students who remain in school and who experience improved attitudes toward self and school and improved academic achievement are not likely to commit delinquency acts.

SYA was initiated by the Michigan Department of Social Services, which awarded an ESEA Title III planning grant to four Michigan school districts to establish an experimental model to address three school problem areas: reintegration of institutionalized youths, viable alternatives to suspensions and expulsion, and creation of a school climate fostering development of responsible citizens.

10. *The Stop Truancy Program,* Joliet, Illinois. The goal is to reclaim dropout students and offer them a meaningful transition back into the regular curriculum. Of sixty dropout students in Joliet's two public high schools, forty-eight completed the program and resumed their normal curriculum.

11. *The Yale–New Haven (Connecticut) Primary Prevention Project.* Begun in 1968, the project initially targeted two elementary schools with a 99 percent black enrollment, using a mental health approach to such problems as low achievement in reading and mathematics, truancy, and severe behavioral problems. The results are remarkable. Students are testing at or above grade level and have excellent attendance, and there has not been a "serious disruptive behavior problem" in the past ten years. Most encouraging, follow-up testing of these students as much as ten years later indicates that all gains have been retained. Dr. Comer, who started the project, comments:

> Children often would become behavior problems because of fears engendered by a totally new environment. A child who has just moved from rural North Carolina and is fearful and anxious, might misbehave, kicking the teacher, attacking other students, etc. Eventually that child is labeled as incorrigible. Needed to prevent such patterns from developing is a basic understanding of what it means to be young and to face a totally new environment. Emotional supports have to be developed for such youngsters. An official welcome by the teacher, combined with a peer buddy system in which the pupil has someone who goes with him and orients him to the school can do much to eliminate future difficulties. We provided insights into how children develop, what makes them anxious, how they act out; getting to the root of many of the difficulties teachers encountered with pupils.

12. *The Boston Student Human Services Collaborative,* Boston, Massachusetts. Instrumental in developing this project was Hubie Jones, dean of Boston University's School of Social Work, who used a pioneer program originated earlier at Madison Park High School as the model for the Collaborative. The Collaborative is designed to bring psychologists and social workers from the private sector into the schools to help school personnel shoulder a large counseling load. This undertaking serves such secondary purposes as reducing interagency conflict, bringing additional expertise to bear on especially difficult cases, lessening educator isolation, and expanding the school's response repertoire vis-à-vis difficult-to-handle students.

13. *Maine's state-mandated health education.* Ten subjects, ranging from first aid to substance abuse to sexuality (e.g., teen pregnancy), must be covered in elementary and high school classes. Local school districts are charged with developing specific course content. Although the program has met with some criticism by private citizens, the state counters that the bulk of the citizenry is supportive because of increasing awareness "of links between life styles and disease, of rising medical costs, and of 'typical crises' such as pregnancy, drunken driving and suicide among teenagers."

14. *Office of Juvenile Justice and Delinquency Prevention's Call for Research:* "To enhance our ability for early identification and intervention with high risk children for the prevention of delinquency." (Washington, D.C., 1985)

15. *Dade County (Florida) Interagency Consortium,* made up of representation from the city government of Miami, the Metro-Dade Police Departments, the Department of Human Resources, the Department of Health and Rehabilitation Services, and other community-based agencies. We quote:

> Recognizing that drug usage and patterns of delinquent behavior often begin in late elementary and junior high grades, the Consortium began an early intervention program for children in kindergarten through fourth grade who exhibit behavioral and emotional problems or are academic underachievers. The Consortium has targeted a number of elementary schools in a high poverty section of Miami to receive the program's services. Considerable emphasis is placed on both an after-school remedial education and treatment of emotional and behavioral problems. A local mental health agency conducts individual and group counseling sessions with these children. Because of Dade County's concern for reducing epidemic-level drug use, treatment in this program, as one of its objectives, makes a concerted effort to deal with problems and educate these predelinquent youngsters about the dangers of drug abuse.

16. *Community task forces on child abuse.* See, for example, "The Community Task Force on Child Abuse: Tips for the Organizer," developed by staff at the Family Life Development Center at Cornell University, 1984.

17. *A Medical Passport,* designed to track the health history of approximately 8,000 children in Massachusetts foster homes and group residences to ensure that these children receive preventive health care.

18. *Florida's Model School Adjustment Program Statute.* Pertinent parts of this statute include:

> (1)(a) The goal of this program is to develop and evaluate one or more research-based model prevention programs for grades four through eight students likely to become academic underachievers, failures, truants, dropouts, or severe behavioral problems. Such students shall be currently ineligible or inappropriate for existing educational alternative or exceptional education programs.
>
> (3) *Dropout Prevention*—Effective during the 1986–1987 school year and each school year thereafter:
>
> (a) Every school district shall cause to be established within each school in the district a remediation program under which qualified school personnel, under the authority of school administrators, shall meet with and counsel, and otherwise professionally assist those students who have been identified as potential school dropouts, and where possible, the parents or legal guardians of such students, in an attempt to alleviate the conditions and problems contributing to the behavioral factors which have led to the identification of such students as potential school dropouts.
>
> (b) Every district school board shall take such action as may be necessary to ensure that school counselors within the district are familiar with the student dropout profile, are adequately trained in identifying those students who fit such profile, and are well grounded in appropriate counseling techniques and procedures deemed effective in such cases.
>
> (c) School counselors shall report any student deemed to fit the student dropout profile to the school principal or his designated representative so that steps toward initiating procedures may be immediately taken by the school administration.

Florida Atlantic University has been charged with developing a data base for use in identifying at-risk students in grades four to eight.

19. *Impact,* Chicago, Illinois. Developed in 1963 for early identification (in elementary schools) and rehabilitation of potential school dropouts. Characteristics of the children involved include: serious conflict with authority, inattentiveness, withdrawal, poor peer relationship, destructiveness, and a gradual pattern of increased absences. A unique feature of the program from the outset was use of a school social worker, who provided services in the school and home.

20. *Children: New York's Greatest Resource, The School's Role in Preventing Abuse and Neglect*—a manual prepared by the New York State Education Department. This is the best state department of education manual on child abuse we came across. Copies may be obtained by writing Ms. Maria Ramirez, Assistant Commissioner of General Education, New York State Education Department, Albany, NY 12234. We cite several excerpts:

> Sometimes educators are overwhelmed at the thought of taking on yet another responsibility. However, child abuse and neglect are clearly related to learning. Research indicates that abused and neglected children often demonstrate significant learning problems and below-grade performance in academic areas. Educators cannot ignore the reasons why children cannot learn. The abused or neglected child, as any other child who has difficulty, is entitled to special help in an effort to enhance learning.

> Academic difficulties may have a variety of causes, and the presence of an academic problem does not prove that child abuse or neglect exists. But, the possibility of child abuse and neglect must be considered—along with other possible causes—when the problem is assessed.

> Behavior can often be a clue to the presence of child abuse and neglect. Behavioral indicators may exist alone or may accompany physical indicators. They range from subtle clues, a "sixth sense" that something is amiss, to graphic statements by children that they have been physically assaulted or sexually molested.

> Reporting is not the end of the child protective process; it is the beginning. Treatment, rehabilitation, the strengthening of family life and prevention still lie ahead. Schools and educators can provide assistance and support to child protective services by sharing relevant information about specific families and children after they have been reported; by providing services for the child and the family; and by participating on a multidisciplinary school-agency team. Schools can also become actively involved in community coordination efforts to reduce the incidence of child maltreatment.

21. *School and Agency Child Abuse Prevention Coordination Teams*—a new project involving the New York State Departments of Education and Social Services, three county child protection units, twenty school districts, and the Associated Board of Cooperative Educational Services. Features include county child protective services personnel participating with school-based child study teams, early intervention strategies in the home and school, improved feedback to school personnel from child protective services units, and an interagency coordinating committee.

22. *Parents and School Partnerships for the Prevention of Child Abuse and Neglect*—cosponsored by the Bronx (New York) Community School District #10 and Cornell University's Family Life Development Center. District #10 has previously been singled out for

praise for its work with families of court-related youth and its parent training approach in a drug prevention program. Its child abuse efforts were sparked by the superintendent of schools for District #10, who in 1980 initiated the Superintendent's Task Force on Child Abuse and Neglect. The task force consisted of Parents Association leaders, administrators, and guidance counselors, working with members of the Family Life Development Center to become educated on maltreatment issues. In turn, the task force has provided training for many educators and parents, has established a parent hotline, and has formed a network with community agencies serving abusive and neglectful families. The task force is the model for Partnerships, which has been designed for replication elsewhere in the country.

23. *Student Ombudsman.* A Children's Defense Fund publication identifies Stephen R. Kaminsky at the William O'Shea Intermediate School 44, New York City, as one such person. Mr. Kaminsky serves as an advocate for at-risk children in the school, home, and community. He also takes some strain off classroom teachers: "There are some kids who just can't sit in a classroom for forty minutes . . . so if they need a break, they will ask to speak to [me]."

24. *District Diagnostic Centers,* Chicago, Illinois—utilized by Chicago schools to determine the precise nature of an emotional, physical, educational or psychiatric problem.

25. *Administrative Advisor for Discipline,* Columbia, South Carolina, school district. This innovative position assigns to one staff person the task of developing better ways to handle disruptive students. The job entails analysis of the types of classroom discipline problems and factors influencing them. Much of the advisor's efforts go toward working with parents of disruptive students.

26. *School Attendance Review Boards (SARBs),* currently in use in San Joaquin County, California. Truancy cases are referred to a multiagency, multidisciplinary group including representatives from law enforcement, the public schools, and mental health, public health, and welfare. Parents also are members. The boards consider all available information, including child abuse and delinquency reports.

27. *A Comprehensive Stress Management Program for Elementary and Secondary Students and Their Families,* developed in Vermont by Northwest Kingdom Mental Health Services, Inc. This school-based program is intended to decrease levels of stress, thereby reducing the incidence of maltreatment.

28. *The Children's Advocate Program,* another school-based program designed to assist elementary school children to respond to threatened or actual abuse.

29. *COMPASS,* a child abuse prevention program in Tennessee for students that consists of four components: personal safety, a hotline, parent involvement, and training and community awareness. Funded by NCCAN, the program has principally targeted grades three through five. Pre- and posttesting indicated that the personal safety curriculum, which is taught by the regular classroom teachers, did not cause children to be disturbed or fearful.

30. *School-based health clinics,* most of which are modeled after the St. Paul (Minnesota) program. Clinics are currently operating in Bridgeport and New Haven, Connecticut; Chicago, Illinois; Gary, Indiana; Flint, Muskegon, and Ypsilanti, Michigan; Minneapolis and St. Paul; Jackson, Mississippi; Kansas City, Missouri; New York City; Dallas and Houston; Cambridge, Massachusetts; New Brunswick, New Jersey; and Providence, Rhode Island. School-based clinics respond to a range of student problems, from dropping out to pregnancy to substance abuse. Major advantages are basing services where students are and utilizing staff from different agencies and systems. Reviews of school-based health clinics

have found them to be popular with students, parents, health and community workers, and school personnel.

31. The *National PTA*, Chicago, has developed national programs on drug and alcohol abuse prevention, latchkey children, and other issues that affect students' ability and opportunity to learn. Their written materials may be obtained by contacting the National PTA, 700 South Rush Street, Chicago, IL 60611.

32. The *National Education Association* has a professional library consisting of publications on child abuse, disruptive behavior, and other children's problems that directly affect educators. The maltreatment publications include, for example, "Questions Teachers Ask About Legal Aspects of Reporting Child Abuse and Neglect"; "Profiles of Abusive and Neglectful Parents"; "Talking with the Victim"; and "Setting Up a Program". Interested readers can obtain the 1986–87 Professional library catalog by contacting the NEA at 1201 16th Street, N.W., Washington, D.C. 20036-3290.

33. *Teacher Talks Forums,* begun in New Jersey in 1985 and since used by several other states. Vermont, for example, held a Teacher Talks Forum from March 17 through April 14, 1986. In attendance were the governor, the lieutenant governor, the chairmen of the state senate and house committees on education, the commissioner of education, the chancellor of the state colleges, the dean of the university's college of education, the directors of state advocacy groups for education, and many teachers, who voiced a variety of concerns. Recommendations included the need for more guidance personnel and more guidance training for teachers; more opportunities to overcome institutional isolation, which teachers described as a "severe problem"; and assistance in easing demands on their time.

34. *A school-court project in Georgia with three overriding purposes:*

(a) to develop linkages between schools and courts so that services to youth involved with both systems can be coordinated and early intervention rather than remedial/rehabilitation services can be increased; (b) to assist school and court personnel in reaching out to other human service agencies to develop a community-wide system of service coordination for young people; and (c) to enable school and court personnel to address youth-related community problems with preventive rather than reactive approaches.

35. *The National Alliance of Pupil Services Organizations,* an ad hoc organization in Washington, D.C., whose purpose is to "assure the provision of comprehensive and appropriate services to children and youth within the educational system." Objectives include (a) promoting the exchange of information and improved communication among the pupil-related services; and (b) developing a unified approach to problems concerning pupil-related services.

36. *North Carolina's Willie M. Program,* which features comprehensive interagency service delivery to the emotionally disturbed, mentally retarded, or neurologically handicapped with histories of assaultive or aggressive behavior.

37. *The Child Abuse and Neglect Prevention Training Manual,* a collaborative effort of the New York City Board of Education, the Mayor's Task Force on Child Abuse and Neglect, and the New York City Department of Health and Special Services for Children. This manual is an outgrowth of an interagency effort, mandated by the mayor's office, to train school personnel in early identification, reporting procedures, and follow-up in suspected child abuse and neglect cases.

Certainly, our nation is not bereft of ideas and interest in responding to CACs and maltreated children. No doubt each of the cited projects has shortcomings of one kind or another. A few may even be defunct. But overall, they suggest a tradition of caring (versus punitive) intervention in the lives of troubled children that can and should be built upon.

Part V
Other
Considerations

19
The Role of Special Education

Although all sectors of the public school system feel the strain of trying to contend with chronic acting-out students, special education personnel have increasingly been asked to carry the brunt of the load. In some cases—especially at the elementary level—teachers, school nurses, counselors, and administrators refer troublesome students because of genuine concern about the possible presence of an educational handicap. At least as often—especially at the secondary level—referrals are primarily motivated by a desire to pass irritating students on to someone else. An estimated four million children are currently receiving special education services.

The question thus arises whether Public Law 94-142 (and its companion, Section 504 of the Rehabilitation Act) is a suitable vehicle for handling all or most chronic acting-out students. The answer would seem to be yes if one accepts the proposition that underlying child abuse and acting-out behaviors block children from learning. After all, should it make any difference *what* is preventing a child from learning?

The legal answer is to be found in P.L. 94-142 eligibility criteria, which include a limited number of disabling conditions. Two of the criteria are particularly relevant to our chronic acting-out, often maltreated student: "seriously emotionally disturbed" (e.g., inappropriate types of behavior or feeling under normal circumstances) and "specific learning disability" (e.g., perceptual handicaps). However, both tend to be construed narrowly, except in a small number of enabling states, such as Massachusetts, which have state special education laws broader in scope than P.L. 94-142. Thus, for example, children who are deemed to be socially maladjusted rather than "seriously emotionally disturbed" are not eligible for special education services. And although "specific learning disability" refers to a disorder in one or more of the basic psychological processes involved in understanding or using language, an evaluation must identify a specific disorder for children to be eligible.

Quite clearly, large numbers of abused children and similarly large numbers of chronic acting-out children have major problems in understanding and using language. Our direct service experience tells us, though, that these children often are never coded, or very belated referrals are made to special education, or they are coded but underserved.

The reasons for this are rooted in budgetary concerns and in the limited tolerance CACs engender in their educators. Notwithstanding the noble purpose of P.L. 94-142, special education is expensive business—especially for CACs, who often require placement in private residential treatment facilities. The cost for such services ranges from $20,000 to over $100,000 per year. Just five or so referrals by a school can quickly exhaust its special education budget for an entire year.

Legally speaking, such financial concerns are irrelevant, as P.L. 94-142 mandates a "free and appropriate" public education for eligible students. Yet Congress itself limited special education services funded with federal monies to a maximum of 12 percent of all students age 5 to 17. In 1984, enrollment in special education programs nationally had risen to over 4 million. Some states (e.g., Connecticut, Maine, Maryland, New Jersey) are already very close to the cap. Others, (e.g., Massachusetts) have exceeded the cap, resulting in recent action by the U.S. Department of Education to retrieve some of its federal allocations to such states.

Another limiting dynamic is our students' disruptive behavior, which spawns a common attitude among adults that these young people are recalcitrant by choice rather than because of an inherent condition. Consequently, a response repertoire with punishments at the center often leads to students being banished rather than referred for special education services. Or, if they are already coded, there is a tendency to cast the problem more in terms of delinquency and home problems rather than educationally related handicaps. At least if a child is coded, suspensions, expulsions, and other punishments must be more carefully considered. Further, the obligation to educate following suspensions and expulsions continues, which is not the case in most states for noncoded children.

Where does this leave us? Theoretically, a strong argument can be made that virtually all chronic acting-out children are educationally handicapped and therefore should be eligible for special education services. Coding some of these children under current laws is problematic, as forenoted; therefore P.L. 94-142 would have to be amended to eliminate this bar. Certainly the 12 percent cap would need to be raised, with a corresponding substantial increase in federal education monies. It is difficult to imagine these things happening in Washington in the mid-1980s, although the Department of Education has recently conducted a study to determine the feasibility of coding socially maladjusted students.

There are other concerns as well. Ms. Isadore Hare, senior staff associate at the National Social Workers Association, believes that chronic acting-out children are deserving of educational and counseling services in their own right without having to be labeled "educationally handicapped." Her concern is that even with liberal application of P.L. 94-142, the requirement that a specific condition be present will continue to rule out services for many students in need.

Jaclyn Adams, a member of our project and a special education coordinator for years in both the public and private sectors, fears what will happen to special education services if the door is opened wide to allow in all chronic acting-out children. She elaborates on these concerns in the dialogue at the end of this chapter.

A foremost problem that would have to be met head on if special education is to assume a greater role is the present poor relationship between educators and child protection. Although not in as bad condition, the relationship between educators and juvenile court personnel would also have to be substantially improved.

Even the Children's Defense Fund, which has taken a very strong stand against the widespread use of suspensions and expulsions, cautions against special education being used as a catchall for problem students: "Clearly, one program for 'disruptive students'—ranging from frustrated dyslexics to minimally brain damaged to emotionally disturbed to children who settle scores with their fists—will be overburdened and ineffective." Moreover, the CDF and other advocacy organizations in 1980 drafted a public petition citing major compliance problems even for many children who have been coded. These include:

1. Tens of thousands of children who have been identified as handicapped and referred for evaluation and services are either on waiting lists or ignored altogether by school officials for months or even years.

2. Institutionalized children and children in other placements outside their natural homes are routinely denied adequate and appropriate services or excluded from educational services altogether.

3. Handicapped children are frequently denied related services, such as physical therapy, occupational therapy, school health services, and transportation essential to enable them to benefit from special education.

4. Many handicapped children remain unnecessarily segregated in special schools and classes for the handicapped.

5. Black children are misclassified and inappropriately placed in classes for the "educable mentally retarded" at a rate over three times that of white children. Other minorities are frequently misclassified as well.

6. Handicapped children are illegally suspended or expelled from school for periods ranging up to nearly two years.

7. Many handicapped children still have not received an individual evaluation or an individualized education program (IEP). "Canned" IEPs often provide a substitute for truly individualized planning.

8. Severely handicapped children are denied education in excess of the 180-day school year, even when such service is essential to the child's education.

Where do we go if special education is not the answer? First, it must be recognized that significant numbers of chronic acting-out children, whether abused or not, are already being served under P.L. 94-142. By some estimates, more than two-thirds of the nation's "emotionally disturbed" children are receiving special education services. These figures are somewhat misleading in that they reference only those children who are clearly eligible under current laws. Moreover, in our experience, coded CACs are frequently underserved because of their multiple problems, the high cost of appropriate services, and, at times, the absence of needed services.

Nonetheless, we applaud educators who make sincere efforts to extend special education status (versus "bad kid" status) to these children. Of course, legal members of our project who advocate for acting-out children insist that these children are entitled to a good deal more than just a "status" under P.L. 94-142. However, our policy-oriented side tells us that even while we push to get our clients all the educational services we can, more is needed than pursuing a singular strategy that results in overloading of the special education system (just as more is needed than overloading the child protection reporting system).

In a law review article entitled "Enacting Legislation to Identify and Treat Children with Conduct Disorders," Ola and Donald Barnett (1980) contend that conduct-disordered children should be identified at the earliest possible stage in the schools and should benefit by programming similar to P.L. 94-142. The Barnetts acknowledge that whereas some CD children are receiving special education services by virtue of a specific learning disability or being seriously emotionally disturbed, many others are not because of the social maladjustment caveat.

Thus, the Barnetts would have Congress set up parallel programming for these CD children. They rationalize major new costs of such a program by the claim that paying now is cheaper than paying later, when these children become criminals or social misfits. Although we agree with the Barnetts that CACs are deserving of special programming linked to education, we would forgo long-range predictions about later criminality, which raise legal problems when doing early intervention.

Instead, we would cite a child's right to a meaningful opportunity for educational success and the right of those around the chronic acting-out child not to be continually disrupted by his/her behavior as the bases for establishing new programs. In addition, we would forgo a finding of CD as necessary for eligibility, citing a student's repeated disruptive behavior as sufficient to warrant special services. For one thing, not all CACs are CD. For another, many therapeutic personnel are hesitant to make a diagnosis as severe as CD in children.

The New Hampshire legislature, like others concerned about the spiraling cost of providing special education services, recently conducted an analysis of the problem and found that it appeared that special education was being used to respond to all manner of student problems. A committee report concludes:

> Handicapped children should be guaranteed services. However, it is not clear that the state needs to provide—and fund—all of the necessary services through the local educational system. The staff recommends that the legislature consider directing other state organizations to more effectively address the needs of handicapped children. At the very least, the Commissioner of Education and Directors of Mental Health and Public Health should be directed to prepare for legislative review a comprehensive plan by which the three agencies they direct will pool available resources—including financial resources—to provide services to handicapped children.

Although the report adopts a more narrow construction of P.L. 94-142 than we would, the call for other units of government, such as public and mental health, to become involved in a comprehensive plan on behalf of handicapped children makes sense. In an era of fiscal restraint at the federal level, this type of "sharing" strategy among state agencies with a child development mandate may be one of the few viable strategies presently available to affect schoolchildren who chronically misbehave. Even if funds were more readily available, multiproblem children necessarily require the services of multidisciplinary agencies. And perhaps most important, a shared strategy reduces the present tendency of one sector attempting to sluff off the problem onto another to avoid financial and human resources depletion.

Before concluding the narrative portion of this chapter, it should be noted again, that our project is always juggling two phenomenona: chronic acting out and child maltreatment. Whereas the former is always present, the latter is not and therefore is apt to get short shrift at times. Special education personnel openly debate whether CACS should be coded, absent a specific handicap such as dyslexia. The acting-out behavior rides on the surface and is always before the educator.

In contrast, abuse is beneath the surface, and coding decisions seldom, if ever, center on a student's abused or suspected abused condition. Public Law 94-142 makes no reference to child abuse, yet we know from research that many seriously emotionally disturbed and learning disabled children are victims of maltreatment. Until our society finds a more effective way of identifying maltreatment, we simply recommend that special education personnel think possible maltreatment in all referred special education cases, particularly if they are attended by chronic acting out.

We salute the efforts of special education personnel such as those employed by S.A.U. #21 in New Hampshire, who recently invited the Boston Children's Hospital Medical Center Sexual Abuse Team to conduct a training seminar on handicapping conditions related to sexual trauma for its special education personnel and other educators in the region. We also refer the reader to what others are doing (Chapter 18), especially such efforts as Florida's Model School Adjustment Program.

Given the strong emphasis on testing and evaluations under P.L. 94-142—including family histories, albeit with parental permission—it should be standard practice for evaluating personnel to inquire about maltreatment. This must be consistent with federal and state laws, some of which are discussed in Chapter 9.

The special education dialogue that follows involves David Sandberg and two project members from the special education community, Joanne Testaverde and Jaclyn Adams:

DS: Is there an awareness among special education teachers that child abuse is a common problem among coded students?

JT: In my experience, special education people tend to view the students as hyperactive products of divorce and low self-esteem, as lacking in culturally enriching experiences, but seldom as abuse victims. Where I currently work, the treatment people are attuned to the abuse factor, although my teachers concentrate on educational rather than family issues.

JA: They think of it secondarily. Is the child retarded? Is s/he brain damaged? Those are the questions that tend to come to mind first. However, family-related problems are increasingly coming to mind, particularly on the part of preschool teachers who work with the educationally handicapped. Regular classroom teachers are less aware than special education personnel, although obviously some teachers are very sensitive to abuse issues. Unfortunately, many regular classroom teachers see chronic acting-out children as "rotten kids."

DS: Why does brain damage or retardation generally come to mind first as the possible source of a child's educational handicap?

JA: For one thing, these conditions present a clear-cut explanation that is easy to understand. Also, there are specific remedial steps to take when a child has an IQ of 50, for example. You don't have to search for underlying why's of school failure. However, in my experience, sexually abused children, especially the girls, test very low on IQ tests. When I receive a female referral who is withdrawn and tests low, I think sexual abuse as a likely prospect. It just seems to be a recurring pattern. However, exploring for abuse can be troublesome and somewhat frightening. It is not something anyone really wants to do.

DS: Should all CACs, including those diagnosed conduct-disordered, be eligible for coding under the rationale that emotional trauma and related acting out block learning?

JT: Absolutely. And, in fact, some states allow for coding of such students under regulations implementing the federal Act. The Act itself is very general as to behavioral disorders. States that narrowly interpret the Act are saying, in effect, that behavior is home-related rather than educationally related and therefore not within special ed's jurisdiction.

JA: No. Special education as it is now designed under P.L. 94-142 cannot handle all of these children. Conduct-disordered children need treatment and socialization before they can learn. Special education targets a limited number of problems that prevent learning, problems that with some educational supplements can be remediated. Consequently, I would prefer to see the CD children, who are not well served in the regular classroom, handled under a new system involving educational, mental health, and juvenile justice personnel.

Now, as a practical matter, almost all the elementary-level CD children get coded. Principals encourage this to get these children out of the regular classroom, where they are extremely disruptive, and into some special programming. However, if they reach junior and senior high level before they are really acting out, special education personnel resist coding and look to the juvenile justice system. In my experience, 10 percent of the acting-out students get coded seriously emotionally disturbed, 40 percent are coded learning disabled, and 50 percent are never coded.

But again, I do not favor the further expansion of P.L. 94-142 to include coding of all CD children. Another system, geared foremost to treatment and socialization, is needed for these children.

DS: What is the scope of assessments that can be made under the Act?

JT: A wide range, including psychological testing by a licensed psychologist. A home assessment can be made as part of that evaluation—conducted by a school nurse, social worker, or guidance counselor. Virtually any test can be done that is deemed necessary to properly identify a student's educationally related need areas. However, parental permission is required unless the student is in the custody of the state or a guardian.

JA: With a parent's permission, we can do or refer a student for just about any type of testing: vocational, psychological, neurological. Without permission, we are limited to administering only those tests that are given to all children in school.

DS: So, as you read it, parental permission is a cornerstone of the Act?

JT: Yes.

JA: Even if the child is in the custody of the state in which I work, we still need to get permission from the parent or the "surrogate parent."

DS: What happens if the student very much needs services but the parents do not give their permission for an evaluation?

JT: The great majority of parents agree after the reason for the testing is explained. If a parent repeatedly refuses to agree to allow a student to be assisted, we have filed neglect petitions.

JA: The school can also initiate a due process hearing at the state level to override a parent's refusal. In my experience, schools seldom do this, as it can be costly. Also, parents do not often refuse. Where it has happened, it tends to be a parent who will not allow psychological testing because s/he doesn't want the school to know about what is going on in the home. This, coupled with other factors, has led me to file a neglect report with child protection.

DS: What if child abuse is suspected prior to or after assessment and coding?

JT: Child abuse reporting laws require that we file a report, but it's a very touchy situation within the public schools. Often, there is a chain of command up to the principal before a report is filed, which involves a number of people. Teachers are afraid of parental repercussions, as well as of their own superintendent or principal coming down on them, even losing their jobs. There are a lot of pressures to ignore the problem.

JA: If we suspect abuse or neglect prior to coding, we file a report with child protection and alert our psychologist, who can look for it in the psychological testing and interview. I cue this person to what the concerns are. If we come to suspect abuse after a child is coded, we report to child protection. In some instances, we have attempted to discuss abusive treatment with certain parents. It seems that these are the parents who then move suddenly. This is not an uncommon occurrence.

Let me add that my state has recently implemented a uniform procedure for all schools to use in reporting abuse or neglect. This has been very helpful and is eliminating many of the problems Joanne refers to. So I don't believe that our teachers fear repercussions anymore. What does continue to be a major concern is how things are handled or not handled by child protection once we file a report. For example, our experience is that child protection often does little more than investigate by telephone. Also, we seldom get feedback from child protection. What we often see after a report is a child who is more closed than ever.

DS: Is child abuse ever looked into as part of the family assessment segment of an evaluation?

JT: In my experience in the public school system, child abuse was not looked for as part of the regular assessment procedure. If, in the course of doing an assessment, child abuse was suspected, then the law requires us to report.

JA: Very rarely; generally, we do not do family assessments as part of special education evaluations. Mental retardation is the only coding condition that requires collection of home data, and even then only concerning the adaptive behavior of the child. Even with CD children who are coded "seriously emotionally disturbed," special education law does not require a family assessment. Looking at the "social and emotional status" of a child is about as close as New Hampshire regulations come to such an assessment. Underlying all of this is special education's focus on whether a child meets the criteria of being educationally handicapped, not whether s/he is being beaten at home. Special education has no mandate nor policy for dealing with abused children.

DS: Is a chronic acting-out student less apt to be expelled if s/he is coded?

JT: Yes; the mandate to provide educational services continues, although it may need to be in a setting other than the public school.

JA: In general, a child cannot be suspended or expelled for reasons related to the disability. Instead, the IEP has to be modified to spell out consequences for certain behaviors. This may result in home tutoring or residential placement. "Out of sight, out of mind" is not allowed with these children who are coded.

DS: What generic or common educational problems do you see with CACs?

JT: They always seem to be at least two or three grades behind, they hate school, and their parents commonly tell you about years of hyperactivity and prior interventions that have failed—years and years of problems that have affected their ability to concentrate and learn.

JA: Many of the CD children seem to have at least average IQ and have good ability, but suffer from failure to have polished their skills by repetition. In contrast, LD kids tend to have clear-cut deficits in specific subject areas. For those who are CD and also have some learning disabilities, as you can imagine, the problems are compounded.

DS: Why is it that some of these first-generation special education students who ultimately wind up in residential programs have deteriorated after years of interventions?

JT: Unless the student's environment changes, all the school's input is not going to do much good for some of the more troubled students who are coded. Among other things, the parents need to change, and most find this very hard. Some refuse. That's not to put all the blame on them, but it's true nonetheless.

JA: For one thing, I think it makes my earlier point that special education alone cannot effectively handle certain kinds of kids. Also, I believe we've gone too far in trying to mainstream some children who can't be handled in the public schools. My preference would be to place a child outside the school or in self-contained programs within the public schools—a school or program where s/he can get the precise services needed. A lot of our efforts to make some special education students feel "normal" by keeping them in regular classrooms do not succeed. The children know they are different and often feel more comfortable with children who have similar problems and skill levels.

DS: How do non–special education people tend to view the student we are talking about?

JT: "Get him out of the classroom. I can't take him anymore!" That certainly is a common feeling, not so much in elementary as in secondary school. A lot of special ed teachers also come to feel this way. These kids are the biggest cause of special ed burnout.

JA: Again, the "rotten kid" syndrome. Over and over, I hear: "He needs a good spanking"; "I'd enjoy coming to my classes if he was not here"; and so forth. Often, teachers send out messages to all the other students that class would be much better without the problem student. Often, too, CACs never make the field trips or special earned activities, further reinforcing their personal isolation. Of course, if I were in these teachers' shoes, I might feel much the same way. CACs need a lot of structure and need to be handled differently. Some teachers can provide this; most can't.

DS: The residents at your program seem to like school, and most do well academically. How do you explain this?

JT: They are not being constantly stimulated by a chaotic home environment; there are consistent guidelines and positive rather than negative peer pressure; a lot of positive reinforcement is given; there is no alcohol or drug use; and we have skilled therapists right here in the same building. Also, we have a 1:8 teacher–student ratio, allowing us to give each resident a lot of attention, which they need. Most of our residents come to really enjoy schooling, although initially we hear a lot about "I'm stupid" and "What grade am I in?"

JA: They get individual attention, and Joanne's program is designed to allow them to succeed, which most have never experienced. Also, there is a level of caring that the residents respond well to. I have found a similar response with the special education students in the public schools. Also, I find that the more self-contained the special education effort, the better the CAC does. These children should not be mainstreamed. The student's goal should be reintegration into the regular classroom. However, the CAC's first need is to learn how to control his/her behavior and gain the academic skills necessary to succeed in a regular class.

I believe special education teachers are trained the way all teachers should be. They are taught to identify individual differences and to teach to the individual learning style of the child, with a strong emphasis on what is called "mastry teaching." In contrast, regular classroom teachers, especially at the secondary level, are taught to be curriculum-based, with little or no emphasis on the different learning styles children have.

DS: Joanne's comments make me realize that within her building are staff representing the educational, mental health, child protection, and juvenile justice viewpoints and training. And there are no bureaucratic walls between these people. This makes me wonder if CACs can be handled within the public schools.

JT: I think many can be mainstreamed, particularly in the elementary years. Often one school cannot do it, but a collaborative system involving a number of schools can. And yes, I think that mainstreaming is desirable as a principle, so long as there continues to be enough flexibility not to mainstream a child who wants or really needs an alternative educational program.

JA: Let me just add that 9 to 10 percent of any school population is handicapped. Within our NCCAN research project, we are looking at a relatively small number of the 9 to 10 percent who are chronic acting-outers. My reservations about mainstreaming are limited to this subset of children.

DS: Joanne talks about the advantage a private program has over public schools in that the program has full control of the child, the home distress is lessened, and all the needed disciplines are present in one place. Doesn't this suggest the wisdom of placing especially difficult students, as early as the elementary years, in such programs for major intervention?

JT: Ideally, yes. But it's not that easy. It's much more difficult to separate a preadolescent than an adolescent from his/her parent for one thing.

JA: If a specialized program with the needed community services can be provided within a public school system, I believe this is optimal. Again, a self-contained or collaborative program will usually be necessary. If this can be done, we avoid placing children away from their homes, which I fear makes them feel so terribly different. Of course, if a fully developed program cannot be developed within the public school system, then referral to good private programs is necessary and desirable. Also, if the home situation is intolerable, removal must be done, but I would prefer to see the child kept in the same community.

DS: This leads back to the schools and to the schools doing more. It also leads toward other disciplines and systems people providing services within the schools.

JT: Schools must do more. They need to do work with parents; it's essential. But as things stand now in most schools, having use of a social worker is considered a luxury. Most schools don't have them. Also, there is a strong feeling among many educators that our job is to teach—not to be therapists and social workers. We feel a lot is dumped on us by parents and others. And within schools, special education people often feel that classroom teachers and administrators dump all the hard-to-handle cases on them.

JA: Without an effective network with other state agencies, I don't see how schools alone can be responsible for most family problems. Educators should be children's advocates in the sense of providing them with a caring, safe, and fun environment at school. If all manner of family-related problems are to be dealt with by the schools, I am concerned about how safe our environment will be for these children. So I would rather have state mental health agencies, for example, deal with the family problems. But I strongly feel all of us have to know what the others are doing.

DS: Interagency cooperation is contingent, in part, on sharing important information. What are the parameters of P.L. 94-142 confidentiality in your experience?

JT: Release of information about the child is closely linked to parental consent. Even with consent, we often get calls from CPS workers who want information about the child. Unless we know the worker, which we seldom do, we're very hesitant to give this over the phone. Here at my program it is different, as all the disciplines comprise one overall staff working on behalf of the resident. Also, I think we are better able to engage parents, and most of them appreciate our need to have all the information we can get from prior agencies that have worked with their son or daughter. Again, in my experience in both the private and the public sector, very few refuse to sign a release of information consent form.

JA: It also needs to be noted that the Buckley amendment overlaps with P.L. 94-142. As for the Act itself, there is no problem when it comes to reporting suspected abuse or neglect. Also, in the State of New Hampshire, child protection has the right to full access to student records as part of its investigation. Beyond this, the confidentiality doors begin to shut. Absent parental permission, we cannot release information to outsiders, including the consulting psychologist. Yet, away from the special education context, a classroom teacher or administrator can talk with a child about a problem. So, strangely enough, confidentiality mainly targets specialists having access to information.

As a practical matter, P.L. 94-142 confidentiality has not caused me significant problems with gaining or sharing information. Of more concern is the difficulty we have had when trying to obtain information from other agencies that have previously worked with a child. In these instances, counselors often cite confidentiality. My experience is that parents usually will sign a release of information form unless it pertains to psychological-related information and the possibility of abuse is present.

DS: How can CPS and public schools achieve greater cooperation and mutual assistance?

JT: Many teachers are frightened by child abuse. They are not comfortable with dealing with it. These feelings are intensified when schools file child abuse reports and either hear nothing back from CPS or receive a form letter. What we need is some inservice training by CPS, not just copies of the reporting laws and a pamphlet about abuse. More than anything, educators need to know a face at CPS, someone they can get to know and trust. In my twelve years in the public schools, no one from CPS ever came to do inservice training or to get to know us.

JA: First and foremost, we need laws that compel a sharing of information and cooperative agreements, especially as to who is responsible for what, including findings. CPS has to be mandated to provide treatment services for abused and neglected children, just as special education is mandated to provide educational-related services. Currently, far too much time and money is being spent on agencies warring over who is going to pay the bill.

Thereafter, I like the idea of a CPS worker based at each school or, at the least, one CPS worker being designated for each school system. Linking of the systems in such a fashion is essential, as is an ongoing meeting process involving people from both systems. I would really like to see all CPS workers spend one day in a classroom where there is a chronic acting-out student; similarly, all educators should spend one day accompanying a CPS worker. I don't think each really appreciates what the other is dealing with.

DS: Do you have an additional thoughts on how CACs can be handled more effectively and at an earlier stage?

JT: School guidance counselors could be much more effective if they were giving sufficient time. Seeing a troubled student once a week just won't do—and that is often all they can do, given a high case load. These kids need to be seen every day, and there need to be frequent home visits. When I was a guidance counselor and later a psychologist in the public schools, I had eighty-five to ninety kids. I seldom saw half of them; I just didn't have enough time.

JA: Individual and family counseling are so often essential, even with preschoolers. Maltreated children also desperately need a designated advocate, and we educators have to accept responsibility for this. It's not so much a matter of our needing a lot of services that don't exist. To me, it has more to do with major interventions at the earliest possible point. We wait too long. Often, there is the appearance of a lot of intervention, but in my experience, usually no one is assuming ultimate responsibility to ensure that the interventions are adequate.

We need to remember that direct special education intervention can commence as early as age 3 and identification/screening from birth to 3 years. Much more needs to be done nationally to get parents and other professionals to refer at the earliest possible stage. In this manner, considerable work can be done before a child even gets to the public school. My experience has been that all the children we identified and began servicing at age 3 or 4 as educationally handicapped have been able to be educated later within the public schools. As it turns out, about 40 percent of the children in our preschool group have been maltreated. About 90 percent of our alternative school students (junior high, high school) have been abused or neglected.

DS: It is evident from what Joanne said earlier that her student/residents' desire to learn has not been snuffed out, even after years of failing in the public school. How much do you think their overall treatment success has to do with the success in your classrooms?

JT: I believe the therapeutic part of our program plays the biggest part, but take away the schooling and I don't think you'd see the same level of overall success. Our school provides the residents with much-needed structure, predictability, gratification, and hope.

JA: And absent intensive treatment and socialization, CACs can't learn.

DS: Lastly, what are your thoughts on our Summary Assessment Profile and on the recommendation that there be a required educational transfer sheet?

JT: The educational and family histories are an excellent idea. I would like to see such a picture for all students in difficulty, so that teachers can have a clearer sense of the child, the family, and what has happened to the child over the years. The transfer sheet is also very valuable, as right now we have several residents for whom there are no prior public school records. These tend to be students whose families have moved into the state within the past year or two, and the referring public school has been unable to obtain prior out-of-state records for one reason or another. This puts us in the position of having to rely on the child or the parent to obtain an educational history. There is presently a requirement that the public school have a student's medical/health record. This should be expanded to include a summary educational history.

JA: I believe that a comprehensive profile of a problem student is essential, as is a full prior academic record. Ordinarily, we do not develop a comprehensive profile, as under present law it is not considered educationally relevant. All we are required to record is educational testing results and basic data on postacademic performance. If we did develop such a profile, parents now have a right to know of its existence and could have it removed from the file. I would like to see some legislation to allow for such profiles. As for prior records, we are required to contact former schools for records. However, we never know what a parent or principal of a former school has removed. So, often a file has been sanitized, usually under a "we don't want to stigmatize the child" rationale. I would like to see legislation requiring a parent to have a child's full prior educational file presented to the new receiving school. Otherwise, much valuable time is lost, all to the child's detriment.

20
Corporal Punishment in Schools

As pointedly stated by NCCAN in one of its publications (Broadhurst, 1984): "There is a paradox in discouraging parental use of corporal punishment while permitting educator use of it." We agree and would go on to say that schools cannot serve as meaningful child abuse intervention agents so long as they themselves are administering physical punishments.

One root of the problem is *Ingraham v. Wright*, a 1977 U.S. Supreme Court decision that upheld the constitutionality of state laws approving corporal punishment in schools. The Court's decision does not mean that states may not ban such punishments; in fact, eight have done so (Hawaii, Maine, Massachusetts, New Hampshire, New Jersey, Rhode Island, Vermont, and New York). Instead, *Ingraham v. Wright* stands for the proposition that if a state elects to use corporal punishment it does not offend anyone's rights under the federal Constitution.

The subject is important enough to have engendered a body of case law, a permanent academic focus (e.g., the National Center for the Study of Corporal Punishment, Temple University, Philadelphia), and the long-time disapproval of the nation's largest teacher union—the National Education Association.

How frequently are these punishments administered? A *Parade* magazine survey drawing on U.S. Department of Education data suggests that there were 203 million incidences within the public schools in 1982 (Satchell, 1985). Of these, *Parade* found that more than 90,000 involved mentally or physically handicapped children, "thrashed because they learned too slowly, talked too loudly, wet their pants." In addition to thrashings, the National Center for the Study of Corporal Punishment cites burning, punching, slapping, and whipping. Documented injuries include broken limbs and teeth, gashes, broken blood vessels, and nerve damage, to say nothing of related emotional harm and mental abuse, such as forcing young boys to wear dresses. Often, physical punishments include locking children in closets and tying them to chairs.

In one midwestern city, *Parade* found twenty-eight cases over an eighteen-month period of students being treated in hospital emergency rooms for corporal punishment–related injuries. A professional observer close to the scene noted that the treating physicians were perplexed over the law's different response to school versus parental abuse. The observer also noted that most of the twenty-eight cases involved special needs children.

In the search for rationales for the use of corporal punishment in schools, none can be found within the research sector, which has consistently found positive correlations between such punishment and misbehavior. Reynolds and Murgatroyd (1977) found that attendance was worst in schools that make the greatest use of corporal punishment. Heal (1978) found more misbehavior in schools with formal punishment systems; and Rutter (1980) found, if not a significant connection, a trend of more misbehavior, including delinquency, in schools with high levels of punishment.

Why, then, does corporal punishment persist? Although an in-depth response to this question soon leads us outside the scope of this project, we feel compelled to offer two reasons: It provides a means of expressing anger, and it continues to be supported by people who believe that children can be "straightened out" through this method. We further believe that what is really going on in many cases is educator feelings of inadequacy, educator fears of losing control of a class, and a very limited educator response repertoire. The use of corporal punishment thus says more about the perpetrator than about the student.

Can corporal punishment never be justified? Certainly, some students—a small number—are true provocateurs, intent on deliberately provoking authority figures into explosive responses. Another group of students are behaviorally disordered, but their behavior is benign in the sense that it does not consistently target specific individuals. Yet a third group is those students who are punished in the absence of any serious misbehavior; as noted earlier, this group too often includes handicapped children.

Each of these situations provides its own reason for banning corporal punishment. Child provocateurs need psychiatric help, not violent retaliation, which only reinforces their disturbed need to incite and be punished. As for the large group of more benign acting-outers, Dr. Densen-Gerber explains that their behavior is, foremost, a release from enormous stress. Unfortunately, some educators misperceive the behavior, construing it to be, foremost, a personal affront to their authority. The third situation has nothing to do with any student wrongdoing; it speaks to what is likely a small number of educators who feed their own pathology through maltreatment of students who are slow or different.

In all three instances, it can readily be seen that corporal punishment is not an appropriate response. Moreover, each situation speaks to educators, requiring (1) a certain amount of insight into certain children, (2) an expanded personal response repertoire vis-á-vis student misbehavior, and (3) an opportunity to ventilate feelings of anger and frustration appropriately. Paradoxically, these closely resemble the therapeutic objectives Dr. Densen-Gerber has identified for chronic acting-out students.

Unfortunately, corporal punishment in the schools is part of a larger debate, which includes capital punishment, beating children as a home discipline technique, and the glorification of physical dominance and violence in general. Consequently, it is apt to linger on longer than it deserves.

We conclude that condoning corporal punishment in the schools is incompatible with child abuse prevention and intervention. Also, as has been pointed out, it too often targets special needs children, including chronic acting-out youth, who are in the greatest need of educator care. The National PTA concurs with this position and has prepared an educational program for parents, informing them of the dangers of corporal punishment as well as alternative disciplinary methods.

21
School Crime and Violence

There are at least three reasons for addressing the problem of school crime and violence within a project such as ours. First, it is an educational issue that has received much attention in recent years, indicative of the general public's perception that violence in the schools is a widespread, alarming problem. In 1984, President Reagan stated to a gathering of secondary school principals, "I can't say it too forcefully, to get learning back into our schools, we must get crime and violence out." Of course, much of the crime and violence is committed by students who are the subject of this report, as part of an overall pattern of acting-out behavior.

Second, if we are correct in our assumption that much school crime is committed by these multiproblem, often maltreated children, then a relationship exists between maltreatment and school crime that must be factored into a long-range response strategy.

Third, when the federal Office of Juvenile Justice and Delinquency Prevention (OJJDP) says that "creating a safe and orderly school environment is a prerequisite for students to focus their attention on learning," an immediate parallel arises concerning the essential need for a "safe and orderly home environment" if students are to learn. This is a rearticulation of the important maltreatment at home/crime in school connection. It is also a statement that interventions have to target causes, not just behavioral responses or symptoms. To the extent that the school crime "movement" discussed here takes this approach, we are supportive.

How widespread is the school crime and violence problem? In 1975, a U.S. Senate subcommittee, after conducting a study and public hearings, concluded that it was a serious national problem. In 1978, HEW (HHS) estimated that school vandalism alone cost an estimated $200 million each year. As for the annual total cost of all school crime, $600 million is a commonly used figure.

One of the most comprehensive studies of school crime is the Safe School Study by the National Institute of Education (NIE) in the mid-1970s. The NIE's findings included the following:

Eight percent of the nation's schools, mostly in urban areas, have a serious crime problem.

Approximately 282,000 students are attacked in school each month, with more than two-fifths of the attacks involving some injury.

Junior high students are twice as likely to report being attacked as high school students.

Twenty percent of all students fear being hurt or bothered at school, at least sometimes.

These statistics, as well as the Senate subcommittee's findings, contributed greatly to a sense that order has broken down in the schools and that violence is rampant. However, these findings have not gone unchallenged. For example, the Children's Defense Fund has raised significant doubts about some of the Senate data. As for NIE's study, the National Council on Crime and Delinquency, in its *Facts about Virulent Juvenile Crime* (1982), points to other NIE findings that received less publicity, including (1) that 96 percent of the reported attacks on students did not cause injuries serious enough to warrant medical attention; (2) that petty theft continues to be the most common crime; and (3) that most schools do not have a serious crime problem. This latter finding was also made by McDermott in his 1975 study of twenty-six American cities, which revealed that 81 percent of the criminal offenses in school were theft or larceny; that is, no violence or confrontation with the victims was involved. The Council underscored other NIE findings, such as that school violence increased throughout the 1960s and thereafter leveled off.

The debate over the relative seriousness of school crime is much like the one that goes on about the seriousness of juvenile crime in general. It is a debate of smaller magnitude, yet the issue of school crime is beginning to develop a constituency via researchers studying school crime as formal subject matter and OJJDP, in particular, funding school crime service organizations. Best known is the National School Safety Center (NSSC), a joint venture of the U.S. Departments of Education and Justice and Pepperdine University in Sacramento. The NSSC is spearheading the establishment of similar centers elsewhere in the United States. Additional impetus has been lent by the National Education Association, through surveys of teachers nationally about the number of student attacks against members. And, as forenoted, President Reagan has voiced his serious concerns about violence in the schools.

What can we make of the school crime issue for present purposes? We suggest the following:

1. School crime—particularly school violence—does not appear to be a serious problem in most U.S. public schools. However, where it does occur at a high rate, which seems to be mostly in some inner city schools, it is a problem that obviously must be given top-priority status.

2. Just as students cannot learn in the midst of school environments filled with crime, violence, and intimidation, neither can students learn who come from homes with the same conditions.

3. It is likely that much school crime and violence is perpetrated by students who have been maltreated in the home, pointing out the need to include early child abuse intervention by systems personnel as a foremost school crime/violence strategy. In addition, research is needed to define more precisely the relationship between maltreatment in the home and school crime.

4. All criminal behavior serious enough to warrant expulsion should be referred to the juvenile justice system or to interdisciplinary community groups (e.g., SARBs). We would caution school officials about serving as investigators and judges involving

serious offenses. Further, we caution school boards and the community at large against a response strategy that relies heavily on expelling a student offender.

5.   Every school has a duty and a right to insist upon a climate of safety in order to maximize each student's opportunity to learn, which is the main business of childhood.

22
School Dropouts

In 1983, the dropout rate nationally was 28 percent. This translates to over one million dropouts nationally each year. Common reasons for dropping out include "being discouraged," "doing poorly," "not interested," and "economic reasons." In Massachusetts, poor young women drop out of high school at twice the rate of poor young men. Similarly, nearly four out of five jobless teenage dropouts are female.

As might be expected, dropouts typically have poor grades, poor basic skills, and dismal prospects for future well-being. Most disturbing is the high incidence of serious crime by those without a high school education. Similarly, research (e.g., Bachman et al., 1978) has shown that pupils who drop out of school are much more likely to be delinquent than their peers who remain in school and graduate.

A significant caveat to this body of research, as found by Elliott and Voss (1974), is that delinquency rates may actually fall among certain acting-out youth upon dropping out *if* the dropping out is accompanied by regular employment and/or marriage. However, stability in either connection is not apt to be a characteristic of chronic acting-out youth who drop out.

In job-rich Massachusetts, 78 percent of teenage high school graduates work, but barely half of the state's dropouts hold full- or part-time jobs. Among black dropouts, the number working falls to 26 percent. Another revealing comparison is that dropouts who do work make only sixty cents for every dollar earned by their high school graduate counterparts.

Nationally, failure to complete elementary and secondary schooling is far more characteristic of the poor and minorities, such that some people contend that being poor as well as black or Hispanic predisposes certain children to school failure. To illustrate, in 1980, 78 percent of white 19-year-olds in the United States were high school graduates, versus 61 percent for blacks and 56 percent for Hispanics. The dropouts may or may not be CACs, and there is no evidence that minority children have been abused by their parents at higher rates than white children. At the same time, these children may well suffer from higher levels of institutional abuse than their less poor, white peers.

Perhaps most significant about school dropout for present purposes is that it is the ultimate school failure, the termination of a long, difficult, and (for most) unhappy relationship. For chronic acting-out youth, especially those who have been maltreated, it signifies the second major failure in their short lives, following "failure" in the home in the sense that most young abused children perceive the abuse as their fault. One could almost feel good about bringing an end to such long-term, painful experiences if there were something heartening to move on to. However, statistics on employment of dropouts are not encouraging in this regard, and we are left to guess how successful chronic acting-out dropouts are in putting together their own families.

23
School Suspensions and Expulsions

Some students, teens or younger, are not so easily helped. The behavior of disruptive children may need to be dealt with firmly, but with increased understanding. Unfortunately, the school's frequent disciplinary tool is suspension, one of the worst things that could happen to an abused or neglected child.
—Cynthia Crosson Tower, *Child Abuse and Neglect: A Teacher's Handbook for Detection, Reporting, and Classroom Management* (a National Education Association Publication)

One cannot talk about chronic acting-out students without talking about suspensions and expulsions, especially when adolescents are the focus. They go hand in glove. In fact, society's ability to intervene effectively with these young people is in some respects more severely tested by suspensions and expulsions than by a lack of resources or know-how.

We take the position that expulsions, in particular, are bad public policy for the simple reason that society severely penalizes itself when it prematurely terminates a child's developmental process, which includes formal learning. For many abused students whose development has already been substantially retarded by virtue of maltreatment in the home, removal from a potentially remedial educational framework constitutes additional damage.

It does not require much insight to appreciate that failure in the home, as the result of being a maltreated child, and failure in the school system, for being an oppositional student, are primary ingredients for later dysfunction, be it in the form of substance abuse, unemployment, mental illness, perpetration of family violence, or abuse of one's own children. Not all "double failure" children removed from school are so fated, but can anyone feel optimistic about their chances for success?

A little-known and particularly disturbing element of expulsions in many jurisdictions is that a school's obligation to educate a child terminates with the expulsion. There are two exceptions to this policy. First, students who have conducted themselves in a particularly offensive manner, thereby winding up not only out of school but in reform school, are entitled to a state-funded educational program. Public policy that extends an education to those who behave and those who grossly misbehave but not to those who moderately misbehave is puzzling.

Second, students who are coded under P.L. 94-142 cannot be as easily suspended or expelled as their nonhandicapped peers. The legal boundaries are still not clear, although federal courts have begun to provide some guidance. [See, e.g., *Stuart v. Nappi*, 443 F. Supp. 1235 (D. Conn. 1978), where the court held that absent "endangering" conduct, the proper method of removing an oppositional child from the classroom was through the IEP rather than the expulsion process.]

The most comprehensive analysis of forced removal from school that we are aware of was done by the Children's Defense Fund, the well-known and respected Washington, D.C.– based lobby for children. Although their data are over ten years old, it is informative to note that their national survey, covering 24 million students, identified one in every twenty-four students as having been suspended at least once during the 1972–73 school year. The CDF also discovered that the vast majority of suspensions and expulsions were for nonviolent, nondangerous offenses. And although approximately one-third did involve fighting, all but a tiny percentage involved students fighting students, not faculty or staff.

Other CDF observations/findings include:

Not a single school official interviewed contended suspensions helped children. One principal said: "I just don't think we're helping any if we suspend a kid; we just get the kid out of our hair for a while."

For children who have serious and chronic behavior problems, it is even more important to refer them to alternative programs or services which have the ability to diagnose and prescribe treatment for the causes of the misbehavior. Otherwise, the child simply returns to class again with the same problem.

Temporarily removing truly dangerous and disturbed children from school with no formal responsibility for them vested in any agency is dangerous to the child and to the community.

Seriously disruptive children ought . . . to be removed from a class temporarily. . . . The child, however, should not be discarded. His or her problem should be diagnosed and treated.

That their alleged [serious] crimes took place on school grounds need not remove them from the purview of the juvenile authorities.

Summarizing its position, the CDF concluded:

The great majority of suspensions do not serve any demonstrated valid interests of children or schools. Instead, they harm the children involved and jeopardize their prospects for securing a decent education. Suspension pushes children and their problems into the street, thereby causing more problems for them and for the rest of us. They have become a crutch enabling school people to avoid the tougher issues of ineffective and inflexible school programs; poor communications with students, parents, and community; and a lack of understanding about and commitment to serving children from many different backgrounds and with many different needs in our public schools. Finally, suspensions are not necessary, except in a small minority of cases, to maintain order.

The CDF is not without suggestions about alternatives to suspending and expelling students, based on the actual practice and innovations of schools nationally. We noted some of these in Chapter 18, as well as others, including Michigan's School Youth Advocacy program, which was established in part as an alternative to suspensions and expulsion. Also, we recommend that educators obtain a copy of the CDF report (*School Suspensions: Are They Helping Children*) by contacting the Children's Defense Fund, 122 C Street, N.W., Washington, DC 20001.

Another critic of our educational system's widespread use of suspensions and expulsions is James Garbarino, a national authority on child maltreatment and child development. He states:

> In many instances school seem to discourage the development of accountability and competence in their students. Students are rarely held accountable for their actions. Rather, discipline is usually unrelated to the crime and is almost always punitive. Someone has to be blamed, and many times students are able to sidestep their own responsibility as their teachers and parents point fingers at one another. Often the school's rules themselves become the ends rather than the means. This preoccupation with rules discourages students from examining their own behavior and its consequences for themselves and others. It sets up teachers and administrators as enforcers who must make students toe the mark. (Garbarino, 1981).

The National Association of Social Workers, in its national study of school problems, had this to say:

> Inadequate discipline policies and procedures were identified as the second major barrier to excellence in this category. This suggests the need for the development of a responsive, consistent and comprehensive approach to discipline within our schools. Such an approach would eliminate corporal punishment and implement alternative forms of discipline which exclude violence. Research studies on effective schools have found good discipline to be a significant factor in schools which are effective academically. *A Nation at Risk* also recommended that the burden on teachers for maintaining discipline should be reduced through the development of firm and fair codes of student conduct that are enforced consistently and by developing alternative programs to meet the needs of continually disruptive students. (Mintzies and Hare, 1985)

In the NASW Statement on School Discipline, presented to the House Subcommittee on Elementary, Secondary and Vocational Education in 1984, Judith Byrne of the Fairfax County Public schools in Virginia (the tenth largest school system in the nation) summarized four essential components of its effective discipline system:

1. Early prevention of learning and behavior problems.
2. Timely disciplinary interventions.
3. Fair and consistent discipline policies.
4. Adequate student support services within the school system.

At the state level, Florida's Safe School Act bars suspensions for students with unexcused absences or truancy. On the judicial front, courts have not had much to say about the wisdom of suspensions and expulsions. They have simply required that school officials adhere to certain procedural requirements [see, e.g., *Goss v. Lopez*, 419 U.S. 565 (1975)]. We note, however, the Alabama case of *Lee v. Mason County Board of Education* [490 F.2d. 458 (1974)], involving the expulsion of two sisters for fighting, truancy, and a variety of other infractions. Whereas the presiding federal district court upheld the school board's actions, the reviewing federal circuit court found that the board did not grant the students full due process. More striking, however, was the circuit court's broad assessment of expulsions:

We do not minimize the children's misbehavior. They were undisciplined, defiant, and abusive, and their mother was uncooperative with school officials in attempting to deal with them. Nor are we insensitive to the difficulties faced by school officials in attempting to curb disorderly interferences with the primary task of the school, which is education. But a sentence of banishment from the local educational system is, insofar as the institution has power to act, the extreme penalty, the ultimate punishment. In our increasingly technological society getting at least a high school education is almost necessary for survival. Stripping a child of access to educational opportunity is a life sentence to second-rate citizenship, unless the child has the financial ability to migrate to another school system or enter private school.

24
Case 3:
Larry, Age 16

Summary Assessment Profile

A. CHILD FACTORS
   1. **Academic Performance**
      Public school history: Prior to 1975, Larry did well in school. At age 8 his grades dropped. His school next reported difficulties in attendance, poor work habits, and poor study skills. Larry exhibited no effort and no cooperation and would not complete or pass in assignments. He was unable to keep up with his class because of the frequent absences.

      His grades in public high school for the 1981–82, 1982–83, and 1983–84 school years were consistently Ds and Fs. Public school reports indicate that Larry exhibited low motivation and effort, moodiness, and poor attendance. The teachers noted that Larry lacked parental support and was influenced negatively by peer pressure. On those occasions when he did attend school, he was capable of periods of self-control, but whenever he felt wronged, he responded by being argumentative and fighting.

      a. *Language competency:* Significantly below grade level prior to court placement. Currently, his reading skills test above grade level, his spelling slightly below grade level.

      b. *Areas of success:* Received As and Bs in physical education. Larry asserted himself in gym, he now believes, to offset his view of himself as a "weakling."

   2. **Acting-Out Behaviors**
      a. *Age of onset:* 7.
      b. *Types and places:*
      (1) *School:* In 1974 when Larry was in second grade, he began to fight with peers in school. This is about the time his parents initiated divorce proceedings.

      Larry describes his school behavior as especially difficult after he accidentally shot a 5-year-old girl in the arm. Peers made fun of him (e.g., called him "crazy"), and he states that he started to act crazy by fighting and bizarre antics.

      He also presented serious difficulty for school officials when he was drunk or stoned. He overdosed on drugs while in the school building, drank a fifth of whiskey on the bus, and took acid before entering classes.

He also reports stealing at school (e.g., wallets) and carrying a switchblade in recent years, which he referred to as his "security blanket." On one occasion, he used the blade to puncture the tire of a car owned by a male rival.

(2) *Home:* He became increasingly oppositioned to rules at home and threatened violence on numerous occasions.

(3) *Community:* Larry first was involved in minor infractions (e.g., group vandalism, prank phone calls) at age 10. Thereafter, his offenses became increasingly serious, including numerous breaking-and-enterings, resisting arrest, and check forgeries. Also, on two different occasions while under the influence of alcohol and drugs, he engaged in reckless driving and was the cause of two serious automobile accidents.

Larry was engaged in prostitution for a short time. He was paid $20 an hour to have sexual relations with older females. He said he ended this when his pimp wanted him to go to women customers' homes rather than a hotel. Larry feared hidden cameras and angry husbands. He also resisted his pimp's plans to have Larry involved in ménage à trois relationships.

3. **Medical/Psychiatric Status**
   a. *Size/appearance:* 5'7", 150 lbs., good looking.
   b. *History of injuries, illnesses, handicaps:* Larry was born with an umbilical hernia. He was operated on at age 6 months. At age 1, he had high fever and convulsions. Also, he was enuretic until age 9.
   c. *Neurological impairment:* Larry was viewed as hyperactive since age 2, according to his mother.
   d. *Psychiatric diagnosis:*
      Axis I—adjustment reaction of adolescence with some elements of depression and antisocial behavior.
      Axis II—diagnosis deferred.
      Axis III—none.

4. **IQ**
   a. *Full scale:* 104.
   b. *Verbal:* 98.
   c. *Performance:* 110.

5. **Child Abuse History**
   a. *Source:* Intrafamily, peer, adult community member.
   b. *Type:* Physical, sexual, psychological/emotional.

   Larry's stepfather (his mother's second husband) has been extremely violent toward his stepsons. He beat Larry and his brothers uncontrollably. Often the beatings involved karate kicks and punches. The children learned early on that the more they cried, the more he would beat them. He has promised the boys that when they reach 18 he will find them and beat them the way he has really wanted to.

   When Larry was 13, he was lured into a sexual relationship with a local police officer, who let Larry use his car and boat. He also gave Larry alcohol.

Initially, the pattern was for the officer to show X-rated films, then engage in mutual masturbation with Larry. Following an episode one day, Larry ended the relationship, threatening to tell if the officer persisted. Shortly thereafter the officer was forced to resign from the police force for sexual assault involving two other boys.

A further complicating factor was the police officer telling Larry he had also had sexual relations with Larry's brother. Larry remains highly conflicted and anguished over this and has not asked his brother.

As forenoted, when Larry was 12, he accidentally shot a 5-year-old girl in the arm. He was incoherent for two hours immediately following the incident. Subsequently, his school peers called him a "psycho," and his parents apparently made him feel guilt over what third parties deem an accident. His parents' reaction was inflamed by the girl's parents filing a successful civil suit against them. The parents appear to have treated Larry as a "sick" person, resulting in his further withdrawal from them.

    c.   *Severity:* Physical abuse was especially severe.

    d.   *Frequency:* Physical abuse was constant.

    e.   *Duration:* Physical abuse from ages 5 to 10.

6. **Substance Abuse**

Larry began drinking at age 8, usually with his older brothers and their friends. He began smoking marijuana at age 12. The following year he progressed to amphetamines, LSD, and cocaine. Also at this time, the police officer who lured him into a sexual relationship supplied Larry with alcohol. By age 16, Larry was heavily involved with alcohol and dealt drugs on a small scale.

7. **Suicide Attempts**

In 1982, Larry intentionally took an overdose of Valium. He describes himself as, at times, possessing suicidal feelings, yet maintains he would not act out these feelings.

8. **Educational Handicap**

Although Larry's difficulties in school began on a regular basis in 1975 in the third grade, it wasn't until 1983 that school officials referred him for a special needs evaluation. The referrals were initiated because of poor achievement and poor attendance. He had earned only 2.6 credits in two full years of high school. Larry was coded as a special needs student with serious emotional disturbance in late 1983.

9. **Cultural Factors**

Caucasian, Lithuanian/Dutch, Protestant.

10. **Peer Relationships**

Larry will do anything to be liked or have a friend. He'd do crazy things to gain the acceptance of age peers and adults. In adolescence he was able to have a lot of "friends." His relationships with girls are solely on the basis of sexual exploitation.

11. **Strengths**

Good with his hands (e.g., carpentry). Can be extremely polite. Bright. Good leadership qualities.

12. **Other**
   a. Larry now cites his antisocial behavior as a way to demonstrate strength and capability, rooted in an underlying feeling of being a "runt" or weakling.
   b. His mother admits to yelling and screaming at her children when they violate home rules, which is frequently.
   c. He is very narcissistic.
   d. He is unusually resistant to age-appropriate independence.

B. FAMILY FACTORS
   1. **Changing Parental Figures**
      a. *Divorce/remarriage/equivalent:* The biological parents were married in 1963 and divorced in 1974. This union produced four sons. Larry was 5 years old when his parents divorced. His mother married her second husband in 1975 and they were divorced in 1980.

      Larry's biological father married his second wife in 1975. They were divorced in 1976, remarried in 1978, and divorced again in 1980. They are presently living together but have separated approximately twelve times since last being divorced.
      b. *Adoption:* None.
      c. *Foster parents:* None.
      d. *Deaths/disappearance/abandonment:* After Larry's parents were divorced, his father drifted in and out of the boys' lives for years. In recent years, he began seeing the boys two or three times monthly. However, in the past year, he has made little effort to see Larry.

   2. **Siblings**
   Larry has three older biological brothers. One of his brothers has a kidney disease, and Larry believes he may have to be the kidney donor for his brother's life-saving surgery.

   3. **Economic Status**
   Lower middle class. Both his mother and biological father are regularly employed.

   4. **Spousal/Sibling Violence**
   Larry's mother reports that she has been physically and psychologically abused by both her husbands. The abuse by her second husband was more prevalent. He beat her frequently and on one occasion kicked her while she was on the floor.

   5. **Parental/Sibling Substance Abuse**
   Larry's paternal family has a long history of alcoholism. Larry's great-grandfather and four paternal uncles were all alcoholics. Larry's father is also an alcoholic, and his alcoholism, along with marital infidelity, was the cause of the divorce. At present, he is not drinking.

      Larry's stepfather drank and smoked pot with his stepsons, including Larry, following his divorce from the boys' mother. Larry's oldest brother is alcoholic and jobless and lives at home. In addition, another brother, who lives out of state, is heavily involved with drugs and alcohol.

   6. **Parental/Sibling Perpetration of Child Abuse**
   Although Larry's biological father and stepfather were violent toward Larry's

mother, only his stepfather was abusive toward him. Larry's mother witnessed the beatings of her sons but apparently felt she was unable to intervene.

7. **Relocations**
   Although Larry has lived in the same state all his life, the family moved six times before Larry was 6. Since then, his family has lived in several different places within the same town. This has resulted in Larry's attending five different elementary schools. Since ninth grade, he has attended an additional four schools, including a residential school.

8. **Psychiatric/Medical Status of Parent(s)**
   Larry's parents have no known history of psychiatric hospitalizations or severe mental illness.

9. **Integration/Isolation**
   a. *Family:* Both parents have a fairly good sense of extended family.
   b. *Community:* Larry's mother is community-oriented through work-related interests. However, she is socially isolated.

10. **Advocacy Capability**
    With encouragement, Larry's mother is able to provide some advocacy on behalf of Larry and the other children. She is genuinely concerned and wants to do the right thing. Treatment staff described her as "very open and supportive."

11. **Other:** None.

C. PRIOR SYSTEM INTERVENTIONS

1. **Public Schools**
   The schools initiated three major interventions: coding in 1983, group counseling at the request of the juvenile court in 1984, and suspension in 1984 for cutting classes and truancy.

2. **Child Protection**
   None.

3. **Judicial**
   Larry first appeared in juvenile court for minor infractions. Thereafter, he was apprehended for increasingly serious offenses, all related in some manner to his substance abuse. Of particular concern to the court were two automobile accidents, which miraculously resulted in no deaths. Following the first accident in 1983, Larry was ordered to attend AA. Also of retrospective concern to the court was the accidental shooting of the young girl. In response to that incident, the court ordered psychological and neurological testing.

   The Court made a series of additional mental health orders. First, in 1983, Larry was hospitalized for two months in an adolescent alcohol/drug unit. Following his release, his behavior improved for a while, but in 1984 he was readmitted to the same unit. The precipitating event was the police being summoned to Larry's home to restrain him from being violent. Between hospitalizations, the court ordered individual and family outpatient counseling.

   Given the absence of change in Larry's behavior, coupled with a breaking-and-entering arrest, the court decided to place him at a residential program.

4. **Mental Health**
   Several mental health interventions were attempted prior to placement, as noted. None of the interventions were voluntary until recently. Larry now chooses to remain in treatment in the absence of any remaining court pressure.

Interview with Dr. Densen-Gerber

David Sandberg (DS): What is the core of this case from a psychiatric point of view based on your review of the reports?

Dr. D-G: Larry is essentially a psychiatric case because of the psychosexual pathology. He is beyond the expertise of most school guidance counselors. With traditional one-to-one psychotherapy twice a week with a psychiatrist, he could be maintained within the public school system. George (Case 1) and Susan (Case 2) also needed therapy, but not psychiatric one-to-one therapy.

DS: Could Larry have been managed successfully by the public schools?

Dr. D-G: Yes. Actually, Larry did well in school until the divorce and soon thereafter was confronted with a violent stepfather. These are major stressors. By 1976, the school should have done major intervention, as family changes were clearly causing changes in Larry's school behavior. His school failure set up additional stressors, and eventually there was major stress caused by the sexually abusive police officer. Again, we always have to remind ourselves that during the time children like Larry are being subjected to all this abuse and chaos, they are expected to concentrate on reading, writing, math, and other subjects.

DS: At least there is some of what you call "constancy of place" in Larry's life—at least insofar as not moving from state to state, like Susan in the previous case.

Dr. D-G: Although Larry remained within the same state, he did move numerous times, which necessitated changing schools. These moves are additional stressors.

DS: What is your impression of Larry's mother?

Dr. D-G: His mother's "tolerance" of her husband's abuse of Larry amounts to parental betrayal and almost without question is a significant source of Larry's anger. Often, a non-abusive parent's failure to intercede produces greater anger in victims than the abuse itself. A child can come to understand that a beater was sick or disturbed. It is much harder to understand why the healthier parent did not intervene. However, she might have responded positively to someone reaching out to her and trying to get her voluntary cooperation. Furthermore, her subjecting herself to considerable abuse by her husband suggests that she may have been a child abuse victim herself.

DS: Just how significant in a psychiatric sense is the sexual abuse by the policeman?

Dr. D-G: It is an extraordinary betrayal of trust by a supposedly trustworthy official. Among other things, it reinforced Larry's sense of being a runt, a weakling, and gave rise to severe doubts about his maleness. The experience constituted yet another exposure to exploitative male role models. This forced Larry to choose between patterning himself after a perpetrator or a victim. Larry chose the former, which is the less socialized choice.

DS: Do you perceive the sexual abuse with the police officer as the cause of Larry's subsequent prostitution?

Dr. D-G: No. I see it as the coup de grace, the final betrayal, a last confirmation that the world was filled with nothing hopeful or positive. Certainly, it is in part Larry's attempt to have a relationship with a supposedly respected, trustworthy father figure and to identify with a strong authoritarian male figure to incorporate him in some way.

Also, I strongly suspect that more happened that links to the prostitution, especially before the child was 5, than we know about.

DS: In thinking more about what else occurred prior to age 5, it is noteworthy that Larry's father was alcoholic and beat Larry's mother, who also had three other children to care for. On top of this, both Larry and a brother presented serious medical problems from birth.

Dr. D-G: At the least, it was a very stressful environment to begin life. We also know that Larry was enuretic and hyperactive from a very early age.

DS: The records indicate no mental illness in the family, yet there is disturbance here.

Dr. D-G: Although there is no mental illness, as evidenced by nervous breakdowns or psychiatric hospitalizations, clearly there is disturbance in this family, as evidenced by such things as the mother's pattern of victimization, which is suggestive of a post–child abuse condition. Also, Larry's father's conduct, such as marrying and divorcing the same woman three times and separating twelve times, is evidence of significant pathology. These are not the healthiest parents. One can debate the alcoholism as a "mental illness," but at the very least, it greatly exacerbated other family problems.

DS: Here is another case with a serious early childhood injury and hospitalization.

Dr. D-G: Yes, and there is very little research data on how children handle these situations long term, even where there are caring, supportive parents. The convulsions are fairly normal accompanying high fevers and usually end by age 5. But again, there can be a significant emotional aftermath to the epileptic loss of control, depending in good part on the parent's response. It is extremely important to know how the parents attended to him and whether they reassured him. We see a deep sense of powerlessness in many of our adult patients who experienced early childhood hospitalizations without sufficient parental support. Often, it requires regressive hypnosis to uncover and work through the sense of abandonment and helplessness.

DS: Do you concur with the initial diagnosis?

Dr. D-G: In my opinion, the diagnosis is too mild; Larry is in greater psychiatric difficulty. He appears to have major psychosexual problems, including trouble identifying himself as a powerful male, which has been reinforced by the homosexual experience. Deep down he likely feels, "I am not a normal male." Furthermore, his prostitution with older women needs to be added to the diagnostic and dynamic formulation.

DS: Another extraordinary event in this boy's life was the shooting of the little girl.

Dr. D-G: Here is yet another major stressor. Larry's family having to pay civil damages seems to have created yet another source of parental anger toward him.

DS: I was bothered to see that when the school finally did intervene, it terminated his counseling because the school year ended, notwithstanding his need for continued counseling.

Dr. D-G: Such seasonal termination is obviously not appropriate. The educational system has to ensure that there is ongoing service over the summer. Common sense should tell us this.

DS: The profile notes that Larry, like many chronic acting-out males, frequently fights and is argumentative. His linking this to feeling wronged is also familiar. My sense is that some of these children generally believe they never fight or argue unless provoked.

Dr. D-G: There is an adult diagnosis of agent provocateur—a person who feels more real by stimulating attention through attack, so always sets himself/herself up to be attacked. These people never see that they initially cause the provocation, whereas, in fact, they usually do. However self-justified and paranoid this behavior is, it is one adaptation to feelings of being wronged. Another child might be passively accepting of imagined or perceived wrongs, which is probably a less healthy response. One treatment technique is to tape a group session so that the provocateur child can begin to see that there was initial external provocation. Let us not underestimate the fact that children like Larry, who have been severely physically and sexually abused, often develop an exaggerated sense of the other's negative intent. If your own environment is Attica, you are apt to feel that all other environments are Attica. If your own parents or others who are close to you are not kind, it is difficult to believe that anyone else is kind.

DS: Carrying a switchblade is not all that common where Larry comes from. What do you make of it, including Larry's reference to the knife as his "security blanket"?

Dr. D-G: This, coupled with several other things having to do with a reaction formation whereby he is a tough aggressor, leads me to believe that his abuse was truly life-threatening. He has had a constant need to be physically safe and not to be a weakling.

DS: Do you consider his auto "accidents" suicidal behavior?

Dr. D-G: Possibly, but they were more likely excessive adolescent omnipotence—a Russian roulette equivalent that permeates this case.

DS: We talked in our first NCCAN project about children like Larry whose physical abuse includes the parental demand that they not cry while being assaulted. What is the effect of this?

Dr. D-G: Mounting rage that will be displaced somewhere else and generalizing one's non-feeling condition to all relationships. It is an ingredient for future trouble.

DS: How is being his brother's kidney donor apt to affect Larry?

Dr. D-G: This is difficult for me to comment on as I am not acquainted with the brother's medical history. However, there is no reason that he, any more than his other siblings, will be chosen to be the kidney donor for his brother. His belief to the contrary is symbolic of other dynamics.

DS: Please comment on adults drinking and using drugs with children. This type of thing seems to be on the increase.

Dr. D-G: Such parental actions condone and reinforce the children's acting-out behavior. More significantly, generational distance, which is critical to essential role modeling, is destroyed. In general, it feeds a cynical view that adults are not a source of strength and guidance. The world is now viewed through a skeptic's eye.

DS: Despite Larry's projected toughness, treatment staff observed an overdependence on his mother.

Dr. D-G: This is not uncommon among violent and/or acting-out types. For example, at autopsy, many drug addicts have elaborate "Mom" tattoos.

DS: Are there incest equivalents in this case?

Dr. D-G: Certainly the prostitution with older women. Also, Larry's reluctance to prostitute in women's homes out of fear of the husbands is Oedipal. This lends further support for the view that this case, basically, is psychosexual in nature. This doesn't necessarily mean that Larry was sexually abused in the home, but there are many unanswered issues with a strong sexual or sexual identity component.

DS: It occurs to me that we know a lot of the child abuse specifics in this case, yet they alone do not explain what is going on with Larry.

Dr. D-G: Yes, it illustrates why, from a psychodynamic point of view, we need more than abuse information to develop a clear sense of who a child is and what s/he needs.

DS: Do you have any other thoughts about Larry's case?

Dr. D-G: I still have a strong feeling that although his case is psychosexual at the core, there is a missing element in the sense that all the data do not seem to add up. There is a great deal of information about guns, knives, shooting, prostitution, acting tough—all of which point toward psychosexual issues. But I suspect that he had crucial experiences prior to entering school that we don't know about. I believe he is literally fighting for his very survival. One explanation for the incomplete data may be that his homosexual experiences and prostitution distanced him from even the mental health people, in the sense that at one level they don't feel comfortable dealing with Larry's pathology.

After reviewing the material, my own inclination was not to use this as a case in the Handbook because I was, and continue to be, unable to get a solid handle on Larry. I'm uncomfortable with the initial diagnosis and the conflicting as well as the missing data. I know where the lesion is—it's psychosexual—but I don't know what type of lesion is involved. We professionals don't like not knowing, and sometimes we simply don't know.

DS: It seems to me that Larry's case can illustrate the need for intervenors to keep digging for enough information until a case makes sense and not to give up on a case or subconsciously avoid it.

Dr. D-G: I would particularly like for Larry's mother to be interviewed. Again, I believe the focus should be psychosexual. For example, did his mother really want Larry to be a daughter? I believe she is the key to understanding Larry; there is much more of critical importance about her that we don't know. This information is very much needed in view of Larry's extreme reluctance to move toward independence and his bizarre symbiotic Oedipal needs.

Part VI
Conclusions and Recommendations

25
Conclusions

Ordinarily, handbooks provide basic "how-to" information, and we believe we have done this on behalf of a very difficult type of child. In other respects, our Handbook is pioneering and goes beyond "how-to's." Thus, there is a flavor of advocacy and calling for change that is not usually present. In the end analysis, we are satisfied if the Handbook effectively explains, illustrates, and supports a small number of points, including the following:

1. Chronic acting out is a coping response some students make in the face of individual, family, and socioenvironmental stressors.

2. Child abuse/neglect is frequently associated with chronic acting out, is a foremost stressor, and should be considered whenever CAC assessments are made by educators and others.

3. Chronic acting out and child abuse/neglect are the proper business of educators because they seriously interfere with the child's opportunity to learn.

4. A K–12 continuum of remedial intervention is needed for chronic acting-out students, with particular emphasis on K–6 because:
   a. It is consistent with early childhood abuse/neglect reporting and intervention.
   b. It prevents ingrained patterns of antisocial behavior from developing.
   c. It predates children "turning off" helpers.
   d. It prevents children from being labeled later on as "losers."

5. Chronic acting out and child maltreatment are both multiproblematic in nature and beyond the ability of any one system to handle effectively; therefore, public schools have to forge new alliances with the mental health, child protection, and juvenile justice systems.

6. Failure at home (and it is to be remembered that most maltreated children perceive the abuse/neglect as their fault) and failure in school are primary ingredients for later delinquency and dysfunction in adulthood.

An important theme in this Handbook is that all the chapter materials have substantive interrelationships. Thus, for example, corporal punishment in the schools, suspensions/expulsions, educational handicaps, and child abuse are not isolated topics, although they are often viewed as such. They are closely related, and these connections must be understood if

CACs as a group are to be helped and educated, rather than punished and cut off from the educational process.

This approach is most evident in Part II, "Description of Chronic Acting-Out Children." Chapters 5 through 7 are an attempt to get past the tendency to discuss these children in terms of a single identifier—be it a behavioral problem, a learning disability, substance abuse, or even child abuse. To the extent that these children's multiple problems are not understood, they continue to be at risk for institutional and other forms of maltreatment.

As for barriers to improved school interventions, Chapters 9 through 12 suggest that public schools can, indeed, adopt more expansive intervention roles. These chapters, as well as Chapters 13 through 18 offer a mixture of specific and general "how-to" advice. Additional specific strategies remain to be developed, and we are confident that educators have the ability to do this.

The last set of materials, in Chapters 19 through 23, are especially important. For example, schools that continue to rely heavily on suspensions/expulsions as the primary intervention strategy offer no hope. They merely ensure that someone else in the community will have to deal with a problem made worse by cutting the child off from the educational process. In contrast, school social workers offer a great deal of hope. The only thing difficult to understand in this era of multiproblem students is why every school system in the country does not have a social worker—not to replace other school personnel but to provide essential supplemental assistance, including all-important contacts with the home and other agencies.

Public Law 94-142 also offers CACs hope because it places their acting-out behaviors within the context of a handicapping condition that is deserving of remediation. However, many CACs who are eligible for P.L. 94-142 services have not been coded. Many others are not currently eligible because they are construed to be "socially maladjusted" rather than educationally handicapped. If all CACs are not to be made eligible for special education services under P.L. 94-142, then new policies have to be developed to maximize educational opportunities for those CACs who are not eligible.

Service gaps do presently exist within the public schools. This explains, in part, why so many CACs, whether coded or not, continue to deteriorate until they are expelled or drop out. Another explanation is the right of parents to move at will, even when this results in their children enrolling in two or more new schools in a single year. When the children are CACs, multiple relocations virtually eliminate any opportunity for the children to receive the services they need to have a chance to succeed educationally. We can't help but wonder how many of these moves could be prevented if a school social worker or similar person was engaged in a parallel process, helping to educate the parents of CACs.

Most significantly, our research indicates that educators, notwithstanding all the pressures they currently face, are committed to assisting the larger community in child maltreatment intervention and treatment. Quite clearly, if we expect them to do more, it will be necessary for better alliances to be forged with other key systems. In fact, the educational, mental health, child protection, and juvenile justice systems have inherited much child rearing previously done by family, church, and community, where everyone knew each other. We also have to better prepare educators. Cynthia Crosson Tower (1984), herself an educator, puts it this way:

I would be proud to report that schools of education or most schools of education or even my own school of education, adequately prepare teachers to recognize these problems and to act effectively. I cannot make this claim. Schools of education are overburdened preparing teachers to instruct in the "basics," to solve other problems, or simply to survive teaching. But truly, is there anything more basic than helping to stop the destruction of children's bodies and the warping of their minds?

The so-called helping professions, we point out, are not the only ones concerned about the growing problem of children in difficulty. For example, a business subcommittee of the Education Commission of the States estimates that there are 2.4 million youth who are unlikely to become productive citizens. Subcommittee members view these young people as "disconnected" from society because of such problems as drug abuse, delinquency, pregnancy, unemployment, and dropping out of school. Members are most alarmed at the mounting numbers of such youth.

National business and education leaders such as Alan Campbell, former head of the Office of Personnel Management during the Carter administration, and Mary Futrell, president of the NEA, have called for a "profound restructuring of schools," heretofore ignored by reformers. Their recommendations range from such programs as Cities in Schools (see Chapter 18) to after-school care to allowing secondary level students to remain with the same group during the school day to foster self-confidence and interpersonal skills.

And lest we become too problem-oriented, we need to remind ourselves on a regular basis that multiproblem CACs can and do get better. A few get better in spite of system interventions; many get better because of intercessions by knowledgeable and responsible caregivers, including educators.

Finally, we hope that this Handbook will serve as a foundation for drawing new attention to CACs and how public schools and others can better deal with them. If we address CACs primarily in terms of their abuse/neglect, their attention deficit disorders, learning disabilities, and other noted stressors, humanitarian concerns alone are ample motivation to effect improved interventions. If we address them in terms of their chronic acting-out behavior, sufficient motivation should lie with the extraordinary amount of "crisis" time educators spend each day responding to CACs—often without benefit to anyone involved. In any case, it is a subject well worth our time and attention.

26
Recommendations

Public schools currently have access to many resources that can be (and are being) used on behalf of CACs. These resources include, for example, guidance counselors, school nurses, school psychologists, special education personnel, caring classroom teachers, and access to the child protection system and even the courts in some cases. Consequently, the call for new action on behalf of CACs is not preconditioned on the availability of all-new resources.

Nevertheless, some new resources will be needed if a significant reduction in the adverse impact of CACs on school (and other) environments is to be realized. Similarly, it will also be necessary to lessen the public schools' isolation and to find new ways of doing some things.

With this in mind, we present the following recommendations for schools, legislatures, and involved agencies and organizations.

For Schools

1. Develop new policies to ensure that CACs who are eligible for P.L. 94-142 services are coded and provided with needed services.
2. Develop new policies to ensure that CACs who are not eligible for P.L. 94-142 services are responded to in a way that offers more chance for educational success than for educational failure.
3. Utilize the Summary Assessment Profile for CACs or a similar form that accounts for individual, family, and socioenvironmental factors bearing directly on the student's status as a CAC, including child abuse and neglect.
4. Confront the problems of student (peer) abuse, teacher abuse/insensitivity, and institutional abuse and neglect.
5. Screen for child abuse/neglect in all CAC cases, through use of pupil review teams, when a child is being assessed for proper class placement.
6. Advocate for widespread use of school social workers.
7. Provide time for teachers to interact with other systems' personnel who are working with children as a means of promoting interagency cooperation and lessening teacher isolation.

8. Hold CACs accountable for unacceptable behaviors, and designate an educator to receive training in effective ways to set limits.

9. Designate one person within the school system or superintendent's office who will oversee quarterly review of each CAC.

10. Promote teacher training in identifying and servicing maltreated children through both public school inservice programs and preservice instruction in colleges/universities at both the undergraduate and graduate levels.

11. Instruct parents of learning-disabled CACs that multiple relocations are ruinous to their children's chances for academic success.

12. Make greater use of special education personnel to help parents of CACs develop realistic expectations of their children and better ways to respond to their behaviors.

13. Lead the way in calling for new alliances with other child protection and care agencies.

14. Develop "bridging" techniques to aid CACs and other children in making the transition from elementary to junior high school.

15. Sharply curb the use of suspensions and expulsions.

For State Legislatures

1. Ensure that all educators directly involved with problem students are legally entitled to a full feedback from child protection agencies following educator filing of a report for suspected abuse or neglect.

2. Require an educational transfer sheet, summarizing prior intervention efforts on behalf of problem students, which a parent must present on enrolling a child in a new school district.

3. Ensure that confidentiality sections of abuse/neglect statutes allow access to maltreatment information by multidisciplinary evaluation teams, including school placement teams, and by other agencies serving CACs.

For State Agencies

1. State agencies for education, child protection, juvenile justice, and mental health should pursue interagency agreements to facilitate interventions on behalf of CACs and to ensure an exchange of essential information.

2. State agencies for child protection, juvenile justice, and mental health should promote staff exchanges with educators to enhance interagency cooperation and understanding.

3. State agencies for education should put increasing emphasis on K–6 interventions without abandoning secondary-level interventions.

4. State agencies for child protection (CPS) should base field workers in the schools on a full- or part-time basis.

5. State agencies for education should develop meaningful vocational training alternatives for those CACs who are unable to benefit from traditional academic and vocational training programs.

For the National Legislature

Legislation should be enacted that specifically targets students who are not eligible for P.L. 94-142 services and that serves to encourage intervention efforts, particularly at the elementary level, on behalf of chronic acting-out children and their families.

For National Organizations

1. The NCCAN and other national child abuse/neglect organizations should give greater attention to expansion of the public schools' service role for all maltreated children, including those who chronically act out.
2. The NEA's "Plan for School Reform" should serve as one blueprint for improved school-based services for CACs and other at-risk students.

Selected Bibliography

Ackerman, R. (1983). *Children of Alcoholics: A Guidebook for Educators, Therapists, and Parents.* 2nd ed. Holmes Beach, Fla.: Learning Publications.

Alfaro, J. (1981). "Report on the Relationship between Child Abuse and Neglect and Later Socially Deviant Behavior." In R. Hunnan and Y. Walker (eds.), *Exploring the Relationship between Child Abuse and Delinquency.* Montclair, N.J.: Allanheld, Osmun.

———(1984). "Child Abuse and Neglect Issues for Preventative Services Agencies." Unpublished manuscript. New York: New York Mayor's Task Force on Child Abuse and Neglect.

———(1985). "Impediments to Mandated Reporting of Suspected Child Abuse and Neglect." Paper presented at the Seventh National Conference on Child Abuse and Neglect, Chicago.

Bachman, J.; O'Malley, P.; and Johnston, J. (1978). "Adolescence to Adulthood—Change and Stability in the Lives of Young Men." *Youth in Transition,* Vol. VI. Ann Arbor, Mich.: Institute for Social Research, University of Michigan.

Barnett, D., and Barnett, O. (1980). "Enacting Legislation to Identify and Treat Children with Conduct Disorders." *Pepperdine Law Review* 7: 827–64.

Broadhurst, D. (1984). *The Educator's Role in the Prevention and Treatment of Child Abuse and Neglect.* Publication No. (OHDS) 84-30172. Washington, D.C.: U.S. Department of Health and Human Services.

Brown, A.; Pelcovitz, D.; Kaplan, S.; and Kaplan, T. (1985). "A Comparison of Child Witnesses and Child Victims of Family Violence: A Controlled Study." Paper presented at the Seventh National Conference on Child Abuse and Neglect, Chicago.

Burgess, A. (1986). As reported in *Children and Teens Today* (May): 2–4.

Burgess, A; Groth, A.; Holmstrom, L.; and Sgroi, S. (1978). *Sexual Assault of Children and Adolescents.* Lexington, Mass.: Lexington Books.

Cantwell, D. (1980). "Hyperactivity and Anti-Social Behavior Revisited: A Critical Review of the Literature." In D. Lewis (ed.), *Biopsychosocial Vulnerabilities to Delinquency.* New York: Spectrum.

Carmen, E.; Reiker, P.; and Mills, T. (1984). "Victims of Violence and Psychiatric Illness." *American Journal of Psychiatry* 141:3, 378–383.

Conte, J. (1985). "The Impact of Sexual Abuse on Children." Paper presented at the Seventh National Conference on Child Abuse and Neglect, Chicago.

Csapo, M., and Aag, B. (1974). *Operation Step-Up.* Vancouver, B.C.: Vancouver Association for Children with Learning Disabilities.

Del Bello, A. (1984). "A Message from Lieutenant Governor Alfred Del Bello." In *Suicide Among School Age Youth.* Albany, N.Y.: State Department of Education.

Diamond, L., and Jaudes, P. (1983). "Child Abuse in a Cerebral-Palsied Population." *Developmental Medicine and Child Neurology* 25: 69–174.

Douglas, J.; Ross, J.; and Simpson, H. (1968). *All Our Future: A Longitudinal Study of Secondary Education.* London: Peter Davies.

Dunivant, N. (1982). *The Relationship between Learning Disabilities and Juvenile Delinquency.* Williamsburg, Va.: National Center for State Courts.

Elliott, D., and Voss, H. (1974). *Delinquency and Dropouts.* Lexington, Mass.: Lexington Books.

Elmer, E., and Gregg, G. (1967). "Developmental Characteristics of Abused Children." *Pediatrics* 40: 596.

Elmer, E. (1977) "A Follow Up Study of Traumatized Children." *Pediatrics* 59(2): 273–279.

Erickson, E.; McEvog, A.; and Colucci, N., Jr. (1979). *Child Abuse and Neglect: A Guidebook for Educators and Community Leaders* Holmes Beach, Fla.: Learning Publications.

Ferri, E. (1976). *Growing Up in a One-Parent Family.* Slough: N.F.E.R.

Finer, M. (1974). Cited in Rulter, M., and Giller, H. (1984).

Finkelhor, D. (1986). *A Sourcebook on Child Sexual Abuse.* Beverly Hills, Calif.: Sage Publications.

Francke L. (1983). *Growing Up-Divorced.* New York: Fawcett Crest.

Garbarino, J. (1979). "The Role of the School in the Human Ecology of Child Maltreatment." *School Review* (February): 190–213.

———(1981). *Successful Schools and Competent Students.* Lexington, Mass.: Lexington Books.

———(1984). "Child Maltreatment and Juvenile Delinquency: What Are the Links?" In *Child Abuse: Prelude to Delinquency.* Findings of a research conference conducted by the National Committee for the Prevention of Child Abuse, Chicago.

Garbarino, J., and Gilliam, G. (1980). *Understanding Abusive Families.* Lexington, Mass.: Lexington Books.

Gibson, H. (1969). "Early Delinquency in Relation to Broken Homes." *Journal of Child Psychology and Psychiatry* 10: 195–209.

Gill, D. (1969). "What Schools Can Do About Child Abuse." *American Education* (April).

———(1970). *Violence Against Children: Physical Child Abuse in the United States.* Cambridge: Harvard University Press.

Glueck, S., and Glueck, E. (1968). *Delinquents and Nondelinquents in Perspective.* Cambridge: Harvard University Press.

Goodlad, J. (1984). *A Place Called School.* New York: McGraw-Hill.

Graham, P., and Rutter, M. (1973)."Psychiatric Disorder in the Young Adolescent: A Follow-up Study. *Proceedings of the Royal Society of Medicine* 66: 1226–29.

Gregory, I (1965). "Anterospective Data Following Childhood Loss of a Parent. *Archives of General Psychiatry* 13: 110–20.

Gross, B., and Gross, R. (eds.) (1985). *The Great School Debate.* New York: Simon & Schuster.

Hagan, R. (1985). "The Children of Alcoholics: Family Dynamics, Developmental Problems, and Treatment Issues." Professional symposium. Hampton Beach, N.H.

Heal, K. (1978). "Misbehavior Among School Children: The Role of the School in Strategies for Prevention." *Policy and Politics* 6: 321–2.

Hirschi, T. (1969). *Causes of Delinquency.* Berkeley and Los Angeles: University of California Press.

Jacob, J. (1985). Quoted in "National Urban League Initiates Male Responsibility Campaign." *Children and Teens Today.* June, 1985.

Kempe, H. (1962)."The Battered Child Syndrome." *Journal of the American Medical Association* 17: 181.

Kempe, R., and Kempe, C.H. (1978). *Child Abuse.* Cambridge: Harvard University Press.

———(1984). *The Common Secret: Sexual Abuse of Children and Adolescents.* New York: W.H. Freeman.

Kent, J. (1976). A Follow-up Study of Abused Children. *Journal of Pediatric Psychology* (Spring): 25–31.

Kline, D. (1977). The Consequences of Neglected Cases. In A. Thomas (ed.), *Children Alone: What Can Be Done About Abuse and Neglect.* Reston, Va.: Council for Exceptional Children.

———(1982). *The Disabled Child and Child Abuse.* Chicago: National Committee for Prevention of Child Abuse.

Krugman, R. (1985). Personal communication concerning the roles of educators in child abuse and neglect.

Lewis, D.; Shanok, S.; Pintus, J.; and Glaser, G. (1979). "Violent Juvenile Delinquents." *Journal of the American Academy of Child Psychiatry* 18: 307–19.

Lindholm, K. (1985). "Consequences of Abuse on Children's Development and Mental Health: A Conceptual Model." University of California, Los Angeles, unpublished paper.

Lynch, M. (1984). "A Follow-up Study: Implications for Preventing Longterm Consequences of Child Abuse." Paper presented at the Fifth International Congress on Child Abuse and Neglect, Montreal.

Maisch, H. (1972). *Incest.* New York: Stein and Day.

Martin, H. (1976). *The Abused Child.* Cambridge, Mass.: Ballinger.

Martin, H.; Beezley, P.; Conway, E.; and Kempe, C. (1974). "The Development of Abused Children." In I. Schulman (ed.), *Advances in Pediatrics* 21: 25–73.

McDanal, C., and Belman. W. (1979). "A Study of the Cognitive Status of Abused Children Admitted to a Child Psychiatric Ward. *Hawaii Medical Journal* 38(6): 159–60.

Mintzies, P., and Hare, I. (1985). *The Human Factor: A Key to Excellence in Education.* Silver Springs, Md.: National Association of Social Workers.

Molnar, B., and Cameron, P. (1975). "Incest Syndromes: Observations in a General Hospital Psychiatric Unit." *Canadian Psychiatric Association Journal* 20: 1.

Morse, C; Sahler, O.; and Friedman, S. (1970). "A Three-Year Follow Up Study of Abused and Neglected Children." *American Journal of Diseases of Children* 120: 439–446.

National Commission on Excellence in Education (1983). *A Nation at Risk: The Imperative for Educational Reform.* No. 065-000-00177-2. Washington, D.C.: U.S. Government Printing Office.

Newberger, E.; Newberger, C.; and Hampton, R. (1983). "Child Abuse: The Current Theory Base and Future Research Needs. *Journal of the American Academy of Child Psychiatry,* 22: 262–68.

Nicholi, A., Jr. (1983). "The Nontherapeutic Use of Psychoactive Drugs." *The New England Journal of Medicine* 308: 925–933.

Nicholson, G., et al. (1985). *School Safety and the Legal Community.* Sacramento, Calif.: National School Safety Center.

Osman, B. (1979). *Learning Disabilities: A Family Affair.* New York: Warner Books.

Petit, M., and Overcash, D. (1983). *America's Children: Powerless and in Need of Powerful Friends.* Augusta: Maine Department of Human Services.

Reynolds, D., and Murgatroyd, S. (1977). "The Sociology of Schooling and the Absent Pupil: The School as a Factor in the Generation of Truancy." In H. Carroll (ed.), *Absenteeism in South Wales.* Swansea, Wales: University of Swansea, Faculty of Education.

Robins, L. (1966). *Deviant Children Grown Up.* Baltimore, Md.: Williams and Wilkens Co.

Roden, S., and Wright, N. (1982). *Ounces of Prevention: Toward an Understanding of the Causes of Violence.* Sacramento, Calif.: Commission on Crime Control and Violence Prevention.

Ross, R. (1980). "Violence In, Violence Out: Child Abuse and Self-Mutilation in Adolescent Offenders." *Juvenile and Family Court Journal* 31: 33.

Rutter, M. (1971). "Parent-Child Separation: Psychological Effects on the Children." *Journal of Child Psychology and Psychiatry* 12: 233–60.

Rutter, M. (1980). *Changing Youth in a Changing Society.* Cambridge, Mass.: Harvard University Press.

Rutter, M., and Griller, H. (1984). *Juvenile Delinquency: Trends and Perspectives.* New York and London: Guilford Press.

Sandberg, D. (1984). *The Role of Child Abuse in Delinquency and Juvenile Court Decision-Making.*

Final report. Washington, D.C.: U.S. Department of Health and Human Services, National Center on Child Abuse and Neglect.

Sandberg, S.; Rutter, M.; & Taylor, E. (1978). "Hyperkinetic Disorder in Psychiatric Clinic Attenders." 20: 279–99.

Satchell, M. (1985). "Should Children Be Hit in School?" *Parade*, 24 March.

Schaeffer, J. (1985). "The Role of Therapy in Foster Care." *National Association of Former Foster Children Newsletter*. Brooklyn, N.Y.: NAFFC Inc.

Smith, C.; Berkman, D; and Fraser, W. (1980). *A Preliminary National Assessment of Child Abuse and Neglect and the Juvenile Justice System: The Shadows of Distress*. Washington, D.C.: Office of Juvenile Justice and Delinquency Prevention.

Smith, P., and Bohnstedt, M. (1981) "School Survey Results: Child Victimization Study." California State University at Long Beach (unpublished).

State Department of Education (1985). Children, New York's Greatest Resource: The School's Role in Preventing Child Abuse and Neglect." Albany: The University of the State of New York.

Stewart, M; De Blois, C; and Cummings, C. (1980). "Psychiatric Disorder in the Parents of Hyperactive Boys and Those with Conduct Disorders." *Journal of Child Psychology and Psychiatry* 21: 283–92.

Stewart, M.; Cummings, C.; Singer, S.; and DeBlois, C. (1981). "The Overlap between Hyperactive and Unsocialized Aggressive Children." *Journal of Child Psychology and Psychiatry* 22: 35–46.

Straus, M.; Gelles, R.; and Steinmetz, S. (1980). *Behind Closed Doors: Violence in the American family*. Garden City, N.Y.: Doubleday.

ten Bensel, R. (1978). Testimony before the Canadian Senate Subcommittee on Childhood Experiences as Causes of Criminal Behavior, July 4. Issue No. 19. Hull, Quebec: Printing and Publishing, Supply and Services Canada.

Tower, C. (1984). *Child Abuse and Neglect: A Teacher's Handbook for Detection, Reporting, and Classroom Management*. Washington, D.C.: National Education Association.

Wallerstein, J. (1984). "Children of Divorce: Preliminary Report of a Ten-Year Follow-up of Young Children." *American Journal of Orthopsychiatry* 54(3): 444–58.

Washington Research Project (1975). *School Suspensions: Are They Helping Children?* Washington, D.C.: Children's Defense Fund.

Wegscheider-Cruse, Sharon (1976). *The Family Trap* . . . Rapid City, S.D.: Nurturing Networks.

Welsh, R. (1976). "Severe Parental Punishment and Delinquency: A Developmental Theory." *Journal of Clinical Child Psychology* 5: 17–21.

West, D. (1982). *Delinquency: Its Roots, Careers, and Prospects*. London: Heinemann.

West, D., and Farrington, D. (1973). *Who Becomes Delinquent*. London: Heinemann.

West, P. (1979). *Protective Behaviors: Anti-Victim Training for Children, Adolescents and Adults*. Rutledge, Wis.: Protective Behaviors.

Index

About the Contributors

Henry Beyer, J.D., is director of the N. Neal Pike Institute for the Handicapped at Boston University School of Law. He has provided technical and legal assistance to the President's Committee on Mental Retardation, to the U.S. Department of Education, and to state agencies and advocacy groups throughout the country. He is editor and publisher of *Disability Advocates Bulletin* and a consultant to the Eunice Kennedy Shriver Center.

Judianne Densen-Gerber, J.D., M.D.—a lawyer-psychiatrist—is the founder and former executive director of Odyssey House, Inc., the well-known treatment program for drug addicts, which originated in New York in 1967. An authority on acting-out phenomena, she was also a national leader in bringing public attention to the problem of child sexual abuse and child pornography. Currently, she is president of Odyssey Resources, Inc., and Odyssey Institute Corporation, both in Bridgeport, Connecticut.

Cynthia Mowles, Ed.D, is superintendent of schools in Henniker, New Hampshire. She began her professional career as an elementary school teacher, and later became a consultant to the New Hampshire Department of Education. She is a past president of the New Hampshire Task Force on Child Abuse.

About the Author

David Sandberg, J.D., is director of the Program on Law and Child Maltreatment at Boston University School of Law. He has been principal investigator for two major multidisciplinary projects on child abuse/acting-out issues and speaks on these issues nationally. He is also a practicing attorney in his home state of New Hampshire, specializing in representation of abused and neglected children, CHINS, and delinquents. Previously, he was a teacher and director of a residential treatment program for court-referred juveniles.